Imagination Beyond Nation

Pitt Latin American Series

Billie R. DeWalt, *General Editor*
Reid Andrews, *Associate Editor*
Jorge I. Domínguez, *Associate Editor*

Imagination

Beyond Nation

Latin American Popular Culture

Edited by Eva P. Bueno

and

Terry Caesar

University of Pittsburgh Press

Published by the University of Pittsburgh Press, Pittsburgh, Pa. 15261
Copyright © 1998, University of Pittsburgh Press
All rights reserved
Manufactured in the United States of America
Printed on acid-free paper
10 9 8 7 6 5 4 3 2 1

A CIP catalog record for this book is available from the Library of Congress
and the British Library.

Chapter 8, "Tango, Buenos Aires, Borges: Cultural Production and Urban
Sexual Regulation," is reprinted with permission from *Buenos Aires:
Perspectives on the City and Cultural Production,* by David William Foster
(Gainesville: University Press of Florida, 1998).

This book is dedicated to Oscarina Batista Bueno,

uma mulher que sabe muitas histórias do Brasil, and

to Virgílio Paulino Bueno, *que as contava.*

Contents

Acknowledgments

The contributors to this volume are predominantly younger scholars. Perhaps this is one of the reasons it has been such a pleasure to work with them, most of whom we have never met in person. All suffered the various stages of this project with great patience and good humor. Our thanks go to Jeannie Gillespie, Nelson Hippolyte Ortega, Héctor Fernández L'Hoeste, Milagros Zapata Swerdlow and David Swerdlow, James Pancrazio, Oscar Lepeley, David Foster, Jerrold Hoeg, Vincent Spina, and Simon Webb. Without them this book would never have been possible, though we also acknowledge other unnamed colleagues who gave us the opportunity to consider their work at earlier stages of the project.

We want to recognize the official help received from the Pennsylvania State University, especially the Office of Minority Faculty Development and the Office for Research and Graduate Studies, both for release time and financial support. Thanks also to Scott Burns for his fine copy editing earlier in the project, to Silvia Pellarolo for invaluable help with the translations, and to our good friend Marie Novak, who once again did a great indexing job.

We are also grateful for the help of a number of friends from the DuBois campus: Robin Gill and Bob Roman, who solved many computer problems; Sue Waitkus, who helped with class scheduling and positive thoughts; Karen Fuller, Kathleen Bender, and Ann Hummer, who ordered books and found essays. In addition, the encouragement of Mary Dupuis, former dean, was invaluable.

Finally, Eva Bueno wants to thank her co-editor, who has made this project a pleasurable learning experience in more ways than can be expressed. Terry Caesar extends the same thanks to his co-editor, even as he wishes he could extend more to his own institution, where, alas, the sort of research this book represents is simply not acknowledged.

Imagination Beyond Nation

Introduction

The Politics of the Popular in Latin American Popular Culture

TERRY CAESAR *and* **EVA BUENO**

The Art of the People

WE INTRODUCE THIS COLLECTION BY QUOTING FROM an exemplary Latin American genre: the manifesto. We cite this particular one, "For a Popular Revolutionary Art," written in 1962 by Carlos Estevam Martins, for the boldness of its presentation, not because we endorse it. Indeed, the essays is this volume dismantle virtually every one of the manifesto's implications. Nonetheless, we begin with it both because its dismissal of what it terms "the art of the people" and its contempt for "popular art" go immediately to the heart of what commends Latin American popular culture as a fit object for study, either on its own terms or as it is perceived by a North American audience. For this latter audience, a distinction between the art of the people and popular art is, we assume, untenable, if not inconceivable, for a notion of popular art that embraces culture high and low is felt to be simply all there is.

Martins was the executive director of the Popular Cultural Centers established in Brazil between 1962 and 1964 as an attempt to make contact with the masses by staging plays in factories and working-class neighborhoods, producing films and records, and sponsoring literacy programs. Estevam writes:

The "art of the people" is predominantly a product of economically backward communities, flourishing primarily in rural or urban contexts that have not yet reached the life styles that accompany industrialization. In it the artist is indistinguishable from the mass of consumers. Artists and the public are integrated in the same anonymity, and the level of artistic elaboration is so primary that the act of creation does not go beyond the simple ordering of the most patent data of a backward popular consciousness. "Popular art," on the other hand, is distinguished from the art of the people not only by its public, made up of the population of the developed urban centers, but also due to the division of labor that makes the masses the nonproductive receiver of works created by a professionalized group of specialists. The artists thus constitute a social stratum different from their public, reduced to a mere consumer of goods whose labor and divulgation escape its control. The art of the people and popular art, when considered from a culturally rigorous point of view, scarcely deserve to be called art and, from the point of view of the PCC, are neither truly "popular" nor "of the people."[1]

We have in this statement much of what distinguishes the study of popular culture in Latin America, ranging from bold, theoretically sophisticated thinking on the nature of art as a social product to an insistence on the role of intellectuals in fostering its emancipatory potential. Estevam argues for a more authentic third kind, distinct from either the art of the people or popular art, which he terms popular revolutionary art, distinguished principally by intellectuals who inspire and guide the masses to revolution. The Popular Center for Culture was banned by the military regime after it took power in Brazil in 1964.

Compare Martins with one of the most promient Latin American theoreticians of popular culture, Beatriz Sarlo. In *Escenas de la vida postmoderna (Scenes of the Postmodern Life)*, she considers that estimable contemporary site: the mall—a monument to "a new civic order: social space, temple and market," wherein can be seen capitalism "in its purest realization."[2] In this "spatial capsule," she continues, there is no need to know local language, for "the mall offers an extraterritorial culture from which nobody is excluded, even those who cannot buy."[3] Finally, "this space devoid of urban references is replete with neocultural references," with the following result:

"The mall combines the iconographic plentitude of all brand-names with some 'craft' labels of the folk-ecological-natural products."[4]

These products, in turn, are examples of what in Martins's scheme are called popular art. More than three decades after his project, there appears to be no other form of art possible; as Michael Denning bluntly states: "All culture is mass culture under capitalism."[5] The art of the people has now been reduced to a mere commodity inscription as "craft." The idea that there ever was such an art as a distinct practice, much less such a people, is naive. As Tony Bennett explains, "It proves impossible to locate an orginating moment in which 'the people's' culture was ever directly and spontaneously theirs."[6] Furthermore, the very hope for an entirely different, oppositional practice—popular revolutionary art—seems to be futile. Bennett continues, "In the process of the transformation of 'their culture' (if such it ever was), 'the people' have been transformed, too, and are unlikely to move back to those cultural spaces they once occupied, whether originally theirs or not."[7]

In sum, Martins and Sarlo appear to have little in common. Their notions of society are strikingly at odds. In Martins's terms, Sarlo appears to have no notion of class; all people ceaselessly flow into the mall, which recreates the desire even of those who cannot buy, whose sociopolitical location outside the mall has ceased to matter. In Sarlo's scheme, on the other hand, Martins seems to be burdened with nothing more than class. What about the "mirror culture" proposed by television, she asks, "where all can recognize themselves?"[8] Or what about the shattering of this mirror? "Today identities are going through processes of balkanization," Sarlo reflects elsewhere; "they live in a present made unstable by the disappearance of traditional certainties and by the erosion of memory."[9] Martins perspective lacks, in other words, the profoundly social destabilizing consequences of consumer culture.

One of these consequences is that every country in the world has its malls, which is another way of saying that every country is becoming like every other one. Although this volume is arranged in order to address the issue of globalization or postmodernity, the whole logic of *Imagination Beyond Nation* is ultimately designed to contest at least one notion: that there is no longer any compelling reason to regard Latin America as fundamentally different from any other portion of the globe. A variety of theoretical orientations are assembled here, with no intention to exclude any. So we might posit Martins at one end of the spectrum and Sarlo at the other. At any point along this spectrum, the reader may expect to find references to Mikhail Bakhtin, Jesús Martín-Barbero, Paul de Man, or Armand Mattelart. But all these theoretical perspectives have been employed to argue that Latin American popular culture matters in rich and distinctive ways.

In a contribution to a recent *PMLA* "Forum" on cultural studies, Leslie Bary cites John Beverley—from a "virtual speech" given on Latin American subaltern studies—to the effect that "cultural studies now tends to describe but not critique cultural processes, thus eliding subaltern cultural agency and helping to create a 'transnational postmodernist sublime.'"[10] The reader will find little evidence of such a sublime in the following pages, vexed as they are (as any must be today concerning the study of popular culture anywhere in the world) by the spectacle of transnational sovereignty. Instead, this is very much a book about popular culture in one continent, where to describe is to critique, as we indicate by opening with Martins's words.

Martins's manifesto also succinctly highlights a number of other points, none of which proposes (contra Beverley) to hypostatize Latin America as some sort of primitive or edenic site for popular culture, but all of which do assume that this culture abides as a national practice and should be comprehended as such. First, the study of Latin American popular culture proceeds because fundamental political issues about class, power, and art are openly at stake. Second, popular culture in Latin America explicitly raises questions concerning the relationship between cultural production and consumption. Third, the utopian potential of popular culture is provocatively expressed with special force by Latin American examples. We will briefly expand on these points.

Political Issues

Popular culture in Latin America is culture won in the face of its appropriation by urban centers or by those characterized by Martins as "specialists." On this basis, as William Rowe and Vivian Schelling note, "To be of use, the term 'popular' must be distinguished from the products of the culture industry and the mass media. . . . In Latin America, the term is used more broadly, to include rural cultures, and has oppositional connotations."[11] Hence, for example, in their introduction to *The Postmodernism Debate in Latin America*, Beverley, Oviedo, and Aronna note, "The engagement with postmodernism in Latin America does not take place around the theme of the end of modernity that is so prominent in its Anglo-European manifestations; it concerns, rather, the complexity of Latin America's own 'uneven modernity' and the new developments of its hybrid (pre- and post-) modern cultures."[12]

This collection preserves the oppositional connotation of the popular in Latin America and strives to advance it. Granted, few essays consider an art as studiously local and rural as the *cholo* paintings and ceramics examined by Milagros Zapata Swerdlow and David Swerdlow. (No matter that, paradoxically, the art is on this basis inseparable from the international market.) Moreover, most of the contributors see their subjects as deeply embedded in television, cinema, and newspapers—the "popular art" that is the object of Martins's contempt (as well as that of the well-known critique of the "culture industry" by the Frankfurt School). However, the political significance, for example, of even such an unexceptional product of the culture industry as a Venezuelan *telenovela* is, in Nelson Hippolyte's reading, not so utterly mediated by television that the primordial sources of its power are lost; indeed, the *telenovela Por estas calles* becomes an example of a cultural product which, in Jesus Martín-Barbero's words, "touches daily life, connects with it not just as a counterpart or as its substitute, but as something of which [life] is made."[13]

Of course, Radio Caracas Televisión, like any network, makes art for the masses. But the masses do not consume it without resistance—and most South American countries experience the enduring presence of rural culture, notwithstanding the fact that, as Rowe and Schelling state: "It is no longer accurate to make sharp or fixed distinctions between rural and urban cultures in Latin America."[14] Thus, for example, George Yúdice (like Beverley et al.) cautions that we misunderstand modernization in Latin America if we think of it as necessarily eradicating "traditions [of] 'enchanted' or 'auratic' modes of life," despite the fact that these modes "may prove inimical to coexistence with others or to the projects of elites and their allies."[15] (On one such tradition, the *caipira* culture of southern Brazil, see Cândido, *Os parceiros do Rio Bonito*.) It is precisely these traditions, of course, that Martins—as well as Sarlo—see as hopelessly unenlightened and effectively lost. Most of our contributors, however, accord these traditions more power—no matter how naive—to insist upon their own constructions, if only because the very category of the masses, or the public, is more heterogeneous than the standard Anglo-European critique of popular culture allows.

This last point cannot be emphasized enough. Society in Latin America differs from that of North America not only because of its greater racial mixture—mestizo and Indian, especially. Latin America also differs because its popular culture is shaped by what is known in more technologically advanced societies as *folklore*, a term less mystified and romanticized in a South American context, where, as Rowe and Schelling explain, it is "more highly charged politically," since "its referent—the cultures thought of as folkloric—can be as much part of the present as of the past."[16] In this respect, cultural history itself becomes yet another category that must be rethought in a South American context, in which, as Yúdice phases it, modernity "is a series of necessarily unfinished projects" where the past remains not so much available to the present as simply one condition of it.[17]

In this respect, each of these essays, from first to last, features the spectacle of popular energies—whether represented as mythic, regional, resistant, or marginal—that are not past recovering, and yet which are ultimately worthy of care and reflection because something preceding the advent of mass culture has either been lost or is in danger of being lost. Precisely what? In the first essay in this collection, by Jeanne Gillespie, it is the figure of a woman whose iconic status in the national imaginary of Mexico necessarily confuses the intersection of class, gender, and religion still traceable in what can be recovered of her history. In the penultimate essay, by Vincent Spina, the popular again appears in the figure of woman, this time as occupying a mythic space in the fictional texts of two writers, Mexican and Peruvian, whose inscriptions of the female as destructive and creative, as well as present and absent, respectively, enable her to function in a realm necessarily prior to established discourse.

Cultural Production and Consumption

Martins's PCC manifesto also discloses much of the populist character of Latin American popular culture—populist, that is, not so much in its rural origin (real or putative) as of some manifestation that confounds the division of labor under capitalism. Once again, in many of the essays in this collection this question does not appear to be at issue, except perhaps for Oscar Lepeley's study of a Chilean drama staged by a leftist theatrical group and based on attempts by a worker's collective to overcome the alienation resulting from the conditions of its own production. And yet, consider Simon Webb's study of the *pachuco* and the *malandro*. In both the United States and Brazil, the subcultures that gave rise to these figures arose as a direct response to the labor market in which Mexicans and blacks were being enlisted and therefore alienated from their cultural identity. Part of what Webb studies as the "uncontained energy and difference" of the two figures has to do with how each situates himself at a moment at once before and beyond "industrialization."

Or consider David Foster's discussion of the tango, whose lyrics frequently speak of a speaker's lost community: the neighborhood and, most particularly, the café become sites where identity can be seen as homogeneous and absolute—thereby granting men what Foster concludes to be "the symbolic power" that is "no longer that of the lived social text as such." In other words, the populist aspirations of tango are locatable in the loss of its world to the imperatives of the modern state, which is founded on the division between work and play as much as the division between urban and rural life. In Eva Bueno's essay on Mazzaropi, this world—unregenerately rural and preindustrial—is represented, over and over again, in films that arose as the result of a practice where, contrary to Martins's claim, the artist was not apart from the "social stratum" that consumed him. Indeed, Bueno compares Mazzaropi to the Cinema Novo intellectuals who might have attacked Martins's political position as elitist but who would have ignored Mazzaropi's cultural position as populist.

Héctor L'Hoeste, in discussing the peripatetic figure of the child in the work of the Argentine cartoonist Quino, while citing the work of Ariel Dorfman and Armand Mattelart, glosses Quino's work as follows: "In a world of infants, according to both authors, all objects are detached from their origin; everything seems to have been accomplished effortlessly." Nothing could be further from the cultural production in this volume, whose populist character is often the result of an enormous effort against hegemonic representations, as well as state policies or political divisions. The populist character of this effort varies widely. Possibly, some of it can be justly comprehended by Martins's dismissal of popular art (while none of it can be recuperated through his advocacy of popular revolutionary art). The most vital examples treated here, however, not only elude such comprehension but also contest it, by indicating how the originary sources of populist practice might survive more or less whole, despite both the economic conditions and the social formations that divide them, or can only process them as divided.

Utopianism and Popular Culture

Finally, Martins's statement is valuable because it expresses something of the utopian potential of Latin American popular culture. This is in one respect no different for Latin America than for anywhere else. For example, the last of the three "interpretive narratives" that Rowe and Schelling specify for the study of popular culture is the utopian (as opposed to the nostalgic or the progressivist), "whereby the practices of oppressed classes contain within them resources for imagining an alternative future society."[18] None of the contributors to this volume openly tries to imagine such an alternative. There is nothing here of the study of popular culture in terms of what Colin McCabe characterizes as "a way of conducting economic struggle by other means."[19] Even with respect to Lepeley's Chilean theater, what a more politicized idiom might call class struggle is understood and understands itself in strictly cultural terms. If hegemony can be subverted, it cannot be escaped; negotiation must proceed through dominant representations. Foster speaks for all our contributors by stating: "Certainly all cultural production, whether or not it speaks of direct social correlations, depends on the legitimation provided by some version of the hegemonic ideology."[20]

And yet, unrepresentable utopian moments abide in the subjects of all these essays, from Argentine cartoons about urban life to a Brazilian film about a dolphin-man. In L'Hoeste's reading, one cartoon expresses the dream of a casual, uncontested moment beyond cartography, while the other inscribes a more deviant aspiration for somewhere, far away, where all social inequities and taboos could be spoken, and then, it may be, expelled by violence. In Jerold Van Hoeg's reading, *The Dolphin* presents a reflection upon the theme of the social order simultaneoulsy reborn in the natural and recreated in the mythical—not any particular myth, but, impossibly, all. Similarly, Jim Pancrazio's discussion of the quintessentially

Cuban practice of confession rests upon an inarticulable hope of pure confession, in which vindication of oneself and excoriation of the country would be total and undivided.

At one point, Sarlo states: "Nobody is responsible for the loss of an original purity that the popular cultures, since modernity, never had."[21] Granted. But by the same token, few would deny that the dream of original purity—just to call it that—persists as a constitutive feature of popular culture, Latin American included. And there is more: such a dream may persist, quite uniquely, at the center of Latin American culture more generally. Jean Franco's conclusion about "the true originality of Latin American art" in *The Modern Culture of Latin America* is worth recalling: "It has kept alive the vision of a more just and humane form of society and it continues to emphasise those emotions and relationships which are wider than the purely personal."[22] What needs to be discussed now is the precise national accent of this vision, and whether its attendant emotions need be comprehended in national terms.

The People of the Nation

We find a last and most important utopian moment everywhere disclosed in this collection of essays: an imagination beyond nation. It needs to be described with some care. This moment does not take the form of political action within a country, either because of dissatisfaction with its inequities or because of longing for greater union with some kindred country. No one argues that Brazilians want to be Mexicans, or that Cubans are any less Cuban whether they live in Cuba or south Florida. Nor is this moment populist either; the *cholos* in Peru do not contest the nation-state with their art. As Xavier Albo concludes, in his nuanced discusison of collective identity in Latin America, "Except for the very isolated, remote, or fanatic groups, or groups in conflicting frontier situations (like the Central American Miskitos), any citizen from any of our countries has a clear consciousness of his country and citizenship."[23]

Some location beyond nation has more to do with how many of these essays variously see around or see through the country in question. Sometimes this takes place as a result of the subject at hand. An especially striking example: when two of the *arpilleristas* in Lepeley's essay, "The *Cueca* of

the Last Judgment," discuss what to do with the embroidered tapestry to
make it look happier, María Luisa maintains that it cannot be, because the
Last Judgment she saw in a film was not so happy. She is referring to *The
Agony and the Ecstasy,* starring Charlton Heston. Later, the women decide to
add a *cueca* dance to a piece, as well as an angel with the face of Florcita
Motuda, a popular Chilean singer at that time. One woman suggests the
inclusion of her idol, John Travolta.

When the suggestion is rejected, the women argue that the *arpillera* is
supposed to represent Chilean reality. However, the very mention of John
Travolta demonstrates that Chilean culture is not as unproblematic or
knowable as the women take it to be—just as the mention of *The Agony and
the Ecstasy* evokes a Chilean nation already penetrated (if not violated) by
Hollywood. Of course, it is possible to lament the presence of mass art. Our
point, though, would be something quite different: that the presence of
mass art opens up (for better or worse) a space in the national imaginary
beyond the confines of nation. The women cannot help but be influenced,
and in this space some are even pleased to dream; the woman's idolatry of
John Travolta seems all of a piece with the moment in *The Dolphin* when the
fish-man appears in the guise of a gringo, a rich banker who plans to build
a lavish tourist hotel.

Let us put this final utopian dimension another way. Few things surprised us more in collecting these essays than how little explicit criticism of
the United States they contained. This cannot be explained by the fact that
most of the contributors are either North Americans or affiliated with
North American universities and colleges. Nor can the lack of criticism be
explained, we maintain, by the immense influence of U.S. culture on Latin
American popular culture. Several contributors, especially Hippolyte and
L'Hoeste—not surprisingly, given their subjects—discuss this influence.
There is no denying that as far as television and comic strips are concerned,
in many important respects Latin American popular culture is almost
inseparable from North American culture.

Hence, one Argentine cartoonist locates his work in New York, while
another has the principal character of his strip, a child, declare: "The idea
that the northern hemisphere is at the top is a psychological trick invented
by those who believe themselves at the top, so that we who believe ourselves
at the bottom keep on believing we are at the bottom. And the worst thing

is that, if we keep thinking we are at the bottom, we are going to stay at the bottom. But from today, that's it!" However, this is the most direct or explicit criticism of the United States contained in any of the following essays. One might claim, on the basis of these essays, that the moment of the sort of cultural criticism represented, say, by Ariel Dorfman's and Armand Mattelart's famous focus on Donald Duck in order to explicate American imperialism in Latin America (a work published in 1975) is over and has been for some time.[24]

The main reason has to do with the ascent of global capitalism. The critique against it, in turn, has eroded the basis upon which any one nation can mount a confident opposition to the influence of another—even the strongest, richest nation in the hemisphere. The world is now too vastly interconnected. Corporations and multinationals have the economic force, if not the political power, of nations. Once more, David Foster speaks to a belief that all the contributors to this volume seem to share (when he takes up the matter of Borges's internationalist biases): "The point is, surely, that it must be impossible to separate 'Argentinian' culture from global culture, or from the universal cultural principle. Certain cultural icons and clusters of icons may be specifically Argentine, but it is questionable they constitute an 'Argentine' culture in any systematic way."[25]

Regarding Latin America, what to conclude about global culture, if not culture-as-global? The fact can be celebrated, or lamented, or mystified—or just postmodernized, which is often equivalent to demonstrating all three at once, as a number of the contributors to *The Postmodern Debate in Latin America* manage to do. (Anibal Quijano concludes of "Latin American identity": "It is the utopia of a new association between reason and liberation.")[26] Beverley elsewhere puts the matter most sensibly: "Cultural forms and traditions in Latin America are destabilized and/or overrun by centrifugal currents derived from the metropolis, including the tremendous expansion of the mass media, but cultural despoliation is never complete, and new cultural forms emerge that resist, neutralize, or co-opt the forces of terror, abjection, and deterritorialization."[27]

What we ourselves mean by the existence of a utopian moment beyond nation in this collection is something more modest and less aggressively theorized: the continued presence of this question—as a question, sometimes answerable, sometimes not. What exactly *is* a national culture at the level of the popular? Is it separable from the state? Can it be ultimately coherent or not? Is it the stuff of dreams or of nightmare? Another compelling moment from Lepeley's essay has to do with the explanation of Rosa, the newest member of the workshop, that, although her husband is employed, he does not receive a salary. Instead, he is paid with merchandise: plastic toys representing Disney cartoon characters. Then she must go to the streets in order to sell these things; hence, she pleads, "Who is going to buy these ugly, poorly made things when the stores are full of imported toys?" The things represent a second level of cultural and economic subordination; expensive at the first level as imports, they have been produced more cheaply by local industry. And yet, we might ask, are they entirely stripped in the cultural realm of some utopian possibility beyond the nation because solely as economic products of Chile these toys are so wholly degraded?

What to make of such questions? Perhaps the most important subject that needs recovery in a collection of essays on the cultural practices of a group of countries is the very idea of nation. It is of course not past recovering; this volume would have no license if it were. Yet one reason nationhood may be even felt to be in some danger in the first place is illuminated by the popular culture of each. Based on the evidence of these essays, do the nations of Latin America appear to be more different or more similar? We must leave this for the reader to decide. We would only contend— granted that some essays fall more exclusively under the auspices of a single national identity than others—that the national idea recurrently appears in our pages as a divided, problematic one, not entirely illuminated by being wafted into the realm of postmodernity. Argentina may provide the most vivid example. But it is not alone in its concern about how to work itself out on a global stage, where how it is influenced, aligned, and regarded by other nations (notably, the United States) is absolutely crucial to its constituent form as an imagined community.[28]

In this connection, we wish we could have included some more substantial treatments of the culture of Indian populations. We also regret the absence of anything on Bolivia, Colombia, and Ecuador. But this volume is not intended as a comprehensive survey but rather as an inquiry into the idea of nationality that the study of popular culture in Latin America makes simultaneously possible and urgent. Therefore, we do not regret that there is no essay on Brazilian Carnival—perhaps the preeminent example of popular culture in the world—or on the *testimonio*—easily the most important populist literary practice to have come to world attention during the past decade.[29] On the other hand, we hope that this collection stimulates more work on subjects which we had neither space nor luck to include, ranging from sport and music to radio serials and religious art or festivals.[30]

We have deliberately not organized these essays in terms of national origin. Instead, they are presented as a series of investigations into the problems, contradictions, and dislocations of what Colin McCabe calls the "national grid."[31] Thus, we begin with Gillespie's essay on the China Poblana, the national archetype for Mexican women, not only because it constitutes the deepest historical exploration of all the essays but also because it provides the most direct model for the concerns of the volume as a whole. The connection of a twentieth-century figure dressed in embroidered blouse, fringed shawl, ribbon-adorned skirt, and patent leather shoes is very remote from the historical figure of Catarina de San Juan, a seventeenth-century Asian woman whose specific historical valence is virtually past recovering.

The essays in part II, "Medianation," focuses on the role of the mass media in the formation of national identity: cinema, television, and comic strips. Bueno concentrates on how the regionalist, provincial stance of the films of Mazzaropi comprises a rebuke both to the pretensions of the internationalist Cinema Novo avant-guarde and to the very dignity of the Brazilians who see themselves as securely urbanized and modern. Hippolyte, on the other hand, discusses how Venezuelans have tried to adapt to their own needs during a turbulent moment in their recent history a wildly popular example of another premier South American genre, the *telenovela*. Finally, L'Hoeste compares the politics in two Argentine artists working in another staple of Latin American popular culture, the comic strip. If in Venezuela the nation—or at least, Caracas—becomes for a time united, in Argentina the nation—that is, Buenos Aires—becomes at once mystified in one urban form and displaced in another nation, in a comic strip located in New York.

In Part III, "Nation as Idea," Milagros Zapata Swerdlow and David Swerdlow make a wide-ranging investigation into a Peruvian racial category, the *cholo*, and what is at stake to the national idea when this figure

14   Introduction

becomes available for artistic representation. By contrast, Pancrazio's discussion of the trope of confession and how it functions in Cuban culture demonstrates a practice that closes the national idea in on itself, rather than opening it up, as in the Peruvian case, to an international frame. Lepeley's explication of a Chilean play about another consummate Latin American form of art, the embroidered panels known as *arpilleras* is in even sharper contrast to the last essay of this section, Foster's reflection on tango lyrics in Argentina. Lepeley emphasizes the politics of class resistance; Foster the politics of heterosexist mythologizing. Different as these essays are, each finds the national idea set in a larger relief—Lepeley because his workers, no matter how localized, participate in a global economy, and Foster because his songs, no matter how romanticized, contribute to the global imaginary.

Essays in part IV, "Beyond Nation," endeavors to visit this paranational site more directly by arguing that their respective instances of popular culture do not find their deepest realities at the national level. For Van Hoeg, a Brazilian film becomes an occasion to consider the limitations of a postmodern world view that celebrates multiple contacts with various cultural worlds through narrative and myth. He argues instead for an "ecosystemic" solution to the "tragic" moment presented by *The Dolphin*—the crisis of differences in world views, the strictly national narrative among them. Myth is once again seen by Spina as a way of mediating social relations, although his comparison of *Like Water for Chocolate* and *The Silent War* pentology finally emphasizes the figure of woman as representing a space in which the vital, resistant practice of popular discourse can take place. In contrast, Webb's subject is the cultural work made possible while tracing the inscription of the male figure, but he shares Spina's interest in gender as a transnational category that opens up the cultural text to deeper commonalities than those comprehended by the national narrative. Indeed, there is some aptness (if not justice) in ending this volume with an essay that discusses the cultural location of the Mexican *pachuco* in the United States and concludes by gesturing at how the zoot suit of this marginal male figure, along with the Brazilian *malandro*, intersects with fashions of resistance to "hegemonic masculinity" in France and elsewhere in the world.

In "Brazilian Culture: Nationalism by Elimination," Roberto Schwarz criticizes the simplistic idea of nation as that which is left once its artifical or inauthentic components are subtracted, and he argues for the pragmatic importance of the national idea of imitation, or copying. Counterposing the national and the foreign, or the original and the imitative, he maintains, comprises "unreal oppositions which do not allow us to see the share of the foreign in the nationally specific, of the imitative in the original and of the original in the imitative." Presupposed by these oppositions are three elements: "a Brazilian subject, reality of the country, civilization of advanced nations—such that the third helps the first to forget the second."[32] Once again, as in so many considerations of Latin America, we return to the question of memory. It is our hope in this volume that highlighting the significance of—to put it lamely—the larger framework beyond the national does not help those in any one national context to forget the reality of the country.

Indeed, our conviction is that nothing more than the study of popular culture recovers the reality of a country—no matter that part of this reality (depending of course upon the country) is now irremediably open to copying. In the end, popular culture in Latin America occupies a sort of middle stratum between an adopted paradign of national identity and a lived complexity of social reality. We offer the following pages as a testimony to the multiplicity of cultural forms that this tension can generate in Latin America. Its popular culture may not be more problematic and varied than cultures anywhere else in the world. And yet, precisely because its practice everywhere provokes some direct dispute about the national privilege to narrate all forms of identity construction, Latin American popular culture strives like no other to secure some space in which it can organize and define the politics of the popular. "It's been said," remarks Sarlo, "that interest for the popular culture is contemporary with its disappearance."[33] On the contrary, we hope this collection of essays demonstrates that Latin American popular culture remains as vital as any in the world.

I

Nation as Icon

1/Gender, Ethnicity and Piety

The Case of the *China Poblana*

JEANNE L. GILLESPIE

T HE MENTION OF THE *CHINA POBLANA* IN MEXICO TODAY evokes images of a dark-haired, dark-eyed young Mexican woman dancing the *jarabe tapatío* (Mexican Hat Dance) and wearing a white embroidered blouse, a full green skirt adorned with ribbons, and a red *rebozo* (shawl). In fact, this image was officially adopted in 1941 as the national archetype for Mexican women. Luís Andrade explains that a monument was erected to commemorate Catarina de San Juan as the creator of the national archetype, the *china poblana*:

> Se perpetúe en un grandioso y simbólico monumento público la inmortal figura de CATARINA DE SAN JUAN, creadora del clásico tipo nacional femenino de la "China Poblana," esa que a través del policromo castor lentejueleado, del rico corpiño bordado y el insustituible rebozo de bolita, forjó para siempre, no el tipo, sino el ARQUETIPO NACIONAL de la virtuosa mujer mexicana, admirablemente simbolizado en la subyugante y airosa figura de la "China Poblana."

> (The immortal figure of CATARINA DE SAN JUAN, creator of the classic national feminine icon: the "China Poblana," is commemorated in a magnificent and symbolic monument, she who with her multicolored sequined cap, her richly embroidered bodice and the irreplaceable fringed shawl, forged forever, not merely the icon, but the national archetype of the virtuous Mexican woman,

admirably symbolized in the captivating and graceful figure of the "China Poblana.")[1]

Andrade's description reports the proud, nationalistic emotions that this figure evokes, especially when the *china poblana* performs the national dance in festivals at home and abroad. She is

> la misma [imagen] que nos conmueve y seduce en todas las fiestas nacionales, la misma que en tierras extranjeras ha sabido levantar olas de entusiasmo, la misma que nos ha hecho derramar lágrimas de intensa emoción, al verla en Norteamérica o en Europa, en festivales o en teatros, ejecutar maravillosa-mente, con su chapines de seda, el zapateo del Jarabe Tapatío, para concluir rubricando su típico baile con el hábil pespunteo de "El Palomo," dentro el ala soberbia del sombrero galoneado de su charro.

> (the same image that moves and captivates us in all the national celebrations, the same one who in foreign lands has inspired waves of enthusiasm, the same one who has made tears of intense emotion stream from our eyes, seeing her in North America or in Europe, in festivals or in theaters marvelously execute the steps to the *jarabe tapatío* [Mexican Hat Dance] in her silk slippers conclude by finishing her typical dance with the ingenious steps of "El Palomo," under the proud wing of the braid-trimmed sombrero of her *charro* [the male counterpart to the *china poblana*].)[2]

While the image of the *china poblana* described by Andrade is well known and widely disseminated, the link to Catarina de San Juan that he cites is incongruous. The image of Catarina de San Juan, a seventeenth-century Asian woman who dedicated her life to ministering to the poor and needy, has been manipulated and permuted to become the festively dressed *china poblana*. The only apparent link between the two figures stems from a semantic confusion regarding the epithet *china poblana*. This essay examines the circumstances that allowed this confusion to occur and how this multifaceted image has been manipulated for religious and commercial purposes, resulting in the loss of Catarina de San Juan's ethnic origin and much of the humanitarian efforts that originally made her famous.

The range of literal interpretations of the term *china poblana* from

"Pueblan servant" to "Chinese woman from Puebla" causes a semantic overlap directly related to the confusion of the two female figures. The term *china* meant servant or slave in the seventeenth century; it changed in the late eighteenth and early nineteenth centuries to designate a well-dressed, independent, *mestiza* woman. Because of this semantic link, the costume of the *china poblana* that was popular at the end of the eighteenth century is attributed to Catarina de San Juan. Although San Juan would have never been referred to as a *china poblana*, she was occasionally referred to as a *china*. Her biographer, Jesuit Alonso Ramos, explains that she was "extranjera china, mogora o india" ("a foreigner of Chinese, Mongol, or Indian origin).[3] While the term *china* was not commonly used to refer to women of Asian origin in the seventeenth century—*asiáticas* was more common—this particular citation indicates a possible Chinese origin, among several others. Most sources, including the description on San Juan's marriage license, "china india, natural de la India" ("Indian servant, native of India"), support an Indian origin, not Chinese descent.[4] Francisco de Aguilera's funeral sermon states that she was from eastern India in the lands under the jurisdiction of the Mogul Empire (Aguilera A2r). In this case, *china* does not signify Chinese, but corresponds to the term *china* or *chinaca* from the Quechua word used in colonial Spanish America for slave or servant. Nicolas León, quoting García Icazbalceta, states that this term could also mean a female animal or a *mestiza* woman.[5]

San Juan's fame stemmed from the fact that she was indeed a very dedicated *china* (servant). San Juan arrived in colonial Puebla at about age twelve as a slave for the household of a wealthy local businessman. Castillo Graxeda describes her work ethic even at this young age: "Descubría ya Catharina en esta edad, que sería como doce a trece años, un juicio, no aquel que pide el verdor de la lozanía, sino el que actúa una prudencial madurez" ("Catarina discovered at that age, about twelve or thirteen, a sensibility, not that which requires the strength of pride but that which acts with prudent maturity").[6] This same ethic was applied to her religious devotion; she was also a dedicated servant of the church. The Ramos biography describes her as "venerable sierva de Dios" ("venerable servant of God"), a vocation she pursued throughout her life. In his ethnographic study of Catarina de San Juan, Nicolas León postulates that San Juan became known as *china* after she married (or was forced to marry) a Chinese slave, or a *chino* (Chinese man).[7] This, too, seems unlikely, since she was called a *china india* in the marriage papers before her marriage. It is more likely that *china* meant servant.

The second part of the epithet, *poblana,* could indicate a woman from the city of Puebla, or from any small town.[8] Thus Catarina de San Juan could be a *china* (servant) and technically called *poblana* for living in the city of Puebla; however, her Asian background probably exempts her from the latter designation. She was called *china india* (Indian servant) and *extranjera china* (Chinese foreigner), but she would not have been referred to as a Pueblan servant, a servant from a small town, or a Chinese woman from Puebla. Since the term *china poblana* can be only tenuously linked to Catarina de San Juan, some other cultural mechanism must have also contributed to identifying her as the model for this Mexican icon.

In one other point of contact, a parallel can be drawn between the manipulation of Catarina de San Juan's image and history by the church and the manipulation of the *china poblana* image by nationalist and commercial interests. Both figures have become pliable subjects for patriarchal causes since they represent dominated aspects of society in terms of sex, race, and class. The manipulation of the image of Catarina de San Juan has developed from the desire of the Mexican Catholic church to offer her as an example of perfect female comportment and as an attempt by the Mexican church to canonize the first Mexican saint. Meanwhile, as illustrated in Andrade's description above, the *china poblana* functions as an icon representing Mexico in both national and international forums.

Norma Alarcón explains the manipulation of this historical figure by the Mexican (and by extension, Mexican-American) patriarchal system:

> In our patriarchal mythological pantheon, there exists even now a woman who was once real. Her historicity, her experience, her true flesh and blood were discarded. . . . Malintzin's excruciating life in bondage was of no account, and continues to be of no account. Her almost half a century of mythic existence, until recent times mostly in the oral traditions, had turned her into a handy reference point not only for controlling, interpreting or visualizing women, but also to wage a domestic battle of stifling proportions.[9]

Sandra Messinger Cypess explains how Chicana feminists have transformed the image of Malintzin into their example of *mexicanidad* (Mexicanness) for them and how she, as the mother of the first *mestizo* (mixed Spanish and indigenous) child, stands for the *mestizaje* (mixed race) created by the fusion of European and Amerindian cultures. For these writers and artists, attacks on Malintzin as one who betrayed her people and as the scapegoat for the horrors of the conquest and colonial rule are perceived as efforts "to sustain male power by treating women as sexual objects and inferior moral entities."[10]

While the image of Malintzin has survived and become a flesh-and-blood voice for Mexicana and Chicana writers, the images of Catarina de San Juan and the *china poblana* continue to serve the patriarchal structures that created them. The manipulation of these two figures stems not only from the fact that they are female, but also from their ethnic origin and social class. San Juan was Asian and a slave/servant, and the *chinas poblanas* were *mestizas*. While the *chinas* were not considered servants in the Mexican context, the original term bore that connotation. On San Juan's part, this racial and class marginalization probably kept her from professing as a nun. She wanted to enter the Convent of the Immaculate Conception in Puebla, but she was denied final vows supposedly because she was raped in a Manila slave camp. The Conceptionist sisters considered waiving the chastity requirement, but San Juan was not admitted. At the same time, Castillo Graxeda, one of her confessors, states that San Juan maintained her vow of chastity even after she married, since the couple maintained separate beds[11] and when the husband died after fourteen years of marriage, Catarina remained *intacta* (intact).[12] However, Electa Arenal and Stacey Schlau point out that indigenous women were not admitted into Mexican convents until the eighteenth century because the convents had *pureza de sangre* (purity of blood) requirements.[13] It was most likely that while San Juan could very well serve the Conceptionist sisters and live among them, she would never have been admitted, *intacta* or not, since she was not of pure European heritage.

Although San Juan was not a Conceptionist sister, she still maintained a position of some power in colonial Puebla. Because of her good works and her devotion as a champion for better treatment of the poor, San Juan held the ear of Bishop Fernández de Santa Cruz. She continually reminded the clergy and the viceregal administrators of the laws that demanded that the native populations be educated and not be forced into the slavery of the *encomienda* system. Her efforts as a champion of the rights of the poor and as a critic of the *encomienda* made San Juan wildly popular throughout the region. This popularity was enhanced as a direct result of the literary space San Juan occupied.

Alonso Ramos's three-volume biography, *Los Prodigios de la Omnipotencia y milagros de la Gracia en la Vida de la V. Sierva de Dios Catharina de San Juan, natural del Gran Mogor difunta en la Imperial Ciudad de los Angeles en la Nueva España (The Wonders of the Omnipotence and the Miracles of Grace in the Life of the V[irgin] Servant of God Catarina de San Juan, native of the Great Mogor Deceased in the Imperial City of the Angels [Puebla] in New Spain)* was the most voluminous work published in New Spain.[14] The first two parts are known. The first contains over 400 pages, while the second part, missing the last pages, contains the earlier known image of Catarina de San Juan. The third part is now lost.[15]

It is within this mass of literary materials that San Juan becomes the subject manipulated by the patriarchal church. In *Compendio de la vida y virtudes de la venerable Catarina de San Juan (Compendium of the Life and Virtues of the Venerable Catarina de San Juan)*,[16] Jesuit José del Castillo Graxeda reproduces the ascetic's "own" words—garbled and often incomprehensible utterances, even though San Juan had lived in Mexico for seventy years. León remarks:

> No sé si por la naturaleza morfológica de la lengua prakrit, nativa de Catarina; por el muy poco trato o conversación con las personas de habla castellana o por un defecto de organización cerebral, nunca pudo hablar el castellano ni medianamente, no obstante su larga vida.

> (I do not know if it is because of the morphological nature of the *prakrit* language, Catarina's native tongue, because of the very little contact or conversation with Spanish-speaking people or because of a mental defect, but she never could speak Spanish, not even moderately, despite her long life.)[17]

Nevertheless, Castillo Graxeda has no problem "recreating" the confessant's utterances and "interpreting" them with comments such as: "As if she were saying . . ." While male confessors frequently "interpreted" the words of their female confessants, this case is interesting because San Juan's historic voice as a woman and as an Asian—her "flesh and blood," to continue Alarcón's metaphor—has been almost totally eliminated.

In one example of this process of interpretation, Catarina de San Juan expresses her despair at the impending death of her close friend and teacher, Madre María de Jesús Tomellín. According to Castillo Graxeda, San Juan reports that Christ asks her, "¿Qué es lo que quieres?" (What do you want?"), to which she responds, in the crude Spanish that he transcribes,

> "Señor, Madri María de Jesús está muy infirmidad, no muera tan presto para ella, yo debo mucho y quiero para mí, y así, lucero mío, mirad para ella."

> ("Sir, Madri Maria de Jesus is very illness, do not die so fast for her, I owe her a lot and I want for me, and so, My Beacon, watch for her.")[18]

Castillo Graxeda interprets: "Como si dijera: 'Señor mío, Padre mío, Dios mío, la Madre María de Jesús adolece al parecer de un accidente mortal; yo le debo mucho; suspende por ahora la muerte alargándole la vida'" ("As if she were saying: 'My Savior, My Father, My God, Mother Maria de Jesus appears to suffer from a mortal accident; I owe her much; suspend for now her death, prolonging her life'").[19]

Several interesting elements appear in this interpretation. First, San Juan's utterances are embellished by Castillo Graxeda. It is a long stretch from "está muy infirmidad" ("she is very illness") to "adolece al parecer de un accidente mortal" ("She appears to suffer from a fatal accident"). Second, it seems that the ascetic "hears" and "reports" Christ speaking perfect Spanish: Castillo Graxeda's hand is constantly felt in the manipulation of San Juan's words, and his interpretations make them all the more palatable as examples of the perfect comportment of women. San Juan became the perfect example of how a woman should behave; therefore, she was the perfect candidate for sainthood: she was a totally pliable subject because she was female, because she was Asian, and because she was a servant.

Carolyn Allen summarizes the tenets of feminist critical thinking as sharing four basic assumptions. These are:

> 1) that the sex/gender system is a primary category of textual analysis, (2) that every act of cultural production and reception occurs in a social, historical and economic context, (3) that within these contexts people in dominant groups

marked by sex, class and race have greater control over their lives than those in dominated groups do, and (4) that because critical acts occur in the contexts of these power differences, they are never disinterested.[20]

In the case of Catarina de San Juan, sex is the primary category for her textual existence; it is because she is an exemplary woman that Ramos and Castillo Graxeda committed her life to text. They appropriated San Juan's words for their own purposes: to encourage other women to emulate her model as a pious servant of the church without questioning or criticizing the social order, and to establish the first Mexican saint— although she was an Asian woman, making this an especially daring and far-reaching operation. Nevertheless, a Mexican saint would mean good "business" for the Mexican church, validating the confessors' and the biographers' participation in the canonization effort as much as celebrating the pious parishioner.

Through San Juan's work on behalf of the poor, she became so idealized that she came to be represented with the same religious iconography as images of Christ. This cult following grew in part from her criticism of the forced labor ranches and other agricultural enterprises called *encomiendas* that were granted to wealthy Spaniards. She and the popular bishop of Puebla, Juan de Palafox y Mendoza, another anti-*encomienda* champion,[21] became cult figures among the indigenous and *mestizo* classes, putting a serious strain on the relationship of the church and the local *encomenderos* (landowners), who depended upon the labor of the lower classes to work their lands.

San Juan's message against the *encomienda* and in favor of indigenous rights would not have made her ideas or her influence popular with the pro-*encomienda* viceregal administration. As with Palafox y Mendoza, documents and biographies describing the life and works of Catarina de San Juan were censored by the Inquisition for "exaggeration" in 1691, and reproduction of images of either of these two figures was punishable by excommunication:

Nos, los Inquisidores . . . prohibimos y mandamos en años pasados, que ninguna persona de cualquier estado, calidad y condición, tuviese, pintase ni vendiese retratos de don Juan de Palafox y Mendoza . . . y por cuanto asimismo, intervienen los mismos en otros retratos y estampas de una mujer llamada

Catarina de San Juan que ha pocos años falleció en dicha ciudad de la Puebla
de los Angeles, con opinión de santa, como asimismo parece de las estampas
ante Nos presentadas, y deberse prohibir y recoger los retratos de la susodicha,
a más de la postura y forma de dichas estampas del retrato de la susodicha en
compañía de la del dicho Obispo (como santos declarados por nuestra Santa
Madre Iglesia . . .) con insignias o señales de bienaventurada, como son los
rayos que salen del Jesús, que están en dichas estampas, guiados al retrato y
pecho de dicha Catarina de San Juan . . . so pena de excomunión mayor.

(We, the Inquisitors . . . prohibited and ordered in earlier years that no one of
any state, quality, or condition would have, paint, or sell portraits of Juan de
Palafox y Mendoza . . . and likewise, the same applies to other portraits and
stamps of a woman named Catarina de San Juan who expired several years ago
in said city of Puebla de los Angeles, considered a saint, as thus she appears on
the stamps that are presented to Us, and these portraits of the above mentioned
in the company of the previously mentioned Bishop [Palafox y Mendoza] [like
saints declared by our Holy Mother Church . . .] with insignias or signs of good
fortune, like those of the rays that emanate from Jesus that are on said stamps,
guided to the portrait and chest of said Catarina de San Juan . . . under the
penalty of major excommunication.)[22]

Later, in 1695, biographies of San Juan must still have been troubling
for the Holy Office because another edict was issued to protest the biographies designed to support this candidate for sainthood. To assure that her
exemplary life made her a candidate for sainthood, Castillo Graxeda
included accounts of Catarina de San Juan's miracles after her death—
proof of the ascetic's piety and saintliness. For example, at the exact
moment of her death, a strange light was said to have flickered in the night
sky above Puebla, and an ailing priest, Jesuit Francisco de Aguilera, was
miraculously cured in order to give the mass for San Juan's soul.

The massive effort exemplified in Ramos's biography contained many
examples of San Juan's "miracles" and religious experiences that displeased
the Holy Office. The Inquisition reiterated its ban on all documents related
to Catarina de San Juan, especially those of Alonso Ramos. According to
the Inquisition, Ramos's volumes were censored "for contenerse en él rev-
elaciones, visiones, y apariciones inútiles, inverosímiles, llenas de con-

tradicciones y comparaciones impropias, indecentes y temerarias y que sapient blasphemiam (que saben o que casi son blasfemias)" ("for containing in it useless and improbable revelations, visions, and apparitions full of contradictions and inappropriate, indecent, and reckless comparisons that *sapient blasphemiam* [that approach or almost are blasphemy]").[23]

Throughout this process, the third tenet of feminist critical thinking becomes painfully clear—that people in dominant groups marked by sex, class, and race have greater control over their lives than those in dominated groups. Although San Juan's biography was "good business" for the colonial church, her efforts and her popularity among the impoverished indigenous and *mestizo* classes as an opponent of the *encomienda* system threatened the business of the colony. This assault on colonial order gave the Inquisition an opportunity to totally eliminate San Juan's written history and her image from popular culture. The European male power structure created her as a textual subject, and then an even higher authority—also European and also male—eliminated her from the printed world because she threatened the economic and religious power centers of the colonies.

Since all documents, portraits, and images of Catarina de San Juan were forbidden, her legend and history endured only in the minds and memories of her devotees. It is not, therefore, the image of Catarina de San Juan, exemplary woman and possible saint constructed by the church that continues in the cultural text, but the image of San Juan as hero of the poor and needy. This situation left a void in the visual representation of San Juan, since all but one of the images were destroyed.

The Jesuits do describe Catarina de San Juan's manner and dress, and it in no way resembles that of a *china poblana*. Aguilera, the priest who officiated at San Juan's funeral mass, states that the ascetic realized that her beauty was the cause of many problems for her so she asked Christ to rid her of it. According to Aguilera: "Desde entonces enflaqueció, perdió el color y quedó desapaciable a la vista, aunque venerable" ("After that she grew thin, she lost her color and became unpleasant to look at, although venerable").[24] Castillo Graxeda explains:

> Era en todo trato Catarina, familiar, apaciable, amigable, querida de todos y respetada. Tenía el atractivo de su apacibilidad, dominio en todas las voluntades, porque se robaba los corazones; enmedio de que era seria, mas no con

extremo, sino con una gravedad modesta, vestida de una blandura cariciosa . . .
siempre gustó de vestidos humildes, modestos y pobres.

(Catarina was casual, gentle, friendly, beloved and respected in every relationship. She possessed the atractiveness of her gentility, the control of all affec-
tions, because she stole people's hearts; additionally she was serious, but not to
the extreme, rather with a modest gravity, cloaked in a capricious kindness . . .
she always liked humble, modest, poor clothing.)[25]

Castillo Graxeda also explains that San Juan wore the *sayal* (cassock)
typical of Capuchin monks and nuns because she eschewed the delicacy of
silk: "El manto con que modestamente se cubría, fué siempre el más
grosero, el más tosco" ("The wrap with which she modestly covered herself
was always the coarsest, the roughest").[26] Only one visual image of San
Juan exists—the illustration in Ramos's biography. This illustration supports the descriptions of Castillo Graxeda and Aguilera. The association of
the *china poblana* costume with Catarina de San Juan stems from the semantic overlap in conjunction with censorship of her image and cult.

In the early nineteenth century, as the power of the Inquisition waned,
it could not continue to suppress the devotees to San Juan's memory. At this
same time, José Puigarri explains in *Monografía histórica e iconográfica del
traje (Historic and Iconographic Monograph on Clothing)* that the fashion
favored by many rural women living in the cities—*chinas*—was similar to
that of the Spanish *maja* or *manola* (young, independent Spanish woman,
like the flappers of the twenties) who "usaban ese traje compuesto de jubón,
brial y basquiña, zapato de seda, muchos colgantes y mantilla de tafetán.
Dominaba este traje en Andalucía y en Castilla Nueva" ("wore this outfit
composed of a bodice, petticoat, and outer skirt, silk shoes, many pendants,
and a mantilla of taffeta. This outfit was popular in Andalusia and New
Castile").[27] The only "Mexican" addition to the costume seems to have been
the *rebozo* in place of the mantilla.

It seems that the only association that can be made between Catarina
de San Juan and Luis Andrade's description of her as the founder of the
image is that of a "virtuous woman," the semantic connection between
china—meaning servant—and the later meaning of *china*—a *mestiza*
woman living in the city without a master—and San Juan's presence in

Figure 1.1 Catarina de San Juan. Drawing by Blair Ziegler.

Puebla. The many differences between the two can be seen in García Icazbalceta's description of the early nineteenth-century Mexican *china*:

> No era la mujer del lépero, sucia y desharrapada, sino una mujer del pueblo que vivía sin servir a nadie y con cierta holgura a expensas de un esposo o de un amante, o bien de su propia industria. Pertenecía a la raza mestiza, y se distinguía generalmente por la belleza de sus formas, que realizaba con un traje pintoresco, harto ligero y provocativo, no menos que por su andar airoso y desenfadado. . . . Actualmente sólo se ve ese tipo en estampas, o en figurillas de cera, trapo o barro. Suele aparecer en la escena cuando se trata de ejecutar bailes nacionales; pero con indespesibles adiciones en el traje.

(She was not the leper's wife, dirty and ragged, but a townswoman who lived without serving anyone and with a certain comfort at the expense of a husband or a lover, or better, from her own industry. She belonged to the *mestizo* race and she was distinguished by the beauty of her appearance that was attained with a picturesque outfit, light enough and provocative, no less than by her graceful and self-assured carriage. . . . Now, one sees this figure only on stamps or in wax, cloth, or clay figurines. The costume usually appears when it is time to present national dances, but with indispensable additions.)[28]

The link between the *china poblana* and Mexican national identity is constantly reinforced. That this free-wheeling, "liberated" woman serves as an example for Mexican women, however, leads to some other interesting sociopolitical implications as the *mestizo* and *criollo* (American-born Spanish) societies interacted. The 1836 lithographs by German Carlos Nebel showing the *poblanas* smoking and talking unchaperoned with a *charro* reiterate García Icazbalceta's remarks concerning the relative freedom and lack of a master characteristic of the *china poblana*. Other early nineteenth-century descriptions of *china poblana* costumes are found in travel texts prepared by visiting foreigners, including the Englishman William Bullock and the Italian Claudio Linati.

On a visit to Mexico in 1837, Fanny Calderón de la Barca, wife of a Spanish minister, describes the Mexican costume sent to her by a general's wife in case she would like to wear it to a fancy ball she was to attend:

This morning a very handsome dress was forwarded to me. . . . It is a Poblana dress, and very superb, consisting of a petticoat of maroon-coloured merino, with gold fringe, gold bands and spangles; an under-petticoat, embroidered and trimmed with rich lace, to come below it. The first petticoat is trimmed with gold up the sides, which are slit open, and tied up with coloured ribbon. With this must be worn a chemise, richly embroidered round the neck and sleeves, and trimmed with lace; a satin vest, open in front, and embroidered in gold, and a small silk handkerchief which crosses the neck with gold fringe.[29]

Calderón de la Barca's intention of wearing the costume, however, was thwarted by the intervention of several viceregal dignitaries, including the president, the ministers of war and the interior, and others, who explained to her that *poblanas* generally were *femmes de rein* (unsavory women), that they wore no stockings, and that the wife of a Spanish minister should by no means assume, even for one evening, such a costume.[30]

Curiously, while the original historical figure upon which the archetype of the perfect Mexican woman was a *mujer virtuosa* (virtuous woman) who dressed very humbly, the costume now associated with her reflects that of an independent, self-sufficient (or at least not controlled by a husband or master) and possibly scandal-provoking woman. This image is not one that the wife of a Spanish dignitary should emulate, nor could it be further from the nature of a seventeenth-century ascetic.

While this image may have been scandalous for the Mexican *criollo* elite, it proved extremely useful in the business world. Another early description of a *china poblana* describes an enterprising restaurateur wearing the typical green skirt, white embroidered blouse, and rebozo to serve Pueblan snacks and *pulque* (an indigenous drink made from the maguey plant) in her establishment around 1838. The *china poblana* was often good for local business, and the connection between the costume and Mexican products continued throughout the nineteenth and twentieth centuries. Here again, social and economic interests enter into the construction of the *china poblana* subject.

In the early twentieth century, the *chinas* were also good for the revolutionary business, as Amado Nervo explains in his poem dedicated to "Guadalupe." In this poem, the characteristics of the *china poblana* are combined with those of another popular archetype—the Virgin of Guadalupe—to form an example of the ideal Mexican woman. In conjunction with the independence of the *china poblana*, the piety and chastity of the Virgin were also a powerful example for female Mexicans. Though Nervo does not draw the connection with Catarina de San Juan, he underscores the religious aspect of the *china poblana*.

In Nervo's poem, the *china poblana* searches for her husband, Pantaleón, as he battles the French in Puebla during the famous Cinco de Mayo altercation:

> Con su escolta de rancheros,
> diez fornidos guerrilleros, y en su cuaco retozón
> que la rienda mal aplaca,
> Guadalupe la chinaca va a buscar a Pantaleón.

> (With her escort of farmers,
> ten robust soldiers and on her spirited mount
> that the rein scarcely restrains,
> Guadalupe the *chinaca* goes to look for Pantaleón.)[31]

Nervo then describes Pantaleón as a daring horseman, a lover, and a worthy soldier who felled a hundred French soldiers in battle. Guadalupe, the *chinaca*, is also involved in the struggle as she treats the wounds of the fallen with remedies learned on the *rancho*. Nervo then expounds upon Guadalupe's religious nature:

> Guadalupe va de prisa, de retorno de la misa,
> que en las fiestas guardar;
> nunca faltan las rancheras
> con sus flores y sus ceras
> la iglesia del lugar.
>
> (Guadalupe hurries, returning from mass
> so that the holy days be kept;
> never are the farm women
> with their flowers and their candles
> missing from the local church.)[32]

As she returns from mass and makes her way to the military encampment, Nervo highlights her beauty in the *china poblana* costume:

> Con su gorra galoneada, su camisa pespunteada,
> su gran paño para el sol,
> su rebozo de bolita,
> y una saya nuevecita y unos bajos de charol;
> Con su faz encantadora más hermosa que la aurora
> que colora la extensión,
> con sus labios de carmines
> que parecen colorines y su cutis de piñon.
>
> (With her braid-trimmed hat, her embroidered shirt,
> her large shade for the sun,

her fringed shawl,
and her new little skirt and patent leather shoes;
with her enchanting face, more beautiful than the dawn
that colors the expanse of sky,
with lips of red
that seem so vivid and her pine-colored skin.)[33]

Finally, Nervo links the *china*'s costume with the colors of the Mexican
flag:

"¡Qué mañana tan hermosa!
¡Cuánto verde, cuánta rosa!
y qué linda, en la extensión
rosa y verde, se destaca
con su escolta, la chinaca
que va a ver a Pantaleón!"

(What a beautiful morning,
how green, how rose-red!
and how pretty in the expanse
red and green, she stands out
with her escort, the *chinaca*
who is going to see Pantaleón!)[34]

Nervo's treatment of the *china poblana* interweaves the multiple messages and conflicting images surrounding the *china poblana*. First, although
he never mentions San Juan by name, he demonstrates that the *chinaca* is a
virtuous, religious woman: she heals the wounded and attends mass. Second, Guadalupe is fiercely independent and extremely patriotic: this *china* is
connected to a male figure, but she is not presented as serving him, but as
saving him with her home remedies and her religious devotion. In this
aspect she also embodies the *mujer guerrillera* (woman warrior) as she literally wears the Mexican flag as her costume. Finally, she is beautiful and carries out these tasks in her typical dancing clothes. This is not a realistic portrait of a woman who has been to mass and ministers to the wounded, but
it makes a very romantic image of what an archetypal Mexican woman
would be.

Nervo's poem follows the tradition, noted by Doris Sommer, of creating romantic literary figures to exemplify the emerging Latin American nation-states in the nineteenth century. In Sommer's words, "Romance novels go hand in hand with patriotic history in Latin America. The books fueled a desire for domestic happiness that runs over into dreams of national prosperity; and nation-building projects invested private passions with a public purpose."[35] Although Nervo's work is poetry, not fiction, by painting this romantic heroine as the embodiment of the Mexican flag, it illustrates that the romanticism associated with the nation-building process was germane to the artistic and intellectual consciousness of the period. The representation of the *china poblana* as a beautiful, faithful, devoted, and virtuous woman helped strengthen and expand upon the evolution of a Mexican national identity especially because she was a *mexicana mestiza*. Despite the

Figure 1.2 China Poblana. Drawing by Blair Ziegler.

romanticized treatment of the *china poblana* subject, she remains in this incarnation *mestiza*, with her "cutis de piñon" ("pine-colored skin").

By 1941 the *china poblana* image had become so popular that the city of Puebla declared an annual China Poblana Day and commissioned a statue and a park to represent this archetype of the Mexican woman. Andrade describes the events surrounding the official celebration, presided over by an executive committee of women. These include a contest to design a monument to house the remains of San Juan; composition of a hymn dedicated to the saint; commemorative postage stamps; a tourism campaign to market the ten-day celebration in Puebla; underwriting a national movie starring María Félix; commissioning a variety of writings, poems, paintings, and other art works; and, finally, a regional exposition in which local industries, ranches, agricultural producers, and makers of other local products participated.[36]

The *china poblana* becomes a "spokes-model" for regional products and for tourism. This development has prompted many more commercial applications of the *china poblana*, including the popular calendars published in the late forties and early fifties. U.S.-Mexican food manufacturers used the same image: the dark-haired, dark-eyed young Mexican woman named "Rosarita," with a white blouse, often decorated with lace, and a full green skirt adorned with colorful ribbons, represents one brand of Mexican food products. The *china poblana* also appears in the Corona beer advertisements and on tavern serving trays popular in the 1950s and 1960s. What is interesting about these representations is that the woman portrayed is not *china*, nor is she *mestiza* or *india*, but very European in her features. This representation is as paradoxical as that of Catarina de San Juan as the "creator" of the *china poblana*, since the fancy costume contradicts Catarina de San Juan's exemplary, ascetic life style and erases her Asian identity, as well as the *china poblana*'s *mestiza* identity.

Though San Juan's popularity survived more than a century of censorship by the Inquisition, her historical reality, unlike that of Sor Juana, who could write her own life story, was completely erased by the church. Representations of San Juan were prohibited under penalty of excommunication. San Juan's biographers "interpreted" her words, and the Inquisition censored those words.

When the Inquisition's power waned, what remained of the story of

Catarina de San Juan was only what existed in the collective memory: she was a devoted and virtuous woman, she was a *china*, and she lived in Puebla. Since the texts and information about San Juan's physical appearance had been suppressed for over a hundred years, few people flocked to uncover the banned documents to recreate her images. Without visual images or textual descriptions, the semantic confusion of the currently popular term *china poblana* linked San Juan to the colorfully dressed, dancing *mestiza* woman who now represents Mexican food and beer throughout the world.

This is perhaps the ultimate example of the patriarchal, social, historical, and class structures so dominant in Mexico and elsewhere. It also demonstrates the fourth characteristic of Allen's feminist critical inquiry: such inquiry is never disinterested because, as Alarcón reminds us: "Even as we concern ourselves with Third World women's economic exploitation, we have to concern ourselves with psychosexual exploitation and pawnability at the hands of one's brother, father, employer, master, political systems and sometimes, sadly so, powerless mothers."[37] Now the image of the *china poblana* serves as an icon for economic interests involved in Mexican agriculture and food products at the expense of those whom San Juan dedicated herself to protect, and the process of exploitation and manipulation continues.

II

Medianation

2/*Caipira* Culture
The Politics of Nation in Mazzaropi's Films

EVA BUENO

> Any attempt to read popular culture politically needs
> to be acutely dialectical. The political cannot necessarily
> be understood independently of the forms of popular
> culture.
>
> **Colin MacCabe,** *High Theory/Low Culture*

HE FILMS OF AMACIO MAZZAROPI PRESENT A PROVOCA-tive site for studying the relationship between cinema and national culture. First of all, they occupy the boundary between this culture and any others; Mazzaropi's films are as unknown outside Brazil as they are known by virtually everyone inside Brazil. Second, and far more important, the films mark a boundary between popular and elite culture. Almost twenty years after his death, Mazzaropi's work remains widely available in video stores throughout Brazil (especially in the south), while it is still disdained as a subject for serious critical consideration.

Mazzaropi started as a circus and radio artist. In 1950 or 1951, Afrânio Catani reports, "Abílio Pereira de Almeida and Tom Payne, sitting at the counter of the Nick Bar, [were] having their habitual drinks and watching a TV show in which a comedian stood out. Right there, in a short dialogue, they decide[d] to invite [the comedian] to work in the Vera Cruz."[1] The comedian was Mazzaropi, and this invitation to work with the Companhia Cinematográfica Vera Cruz was the beginning of his cinema career.

Notice that even this article—the only one ever written about Mazzaropi in a critical work about Brazilian cinema—emphasizes the agency of the two directors, Tom Payne and Abílio Pereira de Almeida: they *saw* the comedian; they *chose* the comedian. It seems that Mazzaropi was totally passive in the process that landed him in the most important cinema industry of the time. To be sure, his participation in cinema, from this point on, was anything but passive.

First, he played the lead in *Sai da frente (Get Out of the Way)*. The film was an enormous success, and the company signed him for two more films, *Nadando em dinheiro (Swimming in Money*, 1952) and *Candinho (Little Candide*, 1953). In 1954 he was in two films—*O gato da madame (Madam's Cat)* and *A carrocinha (The Dog Catcher)*, produced and distributed by Brazil Filmes and Fama Filmes, respectively; from 1955 to 1957 he appeared in three films produced by Cinedistri and directed by different people: *Fuzileiro do amor (The Marine of Love*, 1955), *O noivo da girafa (The Giraffe's Bridegroom*, 1956) and *Chico Fumaça (Smoky Chuck*, 1957). From 1958 on, Mazzaropi starred in films produced by his own company, Produções Amácio Mazzaropi, PAM Filmes. Counting those produced before PAM Filmes, Mazzaropi took part in, directed, and/or produced thirty-two films.

For various reasons, the established critics were indifferent to Mazzaropi's work, focusing instead on the work of another group of filmmakers who coalesced into a movement called Cinema Novo (New Cinema) around the same time that Mazzaropi began his career. The critics' attitude, I believe, does not mean that Mazzaropi can be seen as the negative of Cinema Novo. Rather, their attitude can be read as another manifestation of the political and cultural structures that have made it practically impossible for the idea of the *national culture* ever to be challenged in Brazil. Because of the way the country was colonized, the coastal cities have become Brazil's political and economic centers. Inevitably, they are also the cultural centers; whatever arises from other parts of the country has to pass through the scrutiny of those in charge of labeling the cultural goods.

But every wholesale representation of a country becomes a misrepresentation. Consider an example from one of Mazzaropi's movies. In *O puritano da Rua Augusta (The Puritan of Augusta Street*, 1965), the title character is a millionaire living in one of the most elegant districts of São Paulo. However, his roots are deep in the *caipira* universe. In the story, the hero is shocked to find his children transformed into fun-loving, money-squandering adults who care nothing about the family business, follow the trendiest fashion, and sprinkle their Portuguese with English words. In order to save them, the father pretends to be even more trendy and cool than they are. The children, horrified to see their father doing such silly things and wearing such ridiculous clothes (imitating North American hippies), try to convince him of the correctness of the moral values he used to embrace. As a result, the children realize for themselves how right their father's "previous" beliefs were. In *O puritano da Rua Augusta*, the younger members of the family face a decision: they either embrace their father's antiquated, ultraconservative beliefs or will fall prey to an Americanized, senseless way of life that leads to bankruptcy. Meanwhile, the father, by pretending to be experimenting with his children's life styles, realizes the gaps in his own long-held beliefs.

Just to tell the story of this film, however, misrepresents the depth of the critique it implies. The *puritano* cannot be taken as a portrait of all religious people in Brazil, much less of all possible relations between parents and children. Whereas *O puritano da Rua Augusta* has nothing to do with race, another film, *Jeca e seu filho preto* (*Jeca and his Black Son,* 1978), specifically discusses the complex matter of the relationship between blacks and whites. In this story, Jeca and his wife have twin sons, one white and one black. The boys are raised equally, and only later, when the black son, Angenor, falls in love with and wants to marry Laura, the daughter of a rich landowner, is it revealed that he is not Jeca's son but the product of the landowner's rape of a black woman. When Angenor was born, the landowner ordered the local midwife to kill him. Instead, she took him to Jeca's house, where Jeca's wife was in labor. When she gave birth to a son, the midwife presented the couple with "twins." The revelation of Angenor's origin makes his marriage to Laura impossible, because she is his half sister. Even though it might seem that Mazzaropi avoids the discussion of a racially mixed marriage by making it incestuous, the film can also be seen as presenting an even older problem in race relations in Brazil: the relentless rape of black women by white men. As a further development of the theme, *Jeca and his Black Son* comments on the economic exploitation of blacks and also on Brazil's intricate racial tensions.[2]

Note that Mazzaropi presents these issues in a form that is not usually used for the discussion of serious matters: comedy. That is, all his films contain humorous episodes, jokes, and songs intended to make the audience laugh, or at least smile. In Mazzaropi's films, violence is cartoonish. Sex is only hinted at, and even a kiss is rarely shown. If we compare Mazzaropi's works with Cinema Novo films, the immediate—at least apparent—difference is genre. Cinema Novo films are serious, meant to evoke not laughter but thought, at least at first.[3] Eduardo Leone commented in the early 1990s, in reference to *Conterrâneos Velhos de Guerra (Dear War Buddies)*, that a serious Brazilian film is "the fruit of creativity and invention, directed to a type of public *preoccupied with national problems*." For him, the target public "inhabits the academic atmosphere, the locus of national decisions . . . [and] forms the Brazilian intelligentsia."[4]

Mazzaropi's films, by contrast, try to reach those "simple Brazilians" who, as Mazzaropi once said, "only go to the movies once a year, when a new film [of mine] is released."[5] In other words, the work of filmmakers associated with the Cinema Novo movement differs from Mazzaropi's both in genre (at least during the formative years of the Cinema Novo) and in intended audience. And yet, no matter the audience they reached, and the critics' indifference to their existence, Mazzaropi's films belong to the history of Brazilian cinema. Once that is stated, the first of the many problems related to any study of his work is how to determine what counts as Brazilian cinema in Brazil and what is considered Brazilian cinema in other countries.

Films in Anguish: Mazzaropi in the Context of Cinema Novo

Instead of reviewing or challenging the many excellent studies documenting the history of Brazilian cinema, I will merely present certain key elements of this history as a background for Mazzaropi's career. The subjects of Mazzaropi's films are difficult to present to an international audience that knows Brazilian cinema only through films made by the Cinema Novo group. Brazilian directors known outside the country are Anselmo Duarte (*O pagador de promessas [The Given Word]*, 1962); Nelson Pereira dos Santos (*Vidas secas [Barren Lives]*, 1963); Glauber Rocha (*Deus e o Diabo na terra do sol [Black God, White Devil]*, 1964); *Terra em Transe [Land in Anguish]*, 1967), and Carlos Diegues (*Bye Bye, Brazil*, 1979).[6] Their films have enjoyed some degree of popularity in France and the United States among an educated elite. In Brazil, with very few exceptions, Cinema Novo films are enjoyed by the same college-educated audience. Mazzaropi's work, by contrast, has never left Brazil, because it was made exclusively for an internal audience whose members were not college-educated.

Mazzaropi's films were always popular not only in working-class communities around São Paulo and Rio de Janeiro, but also in countless small movie theaters in the most remote areas of Brazil. When the films were first released, for many people the only time they went to the movies was to see the yearly Mazzaropi movie. Mazzaropi's work thus created an audience that *expected* his yearly films. This audience, to judge from the popularity of the video versions of all the films, now can be found throughout the country, whereas Cinema Novo films, hailed abroad, never appealed to more than a group of intellectuals and students in Brazil. Due to the filmmakers' primordial concern with the political rather than the commercial aspects of the cinema, these films hardly ever reached small-town audiences. There simply were not enough viewers (nor are there to this day) to form an audience of the scope Mazzaropi's films could inspire and create.[7]

Carlos ("Cacá") Diegues offers a more provocative explanation for the lack of broad appeal of the Cinema Novo movement.[8] Looking back on the formative years of the movement, Diegues states:

> We wanted to found a nation through cinema. We sought images, phrases, elements that would make us believe that we lived in a nation that had its own specificity, originality and characteristics that . . . allowed us to create *an ideologically aligned movement with a political-cultural programme that mediated culture and not reality*, like art, literature, and other artistic expressions.[9]

Diegues's words imply that only with the Cinema Novo is Brazil able at last to show itself to itself. *Cinema novistas* aimed to be foundational. The specificity of this nation, as they saw it, had finally found the right medium—"an ideologically aligned movement"—to expose itself to its members. Cacá Diegues does not elaborate on which culture or which reality the Cinema Novo wishes to show. Brazil is simply reduced to one reality and one culture, and (if we are to believe Diegues) Cinema Novo is going to show it. Such a totalizing view of the country still holds for many intellectuals: in 1993 Regina Festa called Glauber Rocha the "greatest genius" of the Cinema Novo, and the one filmmaker to "first . . . make the Brazilian people like to see its own face on the screen."[10]

These statements by Diegues and Festa reveal that, for them, there is a Brazil "out there" that begs for representation, and this representation is made possible for the first time by the Cinema Novo. However, even among the Cinema Novo group, there was some concern with the fact that they were talking at the people instead of to the people. Bernadet writes that even though the Cinema Novo intended to represent the "people," it ended up just presenting "a middle class in search of [its] roots. . . trying to represent its marginality in the screen." Martins takes his criticism even further. Referring to the isolation some of these artists said they felt, he writes that they "are trying to create a new language, [and] what they actually do is to speak [only] to themselves."[11]

The public's indifference to Cinema Novo's films seems to indicate that not all Brazilians see themselves reflected in their presentations. And Festa's statement also ignores an important part of the history of Brazilian cinema, the *chanchada*. Indeed, as João Luiz Vieira and Robert Stam observe, even when Brazilian filmmakers were parodying Hollywood films in the *chanchadas* of the 1930s, they were in search of an elusive Brazilianness, carving it out of the foreign model.[12] That is, the medium—cinema—deeply impregnated by not merely the techniques, but also the ideology of the Hollywood film industry, is yet another instance of an artistic manifestation that has to be made good *in* the country, with the material *of* the country.[13] In other words, if no country can claim total "purity" from outside influences, conditions in Brazilian cinema have been aggravated because of three factors: proximity to the United States, national political alliances with (some would say dependency on) the United States, and North American production and control of the raw materials and equipment needed to make films.[14] Mazzaropi, with his thirty-two films, is one of the best examples of the complex dynamics of accommodation and challenge—in his case, accommodation not only to the conditions set by the international (mostly U.S.) industry, but also by those better connected filmmakers operating from a more prestigious position within Brazil itself.[15] For more than thirty years, Mazzaropi presented an image of Brazil that constitutes another—not to say oppositional—example of the attempt to represent the country, its history, its people, and their struggles.

Mazzaropi's difference, however, is not of intensity, or even of intention; both the Cinema Novo filmmakers and Mazzaropi aimed to be part in the process of revealing a Brazil undergoing profound changes. One was demographic distribution: between 1945 and 1955, the urban population grew by 53.4 percent, and after that, average urban growth was 6 percent a year; furthermore, in 1950–1960, the number of cities with populations between 100,000 and 200,000 went from 9 to 19, and those between 20,000 and 100,000 from 90 to 142.[16] Added to the shift in population, the country also saw an increase in the urban middle classes and the beginning of an urban proletariat composed by those newly arrived from the countryside. Rural Brazil, in the meantime, continued to languish without land reform. For Mazzaropi and the Cinema Novo filmmakers both, the burden lay in deciding, in the face of all these changes, what Brazil was and how to better show it. Their difference consists in how each used the material at hand.

The Cinema Novo films, even when they deal with the backlands of Brazil, approach Brazil from the ideological vantage point of the city. Take, for instance, the examples of two of Glauber Rocha's most critically acclaimed films, *Land in Anguish* and *Black God, White Devil*. In the first, the protagonist is Paulo, a poet who spends most of the time reciting his own poetry in grandiloquent tones. The story of *Land in Anguish* is about Paulo, how he grows from a poet of intentions to a poet of actions; therefore, it is a bildungsroman and not the story of the oppressed people Paulo addresses in his poetry. The oppressed become, in this case, the mere subject of the intellectual's writing. Fernão Ramos writes of *Black God, White Devil* that at its core "one notices the revolt of the urban middle class, where the filmmakers come from." That is, the main character, Antônio das Mortes, "pushes the peasants toward 'history,' thus destroying two contrary ideological universes [in order to] realize the utopian leftist beliefs of the time."[17]

To judge from these two films, the Cinema Novo members derived their political ideas from the standpoint of an urban middle class closely related with the academic elite. Since at the time left-wing thought predominated in the university, one is not surprised at the political coalition of the films.

Thus, in Ramos's opinion, Antonio das Mortes of *Black God, White Devil,* as well as Dr. Paulo of *Land in Anguish,* dramatize the irritation of the São Paulo and Rio de Janeiro intellectuals with what they perceived as the people's "passivity."

An interesting example of this attitude is the text that opens Nelson Pereira dos Santos's great film, *Vidas Secas (Barren Lives).*[18] The text reads:

> Este filme não é apenas a transposição fiel, para o cinema, de uma obra imortal da literatura brasileira. É, antes de tudo, um depoimento sobre uma dramática realidade social de nossos dias de extrema miséria que escraviza 27 milhões de nordestinos e que nenhum brasileiro digno pode mais ignorar.

> (This film is not only the accurate transposition of an immortal work of our literature into cinema. It is, before anything else, a testimonial about the dramatic present-day social reality of extreme misery that enslaves 27 million northeasterners and that no self-respecting Brazilian can ignore any longer.)

Of course, it seems clear that, by representing the extreme misery of the northeast, the filmmaker (or the author of this text) is placing himself in the group of "self-respecting Brazilians" who do not ignore the problem. In other words, it is not enough for the director (as it was for Graciliano Ramos, whose novel the film is based on) merely to tell the story and let the public reach its own conclusions; in this introductory text the director has to distinguish himself from the audience with his reading of the story, should the audience not understand it.

However, even though the Cinema Novo filmmakers understood the public in terms of its capacity for capturing the depth of their political message, they also had to consider the international audience. In contrast, Mazzaropi did not participate in the group of cinema makers who usually met at the Cinemateca Brasileira to discuss their ideas and their plans for films.[19] Mazzaropi's career eventually took a completely individual direction when he built his own studio in Taubaté and started making movies. Luiz Carlos Schroeder de Oliveira writes that Mazzaropi prided himself on never having borrowed money from the government to make his films: he directed everything at PAM Filmes with "quick thinking and finely tuned commercial instincts."[20]

This does not necessarily mean that Mazzaropi and the Cinema Novo members were at odds about what they wanted to accomplish. The polarity between the Cinema Novo filmmakers and Mazzaropi can be comprehended as different struggles to transform the silence of the rural into a voice within the Brazilian nation. Obviously, this is far from a disinterested process: each wanted to secure the ideological weight that such addition to the Brazilian nation would mean. Cinema Novo intellectuals, however, evoked the rural peasant from the point of view of metropolitan intellectuals and, especially after their exposure to European filmmaking, from a renewed sense of authority to speak for the whole country before the outside world. Mazzaropi represents a rural Brazil that is not favored by the Cinema Novo. The *caipira* is either not exotic enough, or not ethnic enough or tragic enough to merit the attention of the Cinema Novo.

Remember that until the third decade of this century the political-bureaucratic entity known as Brazil referred only to the interests and culture of the coastal cities. The interior was terra incognita and the Amazon the "green inferno." It is no surprise that the hegemonic centrist position has gone mostly unchallenged with respect to cinematic history. From the outset, Mazzaropi's work, as well as its reception by Brazilians from every corner of the country, effectively rebuked the certainty of the metropolitan intellectuals' representation of the country. In so doing, it has challenged the hegemonic view of the backlander as only an object of tragedy. Mazzaropi's films refuse to place his characters in this position and instead strive to comprehend them in terms of their complex social life, folkloric knowledge, psychological depth, and even political savvy. Although he never produced films of the epic scope of, say, Glauber Rocha's *Black God, White Devil*, Mazzaropi's work addresses a segment of the Brazilian public in its own language and thus seeks to establish direct contact with the members of a culture from which he himself emerged.

Unlike the Cinema Novo filmmakers, Mazzaropi came from the lower class, lived many years as an artist in an itinerant circus, and enjoyed firsthand contact with the human types he represents in his films. In his circus trips, which he made until the end of his life, Mazzaropi was fond of visiting people's homes, and it was not uncommon to see him chatting with the locals, telling and listening to stories. To say that he was loved by the people of the little towns he visited does not explain his complex relationships with them. In almost all his films, some of the extras, at times even some minor characters, were played by people hired during these trips. It is no wonder, then, that Mazzaropi made his films specifically for the Brazilian market: he had an almost unimpeded contact with the audience and knew how to reach those whose stories he brought to the screen.

Hence, Mazzaropi's work is widely understood as part of a national patrimony that many Brazilians defend to this day. When the films eventually became part of a legal dispute and were in danger of disintegrating for lack of proper storage, in September 1984 Norival Milan Jacob filed a suit asking the city of São Paulo to intervene and to preserve Mazzaropi's work. Milan requested the *tombamento* of Mazzaropi's work (a process in which the artist's work becomes the nation's property), which belonged to the Brazilian people.[21]

Get Out of the Way: Narratives and Resistances

Mazzaropi's more than thirty films fall into several phases. The first eight films—from *Sai da frente* (*Get Out of the Way*, 1951) to *Chico Fumaça* (*Smoky Chuck*, 1957)—constitute the first phase; in this period he developed a distinct physical and psychological type and learned the essential elements of movie making. The frequency of these releases—1951, 1952, 1953, 1954 (two films), 1955, 1956, 1957—show clearly that the cinema companies knew that as a star Mazzaropi was a hit; therefore, he was featured in as many films as possible. These first films established Mazzaropi as a cinema actor and functioned as a laboratory for the development of the character that would become his trademark: the *caipira* (country hick) or, as the character was called, Jeca.

Two of the stories follow a pattern: in *Sai da frente* and *Nadando em dinheiro (Swimming in Money)*, the main character is a truck driver who lives in São Paulo and faces the daily problems of any husband and father of his social class. In *Sai da frente*, he owns an old truck named Anastácio and a dog, Coroné. The three of them work together moving people, furniture, animals, and even parts of a circus. In *Nadando em dinheiro*, a sequel to *Sai da frente*, the hero finds himself the heir to a large fortune. During the story, he has to sort out his feelings for his family, his feeling for his friends, and how to accommodate these to the new life style the money has given him. In his 1953 film, *Candinho*, a version of Voltaire's *Candide*, we already see the prototype of the uneducated country man—the *caipira*—who appears in most of his subsequent films, especially his own PAM Filmes. In *Candinho*, Mazzaropi plays the character of a simpleminded man who, after being expelled from the farm by the man who raised him, goes into the big city in search of his mother, has many adventures and, finally, marries his true love, Filoca, whom he saves from a life of prostitution.[22]

This search for the mother, or the search for origins, also appears in films of the other phases. The *caipira* character needs to know, first, where he comes from, and then what it means to be who he is, so that he can finally reappraise his home, to which he usually returns more aware, if not wiser, than when he left. In these films, Mazzaropi dramatizes a rite of passage through which the innocent Brazilian from the countryside is forced to face the reality of the city, its dangers, its attractions and, most important, its unavoidability. Not coincidentally, in the years when these films were being made and released, a great contingent of Brazilians from the backlands were making the same trip toward the "center," both to escape recurrent droughts and other natural disasters and to find a place in the new, modern Brazil. Most of them, illiterate or semiliterate, were unprepared for the kind of specialized jobs demanded by the urban centers; many ended up in the slums and working in low-paying jobs. Therefore, Mazzaropi's films became, if not a link between these displaced Brazilians and their rural past, at least a window to the idealization of this past. When the countryside is presented—such as in *Candinho*, or even in the 1957 *Chico Fumaça*—it can embody goodness and innocence; however, as the films constantly dramatize, country people are also cunning, intelligent, and able to resolve problems through sheer wit.

But the city-countryside dichotomy also suggests the idea of a vast Brazil unimaginable to those who never leave the certainty of their rural villages. Thus, these films represent moving to the city as more than facing a new job, but confronting a wholly other Brazil—in the faces, accents, and cultural traits of Brazilians from different places in the country. Mazzaropi insistently explores in his films the simultaneous shock of recognition and the feeling of estrangement experienced by these displaced Brazilians when confronted with these "national others," at once similar and different. These differences—such as those presented in *Chico Fumaça, O noivo da girafa (The Giraffe's Groom)*, and *Candinho*—become a way to articulate the concept of a structure that goes beyond individuals. In other words, even though these people are different, their Brazilianness is never questioned when conflicts occur between persons. It is only when the bureaucratic state intervenes that the *caipira* begins to doubt not just his personhood, but his nationality as well.

A scene in *Candinho* is an example. When Candinho is thrown in jail after a street fight, the sheriff asks him to show documents proving that he is a Brazilian citizen. Candinho, who is illiterate and never had a birth certificate, obviously cannot produce any document. He tries to convince the sheriff that the people who helped to raise him can attest to his national identity, but the sheriff insists on documents. To explain his point, the sheriff calls in other "fully documented" Brazilians. One is Japanese, the other German, and the third of indeterminate origin. They can barely speak Portuguese, but all have written proof that they are Brazilians. Candinho then concludes that, since he does not have any documents and cannot prove he is a Brazilian, he probably is a "Turk."[23] Moreover, the other "Brazilians" are well dressed and well groomed. Candinho, on the other hand, is dressed poorly; to make things worse, his Portuguese accent is very different from that of the police officers. In other words, Candinho (and, by association, Jeca) is both the *other* to the foreigners posing as Brazilians and to the police officers representing the state.

The second phase of Mazzaropi's career starts with the foundation of PAM Filmes in 1958. Mazzaropi first bought used and damaged equipment from the bankrupt Vera Cruz Cinema Company. Having repaired the machines, he started making films, and with the profits he bought new machines and equipment and hired more people. The beginning of PAM Filmes represented, then, a hand-to-mouth economy. In time, because his films were so successful and profitable, Mazzaropi built one of the best-equipped cinema studios in the country and purchased his own farm studio in Taubaté, State of São Paulo, where most of his films were subsequently made.

The first film he made with the PAM filmes, *Chofer de Praça (Taxi Driver,*

1958), follows the line of *Sai da Frente* (*Get Out of the Way*, 1951), his first film and one of his great successes in the Vera Cruz Company. The character in *Chofer de Praça* is also a driver, his vehicle is old, and his adventures take him to several places where he meets various people and where he has to use his wits to get out of trouble. However, unlike the character in *Sai da Frente*, who was an established city dweller, in *Chofer de Praça* the main character moves from the country to São Paulo to help a son who is finishing medical school. A closer look at this film reveals again the same anxieties of displacement and fear of loss of identity that appear in the 1951 movie; here again the character explores his identity not just among human beings, but among machines (alarm clocks, trucks, cars) and animals, especially dogs. How to explain this "mechanicist" emphasis?

One way to understand the presence of so many mechanical objects is to see them as reflecting the social atmosphere at the end of the 1950s. Brazil was undergoing dramatic change: the new capital, Brasilia, was being built under the government of President Juscelino Kubitschek, roads were being carved out of the virgin forest to connect the country to the new capital, and industries were being established mainly in and around the city of São Paulo. Just so, Mazzaropi dealt primarily with the preoccupations of Brazilians who were either moving or thinking of moving to the big city, or who were contemplating the rapidity of change in their own lives. The changes were, therefore, more than merely a shift from one place to another: they were moral, spiritual, emotional, and cultural transformations. Accordingly, in *Chofer de Praça*, one son stays on the farm, and the profoundly divided other son settles in the city after finishing his studies. The father and mother—who had moved to the city to help their student son—are rejected by him in the end, and they return to the farm. At the last moment, the son recognizes the injustice he has perpetrated against his parents, runs to the bus station to say good-bye, and to ask forgiveness. He does not, however, ask his parents to stay: his life is in the city now, and a pair of rustic parents will not help him at all. But the film is very clear about one thing: the ties with the countryside are never totally severed, as dramatized in one of the first scenes in the movie. In this scene, the parents arrive in São Paulo from the country, accompanied by their dog, who carries a little suitcase. It falls on the ground and opens, revealing that it is full of bones. Of course, this might mean that the dog was careful to bring with him the means of his sustenance; but it also suggests that every farmer who moves to the city brings in his luggage the past or the rural.

This film and others Mazzaropi made in this period dramatize the fact that Brazilians of the backlands who would reclaim their place in the new order not only have to face the possibility of leaving their rural world and establishing themselves in the big city; in addition, they have to shake off old certainties about themselves as members of a stable religious, linguistic, and ethnic community. Furthermore, they might have to display the same kind of ingratitude exhibited by the urban son in *Chofer de Praça*. Not surprisingly, the themes running through Mazzaropi's films from 1958 to 1963—*Chofer de Praça*, *Jeca Tatu*, *As aventuras de Pedro Malasartes (The Adventures of Pedro Malasartes)*, *Zé do Periquito (Parakeet Joe)*, *Tristezas do Jeca (Jeca's Sadness)*, *O vendedor de linguiça (The Sausage Salesman)*, and *O lamparina (Little Gas Lamp)*—revolve around the characters' search for a place in a universe the displaced *caipiras* cannot fully understand. The most important figure in this phase is the title character of *Jeca Tatu* (1959), who can be seen as a catalyst for many of the anxieties discussed in Mazzaropi's films.

Jeca Tatu was a character first invented by Monteiro Lobato for the agriculture almanac, *Medicamentos Fontoura (Fontoura Medicines)*. The name Jeca is a nickname for José, and *tatu* means armadillo—an animal that, when confronted with danger, rolls inside its shell, forms a ball, and stays there as long as necessary. The name Jeca Tatu thus implies that the character, instead of facing the new, recoils inside himself and refuses to adjust. In this version, Jeca Tatu, or Jeca Tatuzinho, is a lazy, worm-ridden country man who finds happiness when he learns to wear shoes and takes medicine to rid him and his family of worms. Jeca Tatuzinho is merely a pedagogical tool used to explain principles of hygiene and to sell the pharmaceutical products of the Fontoura Company.[24] Here, the "city," in the form of a pharmaceutical company, is presented as "saving" this ignorant Brazilian from himself. His "laziness" is equated with disease; he has no culture to explain or justify his way of life, so the only hope for Jeca Tatuzinho is to give in and adopt the pharmaceutical, and cultural, ways of the city.

In Mazzaropi's version, in contrast, Jeca Tatu is a loving but uneducated father and husband who has to protect his property from a neighbor (an Italian-Brazilian farmer called Giovani) and to protect his daughter from a suitor who keeps provoking incidents between him and Giovani. The suitor plots to reduce Jeca to misery and then save the family by marrying his beautiful daughter. But the girl is in love with Giovani's son. After several adventures, the hero recovers his land, punishes the evil suitor who caused so much trouble, and attends his daughter's wedding to her beloved. Some time later, his farm prospers and, as a final reward, his daughter and her husband come to show Jeca their triplets. So, even though Jeca does not seem to work the land, he wins with his wits and the help of others. His laziness can be seen, then, as a form of resistance to the accelerated system of production that Giovani represents.

From *Jeca Tatu* onward, Mazzaropi's image was forever established in the figure of the *caipira*.[25] The word *caipira*, Antonio Cândido writes, does not refer to a clearly defined racial type; rather, it expresses a cultural aspect prevalent in the interior of the states of São Paulo, Minas Gerais, Goiás, and Mato Grosso, and especially to a person who remains attached to old-fashioned cultural and religious practices.[26] However, Jeca appears with this name only in *Tristezas do Jeca* (*Jeca's Sadness*, 1960), *Casinha Pequenina* (*Little House*, 1963), *O Jeca e a Freira* (*Jeca and the Nun*, 1967), *O Jeca Macumbeiro* (*Macumba Jeca*, 1977, *Jeca e Seu Filho Preto* (*Jeca and His Black Son*, 1978), and in his last film, *Jeca e a Égua Milagrosa* (*Jeca and the Miraculous Mare*, 1980). He also appears in variations such as *Uma Pistola para Djeca* (*A Pistol for Djeca*, 1969) and *Jecão. . . Um Fofoqueiro no Céu* (*Big Jeca. . . A Gossip in Heaven*, 1978). In all of these, the Jeca image is basically the same: a man who wears clothes obviously smaller than his size, has a thin moustache, swings his hips and arms as he walks, and speaks with an accent peculiar to people from the interior of the State of São Paulo. Mazzaropi's moustache has led to comparisons to another Latin American cinema artist, Mexico's Cantinflas, and his way of walking has been considered a variation of the Chaplin gait. In a 1978 interview, Mazzaropi commented that at the beginning of his career, when he still worked with the Vera Cruz, critics compared him to Chaplin.[27]

And yet, even though he is ugly, awkward, and speaks a most undistinguished version of Brazilian Portuguese, Jeca weaves his way through

Brazilian history, Brazilian problems, Brazilian religion, and especially Brazilian popular culture. Some of the films comment on the growing presence of foreign films and soap operas in Brazil's cultural life: *No paraíso das solteironas* (*In the Spinsters' Paradise*, 1968), *Uma pistola para Djeca* (*A Gun for Djeca*, 1969), *Bentão Ronca Ferro* (*Big Iron Blower Bob*, 1970), and *O Grande Xerife* (*The Great Sheriff*, 1971). The first is a parody of the pornographic films that were invading the Brazilian cinema market; if the idea of a paradise for spinsters seems to suggest an orgy in which the spinsters could have every man they want, in fact there is no available man besides Jeca (who is also married).

In 1979 *A banda das velhas virgens* (*The Band of the Old Virgins*) also capitalized on the current pornographic strain in Brazilian cinema, even though the story itself contains nothing pornographic. *A Gun for Djeca* and *The Great Sheriff* are allusions to the very popular Italian Westerns, called "Spaghetti Westerns," in which the hero is called Django. Here again Jeca becomes a hero not because he either desires or is capable of heroism, but simply because the occasion presents itself and he has to take command. *Bentão Ronca Ferro* is a loose parody on the TV soap opera *Beto Rockefeller*, which was enormously popular in the late 1960s. Beto Rockefeller is a direct reference to the name of the millionaire family; in Mazzaropi's film, however, Bentão Ronca Ferro is a circus clown. A thematic unity runs through all these films: in all, the character played by Mazzaropi represents a John Doe type who does not seem destined for greatness but who, when the moment comes, finds ways and invents tricks to obtain justice and reach happiness.

Other Mazzaropi films fall into two different categories, according to theme: the struggle between people of different ethnic, racial, linguistic and cultural backgrounds, and the competition among religious discourses to obtain not just people's faith, but their money as well. The first group includes, for instance, *O lamparina* (*Little Gas Lamp*)—itself a pun on the name of the bandit Lampião ("Gas Lamp"). In *O lamparina* the characters keep getting in trouble because they cannot understand each other; the difference, here, is both linguistic and cultural. In the story, a family of *caipiras* appears in the northeast of Brazil searching for jobs. Their meeting with a group of *cangaceiros* initiates a linguistic comedy.[28] Accents from different regions of Brazil begin to sound like separate languages, and the challenge is to discover not just who is from where, but how one can tell the difference. To make things more complicated, the *caipira* family is accompanied by a Spaniard who insists to the chief of the *cangaceiros* that he is a Brazilian and that Madrid is a city in northern Brazil.

Three other films, *Meu Japão brasileiro* (*My Brazilian Japan*, 1964), and *Caipira em Bariloche* (*A Caipira in Bariloche*, 1972), as well as *Portugal . . . Minha saudade* (*Portugal . . . I Miss You*, 1973), deal with the foreigner within Brazil: Japanese, Argentine, and Portuguese, respectively. In the first two, a foreign element (a Japanese bride, international money) is about to create new alignments within the family. In *Portugal . . . Minha saudade*, the relationship between Brazil and the mother country is dramatized in the twins (both played by Mazzaropi) who are separated in childhood; one is sent to Brazil, while the other remains in Portugal. Both build their lives separately, marry, have children and grandchildren. When they are old, the Portuguese brother invites the widowed and abandoned Brazilian brother to visit him in Portugal. There the Brazilian brother discovers that, even though his richer twin can offer him comforts he does not enjoy in Brazil, the solution for his problems can be found only in the country where he built his life. In all three films, Brazil is never presented as a "pure" entity. As the films abundantly show, the Japanese, the Argentines, the Portuguese— all who have made their lives in Brazil—are Brazilians and should be given the same rights to be respected, accepted, and happy.[29]

In other films, Mazzaropi depicts his increasing interest in religious syncretism. Having dramatized the Catholic church and its involvement with politics in *Little House* (1963), *Jeca and the Nun* (1967), and *The Great Sheriff* (1971), from 1974 on he begins to inquire into the possibility of an afterlife and its effects on life and politics. This phase starts with *Jeca macumbeiro* (*Macumba Jeca*, 1974). In the story, religious manifestations are subdivided as Catholic, represented by a greedy priest who does not pray without being paid first; Espiritismo, headed by a man who uses his "powers" to coerce his neighbors into giving him things and voting for him; and, finally, another (indeterminate) Afro-Brazilian religion. In the end, Mazzaropi's character unmasks the Espiritista leader and saves the community from his extortions. Another film of this phase is *O Jeca contra o capeta* (*Jeca Against the Devil*, 1975), a parody of the Hollywood blockbuster *The Exorcist*. Here, again, the spiritual and demonic phenomenons are the result of corrupt politicians' attempts to force the peasants off their lands. The characters are presented as living between opposing forces that want to win them, their souls, their bodies, and ultimately, all their possessions. It is up to one member of their society—Jeca—to protect them and restore order.

Going Away, Riding a White Mare

The last Mazzaropi film, *Jeca and the Miraculous Mare*, deals with the reincarnation of Jeca's wife in the body of a white mare. The local religious authorities—once again Catholic, Spiritist, and Macumba—battle over the appropriateness of Jeca's long private conversations with a "single" mare, and he is eventually forced to marry her in a Spiritist ceremony. The "bride" then trots down the main street wearing the traditional white veil and orange blossom garland, followed by the acolytes of the Spiritist leader. The end of the story shows Jeca's deceased wife, now no longer using the white mare as her incarnation, following her husband around the town. He holds on to his umbrella, and descends the steps, vowing to not pay attention to her. This was the last scene of Mazzaropi's career.

This scene can be used to try to draw some conclusions about Mazzaropi's relationship to Brazilian popular culture. It is first of all an image of a scandal. It displays, by all accounts, an impossible, unthinkable, marriage between a human being and an animal. And yet, in the logic of the story, the marriage is a sanctified one too, because the mare serves as a vehicle for the manifestation of Jeca's deceased (but lawful) wife. Also in the logic of the story, the mare is "single" (virgin) and it is therefore improper for her to engage in prolonged meetings with a man who is not her relative or her husband. Similarly, according to the same logic, Jeca is a poor man who is being used as a pawn in the fight between two struggling political factions. But finally, the most important point turns on the matter of recognition. This absurd marriage brings Jeca both the recognition that he demands—as a human being, as a political being, and as a cultural being—and the recognition that he receives.

Here Jeca can be seen as a representative of Mazzaropi. The recognition that Jeca receives from the townspeople for being who he was is of the same nature of that Mazzaropi received from moviegoers, who have acclaimed Mazzaropi's work for more than four decades. But as for the other kind of recognition, critical praise, those who write newspaper reviews, as well as essays and books on national culture have almost completely ignored Mazzaropi. A division between how urban intellectuals and the people see Brazil is not new or surprising. The intellectual elite has always had access to the means of representing the nation or even participating in political decisions in the name of Brazil. Therefore, it has been the burden of this elite to comprehend a country it does not fully understand—and sometimes has never seen. It is difficult, if not impossible, for this cultural elite to give Mazzaropi's work the recognition it has long received from so many Brazilian filmgoers, unless this recognition is made through ideology.

In other words, if there is room for differentiation among opposing discourses, the urban elite continues to determine how the country and its cultural manifestations should be weighed, viewed, and appreciated. And yet, if Mazzaropi's work can be characterized as either alternative or oppositional, it expresses a resistance to hegemony that Raymond Williams explains as follows: "Even when they take on manifestly alternative or oppositional forms, [all initiatives and contributions] are in practice tied to the hegemonic . . . ; the dominant culture, so to say, at once produces and limits its own forms of counter culture."[30] Therefore, Mazzaropi's work itself forms an integral part of the ideological construction of Brazil, even when it is most ignored.

Consider Antonio Querino Neto, a member of the established intellectual elite, whose comments on Mazzaropi's films, while they disdain and degrade them, cannot completely reject what they represent. Querino Neto writes that in all of his films Mazzaropi personifies a Brazil that wears "checkered rustic shirts, patched short trousers, awkward boots and straw hat and tight suit" and speaks a sort of gibberish language, far from "the country's official language." He writes that this Brazil "winces [torce o nariz] when it sees the image reflected in the films."[31] What is, after all, the image Brazil wants to see in the mirror? Querino Neto implies that what Mazzaropi portrays in his films is not Brazil. And yet, why comment on it at all? Which Brazil is this, then, that connects with so many who see their reflection in Mazzaropi's films? Even Querino Neto apparently feels connected enough to recognize his image, if only to reject it immediately.

Of course, there is also the possibility that spectators attend Mazzaropi's films not just because they identify with the characters and situation, but to prove to themselves their difference from the *caipira*, or how far they have come from the time they resembled the *caipira* characters. Or these films could possibly be nothing but an exercise in nostalgia for a world unredeemably lost to technology, big cities, and different mores. Nevertheless, as Mazzaropi himself says, his *caipira* is neither an invention nor a caricature: "If you want to see Jeca, you only need to go to the city of São Paulo, in the neighborhoods of Socorro, Santo Amaro."[32]

Indeed, most of Mazzaropi's films are primarily seen by the people who live in the periphery of the big cities and in the small towns in the southern states. Like Mazzaropi's characters, most have rural origins, have known poverty, and have been pressured to surrender their land to banks or richer farmers. To a certain extent, even those who have already moved to the cities also share a general sense that there is an even bigger world "out there" to which they can hardly aspire. Watching a Mazzaropi film in these circumstances attests to a profession of belief in the strength of their *caipira* culture: if Jeca can make it in the big city, so can they. By acknowledging the existence of these films, as well as by watching them, the subaltern, displaced, disenfranchised *caipira*, crowded in poor neighborhoods and slums around the industrial cities, effectively commits an act of insubordination against the official culture of the country that ignores Jeca and what he represents.

In this sense, therefore, Mazzaropi's work dramatizes a complex struggle to set the terms of an alternative reading of the country. But it also represents Mazzaropi's own personal, artistic and economic freedom to make his films as he wanted, without interference from government agencies. The fact that he never borrowed money from the government to finance his films was a matter of great pride for Mazzaropi. He said in interviews that he preferred to please his loyal public. And yet, like any artist, he also must have wanted some measure of critical recognition. In his obituary, the *Folha de São Paulo* quotes his statement that he resented never having been recognized by the critics:

> O que é que eles querem? Que eu perca dinheiro? Só é bom quem fracassa? Se eles querem que eu faça um filme que ninguém assista, isso não farei nunca. Não vou trair esse público só para que a crítica fale bem de mim.

(What do they want? Do they want me to lose money? The only good ones are those who fail? If [the critics] want me to make a film that nobody watches, this I'll never do. I am not going to betray the public just so that the critics can praise me.)[33]

It is tempting to conclude that the thematics of Mazzaropi's films, like his own career as a Brazilian filmmaker treating a subject not privileged by the country's intellectual elite, can be seen as embodying "discursive resources by which people can articulate the meanings of their subordination, but not their acceptance of it."[34] Indeed, in his adventures, the Jeca hero exposes the hypocrisy of priests and other religious figures, the corruption of politicians, and the predatory lust of wealthy men; he is, in sum, the simple man, the John Doe, or the *caipira*, who fights seemingly insurmountable odds and restores peace and order to his universe just by being himself.

Perhaps Mazzaropi's films can also be described as popular melodrama. Laura Mulvey defines the form as depending on "grand gesture, tableaux, broad moral themes, with narratives of coincidence, reverses and sudden happy endings organized around rigid opposition between good and evil."[35] This describes many of Mazzaropi's movies, especially those in which the *caipira* has to face the absolute evil of the landowner whose aim is to obtain power, to be elected, or even to seduce Jeca's daughter. However, the face of the *caipira*, as well as the struggles that this face implies, transcend mere localized, familial problems. It is as varied and as mutable a face as that of Brazil itself.

What is this complex face but that of popular culture? Mazzaropi appropriates syncretic cultural materials current at the time each film was made. For instance, he borrows freely from well-known folkloric components in films such as *The Adventures of Pedro Malasartes* (1959), *Jeca Tatu* (1959), *Little Gas Lamp* (1963), and *Little House* (1962). Another important element is his appropriation—not to say cannibalization—of phenomena taken from foreign mass culture already present in Brazil.[36] However, Mazzaropi's films are not a mere collage of other films and soap operas. Rather, the *caipira* character functions as a unifying element who reads and comments on all these elements as they occur in the national space. The films constitute an extremely complex meditation on folkloric and foreign materials served up as comedy, always with Jeca as most visible figure.

We can see the peculiar strength of Jeca when we compare him to the title character of Mário de Andrade's *Macunaíma, o herói sem nenum caráter* (*Macunaíma; The Hero with No Character*, 1928). Macunaíma is born in the forest, and, although his mother and his brothers are Indians, he is black. Later he becomes white, leaves the forest, travels through time and space, and weaves a commentary on Brazilian culture and history. At the end of his life, "se aborreceu de tudo, foi-se embora e banza solitário no campo vasto do céu" ("he got tired of everything, and went away, and now he wanders solitary in the vast field of the sky").[37] Macunaíma's last adventure, going away to the sky, mirrors the final scene in Mazzaropi's last movie; Macunaíma's constant repetition of "Ai, que preguiça!" ("Oh, what laziness!") can be seen in numerous scenes when Jeca just lies down and lets other people do the work he was supposed to do. Moreover, both Macunaíma and Jeca transcend their humble origins and meet with important people in the big city. Unlike Macunaíma, however, Jeca does not have a specific tribe to which he can attribute his origin; indeed, his existence confounds the idea of origins. Furthermore, unlike Macunaíma, Mazzaropi's Jeca is not "cute": he is ugly, awkward, and does not speak of a "cosmic" Brazil. In other words, if Macunaíma is the "hero with no character," Mazzaropi's Jeca is the hero with too much character. He is a *caipira* character, no less. Furthermore, unlike the mythic, transcendental Macunaíma who can even change his skin color from black to white, Jeca always looks the same and never sheds his class character—the lowest one.

To conclude, it is possible to say that Mazzaropi's career clearly defies known taxonomies in Brazilian culture. Unlike most other filmmakers, he had no formal education: his knowledge of acting, as well as his knowledge of the country, came not from books, but from his travels—his experience in the circus, in the radio, and in the cinema. The genre he used, comedy, can be taken as superficial, unsuited to serious subjects. Finally, he did not seek out the company of other filmmakers, but instead preferred neither to obtain official financial help nor to accept opinions about his work.

At first, Mazzaropi's work belonged, so to speak, in the interior of Brazil and in every small Brazilian town where the release of a new Mazzaropi feature film was anxiously anticipated. With each new film, he became more well known; his work now belongs to the whole country and his films, now released in video form, are among the most popular video rentals in Brazil.[38] In 1993 and 1994, the Rede Manchete de Televisão (perhaps the second most important TV network in the country) aired all Mazzaropi's films in special Saturday night programs that featured interviews with actors, actresses, and technical personnel who worked with him. The popularity of such shows indicates that his work continues to be alive and meaningful to many people.

The interviews also reveal that Mazzaropi was deeply involved with all phases of his films, from first draft to distribution. Indeed, his career as an artist and as a businessman dealing with enormous competition from foreign (mostly North American) products provides an example of how artists in Brazil have had to learn to cope with the inexorable invasion of their market. It offers, too, an opportunity to study the complexity of popular culture, because such an exemplary career at once taps the profound dilemmas of artists posed between their art and commercialism, and exposes the ravages of culture and class divisions. Mazzaropi's presentation—nonofficial, extraintellectual, and unreclaimed by any established Brazilian intellectual group—reaches the screens as if untheorized and unmediated. His films dramatize another facet of the complex Brazilian identity—or Ortiz Ramos's "cultural matrixes"—in profound (and funny) ways. It is up to this generation of students of Brazilian culture to reclaim Mazzaropi and his legacy. This essay hopes to be a first step toward that goal.

3/ Big Snakes on the Streets and Never Ending Stories
The Case of Venezuelan *Telenovelas*

NELSON HIPPOLYTE ORTEGA

THE *TELENOVELA* IS AN IMPORTANT EXPRESSION OF LATIN American popular culture not only because of its success with the public, but also because it reflects this public's symbolic and affective world. The *telenovela* is the main source of support for several television channels in Latin America; hence, it is not surprising that the TV channels have consolidated the popularity of the genre, since they depend so much on them. Oscar López stresses that "*telenovelas* are the basic staple of all Latin American TV programming (day and prime-time) of Spanish-language programming in the U.S., and, to a lesser degree, of TV programming in Spain."[1] This essay will attempt to account for both their commercial significance and cultural role in Venezuela.

The history of the genre in Venezuela is divided into two phases: the proto-*telenovela* (1953–1972) and the modern *telenovela* (1973–1992). In 1992 Radio Caracas Televison revolutionarized the genre with Ibsen Martínez's *Por estas calles* (*Through These Streets*, RCTV, 1992–1994). Since then, the telenovela has become much more permeable to the changes in the genre, in the country, and in the audience. Works of the first phase followed the tradition of the romantic melodrama and of the Cuban *radionovela*, in which frustrated or impossible love coexists with hatred, envy, ambition, and passion. The subject is the premodern society and conflicts related to the characters' origin.[2] These *telenovelas* customarily avoided references to contemporary social life and current history.[3] The second phase uses the same dramatic situations as the first—the pursuit of love, success, revenge—and introduces issues of class, territory, sex, and age. Within it, there are further subdivisions: the cultural *telenovela* (1973) and the urban *telenovela* (1977), which search for other thematic courses inside the genre and attempt to harmonize these new paths and the ever changing myths and reality of the country. According to the *telenovela* scriptwriter and novelist Salvador Garmendia, the Venezuelan *telenovela* needed "to look for themes based on daily life, to incorporate colloquial dialogue in the body of the *telenovela*, because, up to that point, the *telenovela* language was so hard and artificial that there seemed to be no connection between the world it tried to convey and the world of its audience."[4]

There is considerable overlap between these two phases of the Latin American *telenovela*. A more fundamental generic distinction is that between the North American soap opera and the traditional *telenovela*. They are sisters, but not twins. Both coincide, in a general way, in the thematic treatment of family, power relations, the bad woman, the great sacrifice, the mercenary marriage, and the problems of paternity. However, the central motivations of the soap opera are money and sex, whereas the motivation for the *telenovela*, according to José Antonio Guevara, is the continuation of a family: to fall in love, to marry, to have children.[5] Therefore, the soap opera reflects an "artificial" world based on the lives of the upper middle class; the *telenovela*, on the contrary, contrasts rich and poor, good and evil, because of what these opposites can yield in melodramatic content. The soap opera's intention is to entertain; the *telenovela*'s mission is to show "reality" and to teach about the affective, social, and political problems of contemporary society.

Regarding structure, the soap opera remains in a state of eternal development. The final episode does not exist in the soap opera; rather, there are a series of micro-ends—the product of a net of plots and subplots that appear and disappear as the story develops.[6] This is how the soap opera tries to reproduce the timeless rhythm of life: by presenting a succession of events that either can or cannot be solved. The *telenovela*, for its part, has a beginning, a development, and an end, because its goal is to "solve" life and provide it with a happy ending, which is why it is easier to historicize and nationalize the *telenovela* than the soap opera.

The *telenovela*, much more than the soap opera, has evolved so that each producing country could put its unique stamp on it. These differences between the two genres can be explained both by the fact that the *telenovela*-producing Latin American countries compete among themselves for national and international markets, and that a large number of actors and actresses are ready to perform in them. In other words, if the *telenovela* does not offer an interesting plot and a good cast, it will most likely have a short life on the air. There are many other stories, other actors and actresses, available to take their place. U.S. soap operas, in turn, seem to have stagnated, not just in their themes, but also in their placement in the less desirable afternoon time slots. *Telenovelas*, which are broadcast in the evening between 6 P.M. to 10 P.M., reach a more diverse audience.

This study will examine the generic *telenovela*, first within a broad historical background, beginning with a discussion of genres that have been considered its direct antecedents—most especially the the *folletín* (serialized newspaper fiction) and the *radionovela*. Next, I will briefly review the history of soap opera from its inception in the United States to its further development in Cuba, when the elements were set for the extension of the genre to other Latin American countries. This history will then lead to the case of one preeminent Venezuelan example, *Por estas calles*, which embodies both the traditional forms of the genre and recent changes. Finally, I pose the wider question of the future of the genre in Latin America, taking the phenomenon of *Por estas calles* as a defining moment in this new direction.

Genealogy and Development of Latin American *Telenovelas*

Now close to its fiftieth anniversary, the *telenovela* continues to provoke many different reactions regarding its cultural location. Héctor Abad Faciolince writes that "the *telenovela* is the happiness that is possible when there is a lack of culture."[7] Antonio Pasquali says that it is "trash and vulgarity that cannot be aesthetically recovered; it is a genre that did not go to the school of the great Latin bolero."[8] For Marta Colomina, however, the *telenovela* is a form in which commercial language coexists with other languages, those "of the popular culture, of the short story and Latin American myths, of song—bolero, tango, *cumbia, corrido o vallenato.*"[9] Martín-Barbero regards the *telenovela* as "not only a series of products, but of matrices and cultural practices different from the hegemonic."[10] The most important of these matrices is the melodrama.

According to Peter Brooks, melodrama is a popular form not only because it is favored by the audience, but also because it insists—or tries to insist—on the dignity and importance of the ordinary.[11] The *telenovela* incorporates the ordinary without fundamentally changing its character regarding to what Martín-Barbero calls primordial sociality.[12] Watching the *telenovela* is a family ritual organized to maintain the attention of the spectators. Typically, everybody feels involved in the telecast. The story is discussed during and after the performance. Later, viewers even offer possible solutions to conflicts presented in the drama by writing letters to authors and actors. All feel affected by the world created in the *telenovelas,* as long as it raises problems they believe they have gone through themselves.

Martín-Barbero emphasizes that most people in Latin America are acceding to modernity not through the book, but through the audiovisual image.[13] The *telenovela* seems to facilitate an unmediated access to modernity, given the immediacy of its contact with what Colomina calls "the symbolic and affective world of Latin Americans."[14] Its daily broadcast, as well as its duration—usually three to four months—have enabled the introduction and development of a variety of themes that comprehend life in wholly emotional terms; as Colomina further states, "The success of this genre demonstrates that people have not renounced their passions."[15] Up to the moment of its inception in Venezuela, no other TV program before *Por estas calles* had so openly displayed a society not so much plagued by fictional conflicts as plagued by conflicts that are signs of the reality external to the *telenovela* itself.

Of course, the genealogy of the *telenovela* cannot be limited to its melodramatic sources. As William Rowe and Vivian Schelling state, the origins of the *telenovela* "can be traced through a series of popular forms, beginning with the *folletín,* or newspaper serial, itself transitional in that it was a first step whereby traditional oral themes and styles entered the medium of print at the same time as their audience negotiated literacy."[16] Rather than explore any of these popular forms, I will emphasize the most important influence in shaping the *telenovela* for modern audience: the radio soap opera.[17]

Painted Dreams, by Irna Phillips, initiated the era of the radio soap opera in the United States on October 20, 1930. It was a familiar and romantic story, a dramatic serial comprised of fifteen-minute episodes, with little action and much emotion revolving around domestic crisis.[18] The target audience for the new radio show was women; its project was to create in women the habit of listening to the radio, as well as buying food and other products for the home advertised on the program. As is well known, the name *soap* was attached to the radio drama because so many of the commercial sponsors advertised cleaning products for the home. Less note is given to the term *opera,* which appropriates one of the most elite forms of artistic expression to sell a humble commercial product, soap. Thus, the soap opera collapses the distance between the themes of opera (legends, myths, royalty) and bourgeois circumstances.

The form passed from the United States to Cuba in the 1930s, from which point the soap companies started to promote their products not just in the island but elsewhere in Latin America.[19] The North American advertising agencies that sponsored the *radionovela* imposed a series of guidelines. Oscar Luis López writes,

> The massive production of serial shows demands the simplification, the mechanization, the reduction of costs and the limitation of the time of spectacle in favor of the time for the commercial. This is the way the ideas for the programs that always repeat the same scheme are perfected: a simple and superficial argument line; two stars as protagonists surrounded by three or four secondary figures.[20]

Cuba was the first producer of *radionovelas* in Latin America. The Cuban model incorporated earlier forms such as the adventure story (for example, *Tamakún* in the 1940s); the dramatic-historical story *(Misterio de las tres torres);* the peasant story *(Desahucio criminal,* aired in the 1940s).[21] For decades, the Latin American *telenovela* followed the direction established by the Cuban *radionovela.* The Cuban influence is noticed, Carlos Monsiváis maintains, not only in the theme of children born out of wedlock, but also in the exercise of suspense, in the particular use of music, and in the characters' histrionic tone. In addition, the model maintains the same melodramatic scheme in which each episode offers a solution to some previously proposed problem but adds to the infinite possibility that the drama and the interweaving of the plots can contribute to the same pleasure that the *folletín* once produced.[22]

The *telenovela* genre has evolved and acquired different nuances in each country that produces it. At this point, it is not possible to speak about a Latin American *telenovela*, since there are several. In Brazil, for instance, since 1968, with *Beto Rockefeller*, there has been wide experimentation with the genre; in Venezuela in 1977 a similar experimentation started with *La hija de Juana Crespo* and *La señora de Cárdenas;* in Peru it started in 1986 with *Bajo tu piel* and *Malahierba,* and, finally, in Colombia the same experimental phase started with *Gallito Ramírez* in 1986. In a general way, all these *telenovelas* follow the golden rules of the genre: they follow a story in which a man and a woman fall madly in love, but before they can live happily ever after, they have to overcome a series of obstacles. The man and the woman come from different social and economic backgrounds—one is poor and the other rich. One of the characters fights to discover whatever mystery the plot provides, which usually relates to the families of the main characters. Anything can become the source of intrigues, mistakes, surprises, and confusion. Finally, either two men fight for the love of a woman, or two women fight for the love of a man.[23]

In sum, the genre has some invariable ingredients and a series of variables—either in how each *telenovela* makes use of melodrama or how it appropriates new themes, styles, and intertextual material.[24] Thus, in general, Mexican and Venezuelan *telenovelas* are schematic because the central conflicts develop around family relationships and the structure of the characters' social roles is crudely manichean. Brazilian and (to a lesser extent) Colombian *telenovelas* break the rigidity of the scheme both by introducing the subjects of class and territory, sex and procreation, and by incorporating other expressive possibilities borrowed from the movies, advertising, and music videos.[25]

At a structural level, the Brazilian *telenovela* works with a complex series of plots and subplots, whereas Argentine, Mexican, or Venezuelan *telenovelas* are more linear and tend to focus on the male and female protagonists. In the latter there is also what Martín-Barbero calls a "primary orality"; that is, some of what happens in the story is not dramatized but conveyed through exposition. Nora Mazziotti wonders whether this abuse of "orality" reflects each country's cultural characteristics or simply a desire to cut production costs by not filming exterior scenes.[26] Perhaps this is a moot point, although the Venezuelan producer Hernán Pérez Belisario suggests that the great defect of the Brazilian soap opera is the coldness resulting from the greater attention given to outdoor scenes than to the closeup.

Apart from these various technical considerations, the *telenovela* has become more thematically specialized. Now there are romantic *telenovelas*, historical and political *telenovelas*, *telenovelas* with ecological themes, and mystery *telenovelas*. Romantic ones, for example, present the sentimental problems of the classic love triangle in which the principals must undergo certain difficulties in order to consolidate their love. Historical *telenovelas* develop their plot within a clear historical epoch. Gilberto Braga's *A escrava Isaura* (*The Slave Isaura*, 1977) is a mixture of the theme of slavery in Brazil and the story of a slave who loves a white man. In Venezuela, there have been other examples of the use of historical themes, such as *Sangre Azul* (*Blue Blood*, 1979), *Estefanía* (1979) by Julio César Mármol, and *Gómez I* and *Gómez II* (l980), by José Ignacio Cabrujas.

The political *telenovela* appears to have a clear purpose, to caricature or denounce a system of government. Dias Gomes's *Roque Santeiro* (1985), for instance, was a national satire that had been censored in 1975 and was released only after the dictatorship it criticized was over. The ecological *telenovela* seems to have an even more formulaic aim, if possible, to dramatize the deterioration of the environment. *Pantanal* (1990) and *Amazônia* (1992) in Brazil, as well as *Kaína* (1994) in Venezuela are three examples. In sum, since the time of Félix B. Caignet's *El derecho de nacer* (*The Right to Be Born*) until today, *telenovelas* have retained some of their original characteristics—taken from the *folletín* and the radio melodrama—and have developed them in ways that reflect the paradoxical nature of the *telenovela* as art and as merchandise, as anachronism and as modernity, as repetition and as innovation. Of no *telenovela* is this more true than *Por estas calles* (*Through These Streets*, 1992–1994), by Ibsen Martínez, which functioned, for the first time, as a televisual news medium as it reproduced, in daily telecasts, the current political developments of Venezuela.

Reality and Its Mirrors

The "*telenovela* mania" that has spread throughout many Latin American countries is explained by the fact that the *telenovela* makes its own reading of the past and of the present; in addition, it has reinvented, up to a certain point, its own themes, its own dramatic structure, and its own characters. The contemporary *telenovela* is much more dynamic and complex than the *telenovela* of twenty or thirty years ago. Venezuela's *Por estas calles* is a premier example of how the theme, structure, and characters of a *telenovela* can be changed, how it can rank high in national ratings, obtain the approval of specialized criticism, be financially lucrative and, finally, how it can manage to reflect a specific time in a country's history. Furthermore, this can be done with a mixture of comedy, tragedy, bitterness, sweetness, and even black humor.[27]

The phenomenon of *Por estas calles* cannot be understood outside the context of Venezuela's political, economic, and social situation in the last decades of the twentieth century. The "Great Venezuela" evoked by the first government of Carlos Andrés Pérez (1973–1978)—a product of the rise in oil prices—began to fade on February 28, 1983, when the government of Luis Herrera Campíns devalued the bolívar in an attempt to shore up the economy and stave off economic disaster. From that day—dubbed Viernes Negro (Black Friday)—Venezuelans were faced with hunger, malnutrition, deteriorating health, as well as the disappearance of job opportunities, access to education, and social benefits.[28]

The first sign of popular frustration occurred on February 27, 1989, only eight days after the new president, Carlos Andrés Pérez, was inaugurated. The marginal population of Caracas, protesting the lack of jobs, the high cost of living, and the rise in the price of gasoline, took to the streets and looted supermarkets, clothing stores, and other commercial establishments.[29] On February 4, 1992, the military tried to oust the constitutional government after thirty years of representative democracy.[30] The president survived the military rebellions of February 4 and September 27, 1992, but he did not survive the signs of corruption that expelled him from the government on May 20, 1993.

This brief summary sketches the circumstances in which *Por estas calles* was conceived. Until this *telenovela*, no other television program in

Venezuela had so successfully exposed the national reality as, in effect, an
extravagant melodrama consisting of juvenile delinquency, drug trafficking, money laundering, and medical malpractice and corruption, among
other things. The plot did not invent a totally imaginary country. In other
words, it did not represent Venezuela's political and social chronicle through
imaginary characters with imaginary problems; rather, it situated the action
of the *telenovela* precisely in the heart of Caracas, and its characters lived out
dramas that were shared with the whole Venezuelan population.

The people, in turn, experienced a sort of catharsis by seeing the most
important figures in the political system desacralized, brought down to the
level of caricature.[31] The intersection of a climate of national unrest, a
mature dramatic genre, and a politically progressive TV station made possible the realization of something hitherto unimaginable: the transmission of
a "subversive," "destabilizing," and "negative" *telenovela*. However, *Por estas
calles* eventually could not avoid the pressures and protests of the Ministry
of Communications, the Metropolitan Police, the College of Medical Doctors of Venezuela, and the Instituto de Obras Sanitarias, the Institute of
Sanitation, among other private and public entities that felt attacked by the
telenovela.

For instance, the Metropolitan Police complained when a subplot mentioned that a police employee rented his revolver to certain delinquents in
exchange for drugs. The complaint was that the soap opera stressed only
the negative, to which the producers responded that "with the positive side
only, one cannot make a story." A Supreme Court magistrate disapproved of
the behavior of the character Maigualida Casado, an attorney who
accepted bribes. The Colegio de Médicos—College of Medical Doctors—
complained about the character Arístides Valerio because his behavior
impugned the honor of all doctors. The Federación de donantes de órgano
(Federation of Organ Donors) called false and damning the subplot about
doctors who provoked accidents to obtain kidneys in order to sell them later.
The Polar Company, makers of Harina Pan (Pan Flour) confessed its annoy-
ance because a product similar to theirs appeared in the soap opera as a pretext for trafficking in cocaine.[32]

At the same time, newspaper articles supporting the *telenovela* began to
appear. Cárdenas wrote, "*Por estas calles* is an intelligent and destructive
political program."[33] Hugo Prieto said that "*Por estas calles* is sufficiently

sharp and penetrating; . . . there is a certain amount of cynicism, of black humor, of calm that galvanizes the spectator";[34] and Liscano observed, "[The *telenovela*] is a good mirror for us, Venezuelans, who are so inclined to making jokes and to irresponsible superficiality."[35] Since the cultural and urban *telenovela* of the seventies, no other dramatic production had provoked so much debate and audience interest.

The Metamorphosis of *Por estas calles*

Its initial plot could not have been more conventional. Ibsen Martínez, in charge of the project, wrote *Eva Marina*, the story of a neighborhood teacher who in the first chapter appeared to be implicated in a murder she did not commit. When presented with the first filmed chapters, the television directors showed little enthusiasm but continued with the project nevertheless. *Eva Marina* would have become one more *telenovela*, most likely with a *telenovela*'s usual life span, if it had not been for the lyrics of a song on the sound track and for the attempted military coup of February 4, 1992. The lyrics were the inspiration for changing the name and redefining the program's content. The credit sequence was a group of images showing corruption, juvenile delinquency, and the contrast between wealth and poverty in Venezuela. The song lyrics are:

> Por estas calles la compasión ya no aparece,
> y la piedad hace rato que se fue de viaje;
> cuando se iba la perseguía la policía;
> oye, conciencia, mejor te escondes con la paciencia.

> (Through these streets compassion no longer appears,
> And pity has disappeared for some time already;
> It left persecuted by the police;
> Listen, conscience, you'd better take refuge with patience.)

"We are not going to show anything new," remarked Ibsen Martínez, "but I am sure that the spectator will like to see how a judge is bribed and to see that somebody surprises him and says: 'You are corrupt.' The idea is for everybody to have a catharsis."[36] And here was the first original contribution of *Por estas calles*: crossing politics with love, journalism with melo-drama, news with jokes. *Eva Marina* was never aired, and in its place *Por estas calles* was born. The *telenovela* became a panoramic mural of Venezue-lan life that oscillated between critical news events, social and political denunciations, and a sentimental plot.[37] If the logic of North American films of the Great Depression, the Cinema Novo of Brazil, and the cinema of the 1940s in Mexico was to show people's misery, it was felt, why could not the Venezuelan *telenovela* do it too?[38]

The plot of *Por estas calles* does not rest, as Tulio Hernández points out, "in the eternal love triangle, but in a net of interconnected conflicts that are similar to the Brazilian model."[39] The *telenovela* divides its universe into three areas: the good, the bad, and the hybrid. In the first category, there is the protagonist couple: Eurídice Briceño, the victim, a noble, pure and hon-est young woman, like all female protagonists; Alvaro Infante, the agent of justice, a lawyer with solid moral principles and a high sense of justice; Eloína Rangel, the protagonist's best friend, a humble nurse, ignorant about romantic subjects; and finally, Eudomar Padilla, a neighborhood ras-cal who fights to move ahead in the social order.

The unexpected charisma of Eloína, Eudomar, and another character not of this group, Arístides Valerio, makes the protagonist couple uninter-esting, and they disappear from the story; worse still, the hero is murdered early in the series, an unacceptable irreverence in a traditional *telenovela*. Perhaps it can be argued that this murder happens in the story because the plot is not based on the love pursuits of the protagonists, but instead upon the development of political events (especially the caricaturing of a type of Venezuelan who appeared with the democratic regime). Eudomar, for instance, is a stereotype of a marginal young man whose only possessions are his body and his capacity to conquer—and to fool—women; similarly, Valerio is a professional corrupted by forces (specifically having to to with the petroleum boom of the 1970s) beyond his control, and Eloína is the stereotype of the half-clever, half-naive woman who does not know how to resolve the conflicts of her love life.

On the other hand, Elisa Gil and Natalio Vega represent the second group. Elisa caricaturizes the female villain of the proto-*telenovela*; instead of indignation, Elisa's cunning provokes laughter. Perhaps the laughter is the mere reflection of situation in the streets in a country persecuted by so much violence. Natalio Vega, in his turn, seems to be a more recent type of villain, perhaps because he is a policeman rather than an aristocrat.

The third group of characters fall into the hybrid category, because each is a combination of positive and negative, the real and the fictitious. Arístides Valerio, an unscrupulous doctor, is a nouveau riche social climber whose popular appeal and Don Juan techniques neutralize his amorality; Mauro Sarría Vélez is a drug dealer, inflexible and tender at the same time, who falls in love with the protagonist and works for her community; Marco Aurelio Orellana (nicknamed "Don Chepe"), is the figure of the demagogic and corrupt politician; and Luisa Briceño ("Lucha"), is an efficient businesswoman who manages prostitutes. Each one of these characters represents the transition between the "Great Venezuela" and the "Poor Venezuela," or the historical phase during which Venezuelans corrupted themselves and lost their ethical and moral values. Besides the characters in these three groups there is Don Lengua, a character who appears every day at the end of the episode and comments on the country's problems. This character performs the function of a newspaper editorial: he defines his position about the leading items of the day, especially political ones. Don Lengua thus becomes the "father" who scolds the political elite.

The reception of the *telenovela* demonstrated the complex mediations that circulate between the message and its audience. One critic wrote, "Eloína fascinates me because she is similar to me and to all the other Venezuelan women in her purity and ingenuity." Another declared: "I identify with [Natalio Vega] because I would like to seize justice with my own hands." A third remarked: "I like the fact that they took the story to the street, not just in the plot but also in the production," and a fourth said: "All the problems of my neighborhood are there; . . . [*Por estas calles*] is a very funny *telenovela*. . . . Now I read the newspaper every day to see whom the story is talking about."[40] *Por estas calles*, concludes an article in the magazine *Producto,*

> became the communication phenomenon of the latest years: people speak like
> its characters, admire them, identify with them, suffer with their problems,
> relate [them] to daily events, and even use the *telenovela* as a center of infor-
> mation about what goes on in the nation.[41]

It is quite possible that one reason for the success of the *telenovela* in recent years is that it has developed enough to enable it to become both a reflection and a product of social and political changes in the country. Ibsen Martínez's story took a snapshot of a Venezuela polarized between wealth and poverty.[42] The organization of the narrative did not make use of the classic model in which the existence of a secret or a mystery allows the continuation of the story. The important thing in this story was its impact on Venezuelan news broadcasts. Now, instead of the traditional *telenovela* technique, whereby each chapter ends with a character threatening another with a gun (even though usually nothing comes of the threat), in *Por estas calles* a character was assassinated when the public did not expect it.[43] Instead of building suspense at the end of each episode, endings were often an abrupt cut to another topic, since the series was based not on creating dramatic tricks to keep the viewers' attention, but on current news items, which might last two or three days and then disappear.

The characters had real and identifiable referents. Marco Aurelio Orellana (Don Chepe), was a composite caricature of two former Venezuelan presidents, Jaime Lusinchi and Carlos Andrés Pérez, and their respective "private female secretaries." When President Pérez announced his resignation on the TV news, Don Chepe (the fictional character) read a similar speech and resigned his job in the fictional realm of the the *telenovela* the following day. At the time, a story became current in Venezuela about how the popularity of the *telenovela* contributed to Pérez's resignation. According to Alberto Giarroco, producer of *Por estas calles,* the president "met with part of his cabinet and asked them for an excuse to censor the *telenovela.* 'These people are irresponsible. The *telenovela* is an invitation to violence.'" A member of his cabinet said that censoring the *telenovela* could cause disturbances in the country, and there was even the possibility of riots.[44]

However, this mixture of melodrama and news dramatized by *Por estas calles* became weaker after eight months when Ibsen Martínez decided to leave the project. After his departure in February 1993, the group of writers who replaced him began to enrich the plot as it evolved with their own experience and own vision of the world. Carlos Pérez, for instance, decided to have the characters under his responsibility venture out into the neighborhoods of Caracas; accordingly, these characters began speaking and thinking like marginal Venezuelans. To make the characters even more believable, Pérez developed a subplot and hired a group of real delinquents with no dramatic training to play the characters. Thus, this segment of the story acquired an almost testimonial character.

Perhaps even more radically, *Por estas calles*, unlike the traditional *telenovela*, substituted a political and national plot in place of the familiar domestic, sentimental plot. Lost children, the search for identity, or social differences were no longer an impediment to happiness. The only thing that mattered was the collective life in Venezuela. In fact, this can be said to be the great legacy of *Por estas calles* to Venezuela. However, at some point, the commercial exigencies of the *telenovelas* took over. *Por estas calles* became so popular that it reached a plateau in terms of how much revenue it could obtain. The producers, eager to attract more and better paying supporters, encouraged the writers to immerse the story in the old melodramatic polarities; it became populist and demagogic, showing what people wanted to see: corruption versus honesty; downtown versus marginal neighborhoods; hope versus despair. Eventually, the audience grew tired of the show. Nonetheless, the influence of *Por estas calles* can be seen in a number of others, such as *Peligrosa* (*Dangerous*, 1994), *El paseo de la gracia de Dios* (*The Promenade of God's Grace*, 1994), *Amores de fin de siglo* (*Loves of the End of the Century*, 1995), for example, began to work with the contrasts in the country. In addition, Mexican and Peruvian *telenovela* producers started to create *telenovelas* with similar aspirations.[45]

The Legacy of the *Culebrón*

The truculence and the unnecessary lengthening of the plot—a necessity if *telenovelas* were to be successful—once inspired critics of the genre to call it, disparagingly, the *culebrón* (big snake). In 1953, an anonymous letter to a newspaper first used the term because, the writer maintained, *telenovelas* were an offense to good taste, and also tiresome, poorly written, and poorly acted.[46] Nowadays, the letter stated, "*culebrón* has lost its negative connotation and has become synonymous with the term *telenovela*." Even García Márquez used the word: "Hay que hacer culebrones, pero de buena calidad" ("We have got to [write] *culebrones*, but good-quality ones").[47]

Of course, *Por estas calles* is not an example of the traditional *culebrón*. Rather, it can be seen as an innovation, a refreshing change in subject matter and the way of presenting it. However, even though they were once the moving force behind this *telenovela*, its denunciations eventually lost their force, as all news reporting does when then the original events no longer matter. And yet *Por estas calles* has become an important historical document regarding the situation of the country and its inhabitants at a specific time. The plot and its characters, on the other hand, could be summoned back someday, as Don Lengua—the crazy philosopher of the story—threatened to do at the conclusion of the last episode.

The *telenovela* ended with a visual metaphor. While Eloína and Eudomar remember their unstable relationship, several trucks start up toward the Moscú neighborhood, carrying the television company's technical and artistic personnel, apparently about to begin recording a new episode of the story whose final episode has just been shown. This *telenovela* is thus open-ended, because it does not offer any closure. In other words, *Por estas calles* ends, as all *telenovelas* must, while pointing out that the stories it has presented will continue in the world. For this reason, the *telenovela* could theoretically continue eternally denouncing the current social, economic, and political problems of Venezuela. Don Lengua concludes his commentaries by remarking that only when all the country's problems are solved can *Por estas calles* have an end. After summarizing his views about corruption in Venezuela and the need to combat the unequal distribution of privileges, Don Lengua finishes by saying that he cannot tell his audience that the series is ended: "I prefer to say: now you be the actors."

But an intensive viewing of the whole *telenovela* shows that the mixture of melodrama and dramatized news did not always maintain its high pitch of popularity; in fact, the feeling of urgency in *Por estas calles* began to dissipate after the first eight months. In February 1993 the original writer, Ibsen Martínez, decided to abandon the project, not only because of commercial considerations, which required lengthening the *telenovela*, but also because of the program's relationship to the real-life events it purported to represent. For him, *Por estas calles* had become an inconsequential caricature of the initial plan. In his words, "What at first was new, or what was a novel proposition, has become routine and banal; . . . [all] has sunk into the muddy province of ratings, has succumbed to the myopia of the sales department and the carelessness of certain types of executives."[48] In a letter published in a newspaper Martínez asked, "How could our *telenovela* compete with a real air battle that all people from Caracas followed live?"[49] He also recognized that his story had begun to turn in on itself and the characters had became trapped in a neurotic automatism. They "do not learn, do not change; they do nothing besides provide gratification to the worst instincts of the audience."[50]

The relationship between drama and life is a complicated matter. On the one hand, one can say that the *telenovela*'s purpose is not to import "real life" into the genre, but to heighten real life. José Ignacio Cabrujas defines the *telenovela*'s purpose as follows: "In the modest Latin American cultural landscape, the *telenovela* tries to magnify, catapult, exaggerate, hyperbolize the feelings in order to make them absolutely drastic and disturbing for the mass." Furthermore, he argues,

> how can we believe that a person would turn the TV on to see reality? How can we believe that a fictional show can substitute for a news show? This is absurd. Nowadays there are news broadcasts that are sufficiently melodramatic, [which try to be] convincing in order to show us some item of news. . . . The *telenovela* could focus on reality . . . as a texture, as a detail, as a style.[51]

On the other hand, the development of *Por estas calles* proves that more life can be imported into art than one would think. The very end of the *telenovela* can be understood as playing out the energies that determined both the creation and the reception of the story. In their place, the logic of the production of the *telenovela*—after all, a product to be sold—took over. In their discussion of the *telenovela*, Rowe and Schelling state this dynamic as follows:

> Popular reception thus already implies a tendency to resignification, which by mobilizing popular experiences and memories produces a margin of control, not over the ownership of media (this is the province of alternative media), but over their social meaning.[52]

In the case of *Por estas calles*, either the producers had lost the control they needed in order to keep the production going, or Venezuelan public life had become so entangled in the plot that the *telenovela* became indistinguishable from news broadcasts. As if to testify to this slippage into almost trans-

parent topicality, *Por estas calles* did not have much success in the few countries that imported it. Its plot was so interwoven with national events in
Venezuela as to be, in Cabruja's terms, at once too remote for melodrama
and too whole for reality. The Spanish channel Antena 3 discontinued the
show after one week. The mediations between the public and the message,
as Martín-Barbero stresses, play an important role in decodifying and
appropriating these messages. In one respect, *Por estas calles* was transpar-
ently *foreign* to foreign audiences, while in another respect, it was opaque.

How can we judge this *telenovela*, then? It started as if it was a truly revolutionary innovation that even threatened the political life of the country,
but it concluded by becoming just another example of the old formulas. In
one respect, *Por estas calles* may constitute a vivid example of what its producer referred to as the cyclical nature of the *telenovela* genre: "When
everybody thinks that the old schemes are gone, the new proposition also
exhausts itself and it becomes the traditional *telenovela*."[53]

In another respect, however, *Por estas calles* is a striking example of a
very strong Latin American cultural trait: the concomitant use of the old
and the new, sometimes at the same time. It thus passed from an avant-
garde phenomenon to a mere conventional exercise. More to the point,
what does *Por estas calles* represent in terms of Venezuelan *telenovelas* and
popular culture? Utilizing old tricks to tell new stories and the most sophisticated technological apparatuses to recreate the country as fiction, *Por
estas calles* illustrates how the genre in Latin America combines the following heterogeneous elements: the anachronistic and the modern, the melodramatic and the topical, and the commercially produced and the popularly
received. *Por estas calles* could only be about Venezuela, but the *telenovela*
could have been made anywhere in Latin America.

4/ From *Mafalda* to *Boogie*

The City and Argentine Humor

HECTOR D. FERNÁNDEZ L'HOESTE

THERE HAS BEEN MUCH CHANGE IN ARGENTINA DURING
the last decades. Narratives born under a fragile political equilibrium,
rife with the neglect of civil liberties and the predatory execution of
neoliberal policies, are bound to illustrate social and economic upheaval. It
is to be expected that graphic humor should mimic prevailing social
dynamics as well as acknowledge the tacit exchanges of power throughout
society. Given these developments, I propose to study a geographic shift in
Argentine graphic humor: the change from a typical Buenos Aires vicinity
in *Mafalda*, the famed comic strip by Joaquín Salvador Lavado, to the New
York surroundings of *Boogie el aceitoso* (Boogie the Greaser) by the
renowned cartoonist Roberto Fontanarrosa.

This shift happens, in part, as a result of Argentina's transition from a
military dictatorship to its first experience with democracy in the 1980s.
Granted the fluctuating political environment of this era, urban space
marks a crucial site for the consolidation as well as the contestation of dominant ideology. Each of the comic strips I will examine represents a cultural
practice that addresses domestic change by mocking power but also by
adapting and conforming to it in subtle, devious ways. Whether in order to
survive in an atmosphere of censorship or to exist entirely apart from it,
each strip entails a careful recreation of urban space.

First, a word about the genre. The comic strip, developed by North
American graphic artists in the early twentieth century, has achieved broad

popularity in Latin America during the past forty years, largely through the thriving urban press. As cities grew, newspapers seized whatever was within their reach to ensure an audience. An important source of appeal was the comic strip. Mexican, Brazilian, and Argentine comic artists, among others, attracted audiences through an intricate process. From the first drafts by the Mexican humorist Rius, a forerunner in the solidification of the genre, to more recent postmodern attempts, the trajectory of the comic strip in Latin America has been marked by achievement and failure.[1] In time, many strips became regular features in the press, and their widespread distribution brought commercial success. The Argentine artist-authors Joaquín Salvador Lavado (better known as Quino)[2] and Roberto Fontanarrosa[3] are major practitioners of the genre, comparable in popularity to Scott Adams, the creator of *Dilbert,* and Garry Trudeau, of *Doonesbury* fame. Their art is dissimilar, but their obsessions, together with their corresponding approaches, represent a distinct course in contemporary Latin American popular culture.

A measure of the importance of the comic strip lies in its subversive potential. In *De los medios a las mediaciones,* Jesús Martín-Barbero proposes the study of the unfolding or the development of a cultural subject.[4] The comic strip genre, according to Martín-Barbero, is premised on the work of North American social theoreticians of the forties and fifties, a group that conceived of expressions of mass culture as assertions of hope for a democratic society. For Martín-Barbero, the comic strip is a vestige of mass culture, where the term *mass* implies that society is a dispersed community of isolated individuals—that is to say, individuals who live in an urban space.

My argument is that the graphic treatment of space, as illustrated in the work of these two artists, entails ideological statements that both mirror accepted social conditions as well as undermine and subvert the established discourses (whether favored or imposed) about them. Albeit thwarted by irony and distance, respectively, the characters created by Quino and Fontanarrosa serve in a playful, selective manner either to cover or reveal ideology. My interest lies as much in what they presume to accomplish as in the formal means through which they accomplish it.

In Quino's case, the bulk of the *Mafalda* comic strip was produced during the Onganía and Lanusse regimes of 1966–1970 and 1971–1973. Hence, it is reasonable to assume that much of the strip was influenced by self-censorship as well as motivated by a desire to formulate criticism within the limits permitted; Quino's strategy is thus marked by an air of pretense and duplicity, although the outcome basically reinforces prevailing hegemonic forces, treated as inescapable and irremediable. Fontanarrosa, on the other hand, although his first print dates back to 1974, was doubtless simultaneously favored and hindered by the arrival of democracy in 1973—favored by the hypothetical end of censorship, hindered by the absence of an explicit target for criticism. Fontanarrosa's approach becomes the opposite of Quino's: Fontanarrosa never pretends to sketch a full working order but instead thrives upon the failures and shortcomings of the system. In his work, the bourgeois mentality reproduced and finally affirmed by Quino is instead laid bare, discarded, and fragmented. As a result, Fontanarrosa proposes the inescapable deficiencies of society as suitable locations for potential cultural resistance.

The Discreet Charm of Argentine Suburbia: *Mafalda*

The street, in Quino's work, is a spectacular site that exposes a number of subjects to mockery: nationalism ("Are you searching for our national roots?" inquires Mafalda of a pair of workmen trying to locate a gas leak); torture ("What confession are you trying to get from this poor street?" asks the child when she comes upon a road crew [815]); inflation and the state's repressive techniques ("The little stick to dent ideologies?" replies a puzzled police officer, having heard Mafalda describe his club [1207]).[5] Quino takes the street by force, raising his survey of its daily activities to the status of an inquiry into national identity. Furthermore, he changes an ordinary component in the routine of a large city into a reminder of the abuses and betrayals of the system.

For Resnick and Speck, much of Quino's work has a classic narrative structure: first, an established equilibrium is interrupted; second, the conflict sharpens, with the consequent arrival of a climax; and finally, a resolution is obtained, generating a new equilibrium in terms different from those at the beginning.[6] However, the characters' peripatetic wandering through the streets of Buenos Aires lends another kind of structure. *Mafalda* episodes follow four basic schemes unnoticed by Resnick and Speck. After a rearrangement of the narrative structure, a likely result may be expected in the area of graphic syntax. The four basic patterns are as follows: (1) a stationary character observes the passers-by, generating possibilities for criticism; (2) a character wanders till he or she spots a specific target for criticism; (3) a protagonist formulates his or her ideas in an offhand fashion and surprises a nearby spectator; (4) a character juxtaposes several scenes or situations to make a point.

Unfortunately, these dynamics serve as a correlation to an analytical framework supporting cultural dependency. The world of *Mafalda* is plagued by the paranoia of the periphery. To Quino, it is clear that the modernity of Buenos Aires is (as Beatriz Sarlo calls it) a modernity of the periphery. Although Quino means to make a critique of the developed world, the arguments involved in *Mafalda* suggest a peripheral mentality, ratifying the power of a governing center. Hence, one of the characters, Susanita, states with considerable irony, "Nothing is good, unless it is widely accepted in Europe or the United States" (204). Passion for the Beatles, for example, links *Mafalda* with an imported cultural model. The child would rather nourish herself with a formula prescribed by the metropolis—a trait typical of the youth of the petit bourgeoise, who recognize in pop culture an opportunity to identify with the markets of industrialized nations.

In search of a defining moment, Quino sometimes issues mild critiques. Even the cartographic disquisitions of the smallest member of the group, Libertad (the onomastic implication is rather obvious) appear as fallacies—mocking their provincial views. As the tiny child declares, "The idea that the northern hemisphere is at the top is a psychological trick invented by those who believe themselves at the top, so that we who believe ourselves at the bottom keep on believing we are at the bottom. And the worst thing is that, if we keep on thinking we are at the bottom, we are going to stay at the bottom. But from today, that's it!" (1795). Her argument pretends to question the logic of how maps represent geographic location without questioning the logic behind the representation itself, which is not only marginal in global terms but petit-bourgeois in social terms.

In speaking of the rhetoric of walking, Michel de Certeau refers to the path of the pedestrian as a spatial practice that weaves an order.[7] For de Certeau, walking is akin to speech in that it manages to enunciate a meaningful system. Just so, by following the children through their erratic wanderings, Quino emphasizes the tranquil parks, spacious avenues, and immaculate sidewalks of Buenos Aires, the massive apartment buildings, public schools, neighborhood stores—spaces that remain uncontested, while the opinionated gang of children pretend to dispute the way of life of the inhabitants they see around them. Thus, by substantiating the comfortable idea of bourgeois space, *Mafalda* validates the dictates of a hegemony it pretends to challenge.

Quino defines the roles of the characters with a similarly narrow design in mind, whereby the national imaginary is everywhere besieged by multinational corporations, foreignisms, alienation, and pop culture, somewhat in the style of the critiques expressed by Dorfman and Mattelart in *Para leer al Pato Donald (How to Read Donald Duck)*.[8] In their discussion, Dorfman and Mattelart repeatedly discover the all-powerful hand of U.S. imperialism in almost every Disney figure. On occasions, Quino appropriates exactly this kind of reasoning, producing an identical impression. His goal, however, is not to take imperialist aggression seriously but to trivialize it.

The failure behind the pseudo-resistance exhibited in *Mafalda* is the crux of Quino's project. Quino's diminished comment, if anything at all, intends to denounce a strategy of explicit opposition. According to Quino, open resistance would only lead to a perilous extreme. When Mafalda encounters an indigent woman hiding from the rain, the child prefers to look innocently at her (582). Social justice seems to be some extraneous, foreign affair. Would candid concern make any difference? Instead, the child seems to validate the notion of abandoning ideals as we age, or, as Mafalda says: "We are in trouble, guys! It turns out that if one rushes to change the world, it is the world that ends changing one!" (1822).

Pablo José Hernández concludes that *Mafalda* is not a progressive comic strip; on the contrary, the critiques of the central character are made within the boundaries tolerated by the system, not only not questioning it, but helping to maintain "'freedom of the press' with her timid comments."[9] Anyone who mistakes Mafalda for a sworn enemy or a deceitful accomplice of the system is wrong. Her strategy—or rather, Quino's—is faint resistance. If, on one hand, the child or her family complain about left-wing regimes (one recalls rants with respect to China, the Soviet Union, and Fidel, whom Mafalda exploits as an excuse for avoiding soup), on the other hand, she never manages either to dismiss or forgive the excesses of capitalism.

In strip 110, for example, Mafalda assures the reader she is tired of having to choose between communism and capitalism. The abuses and disadvantages of both systems are quite evident to her; therefore, it is senseless to support either. What is really the case, though, is that Mafalda—or Quino—wearied by dogmatism, prefers neither. Rather than choosing between being a child of the bourgeoisie or being the poor shoeshine kid she and Miguelito encounter (59-9), she would simply rather go home. As a result, Quino effectively ends up closer to the establishment than presumably he would like to be; his mockery, although significant, does not manage to distance him enough.

The world of Quino includes a fairly constituted, functional household. Here the adults, who are blatantly absent in many strips of this kind, are clearly visible. The father fears reality. He barely manages to free himself from obstacles and difficulties. Being just another link in the system that leads from his flat to the corporate world, he never admits to sharing some responsibility for social injustice. To him, the prevailing system is an agreeable way of life; hence, he never questions it deeply. Thus, if Mafalda pretends to put her peers on trial, her progenitor appears to conform. Through him, the implicit order of production is recognized haphazardly but is definitely accepted.

Raquel, the mother, spends her days enslaved by housework, trying to live up to an obsessive ideal of cleanliness. Her world is circumscribed to the walls of her abode; on the few occasions when she ventures into the streets, she does not go beyond the grocery store of Don Manolo Goreiro, the local vendor. Mafalda, although she playfully condemns these facts, never recommends an alternative for her mother. The life of a housewife is an end in itself. Even sporadic vacations appear to teem with anguish and frustration—the parents constantly recall the mound of bills awaiting their return—so there are never any authentic options for relaxation. In short, even if adults have superior influence in *Mafalda*, only the children possess the true freedom to circulate throughout the world, although even that freedom is not without problems. Dorfman and Mattelart state, "The imaginary of children is the political utopia of a social class."[10] In a world of infants, all objects are detached from their origins; everything seems to have been accomplished effortlessly. Therefore, any sort of accountability for social injustice evident in Argentine reality is perhaps more wholly absent in the world of children than in that of adults.

The personalities of Mafalda's circle of friends configure the framework that upholds Quino's social vision. Manolito, the vendor's son, is the openly profit-oriented member of the group; his limited intelligence does not hinder his excellent commercial insights. Indeed, Quino celebrates the child's self-assurance; Manolito seems to be the only one who knows what he wishes to become, and the irony of his altogether questionable motivation—blatant, remorseless greed—never detracts from this fact. Manolito becomes the one in charge of proclaiming the capitalist creed: "One cannot amass a fortune without grinding others." His mercantilism is striking, expressed in statements such as "The checks of your scorn bounce upon the bank of my spirit." Manolito is a key element; if Mafalda's critical spirit is the soul of the strip, his repeated blunders serve as comic counterpoint to the gravity of her allegations.

On the other hand, Felipe, Mafalda's toothy sidekick and a model of naïveté, reveals substantial insecurity. His presence in the strip seems to be a tart reminder of existentialism, while Susanita personifies all clichés and incarnates the bourgeois paradigm for the feminine sex. She is an arriviste, with an air of superiority, when in truth there is little that distinguishes her from her friends. In fact, Susanita celebrates and legitimates the status quo. Her opinion as to how to deal with poverty suggests the same strategy as that of the Argentine junta prior to the World Cup tournament: hide the poor.

To complete the assortment of children: Miguelito, another of Mafalda's buddies, serves as Felipe's alter ego: inquisitive, pragmatic, individualistic, and very self-assured. For him, there are no complex truths. Appropriately for one who admires Mussolini (thanks to the dedicated schooling of his grandparents), he dismisses all doubt. Finally, the efficacy of the comments made by tiny Libertad, the maverick of the group, is diminished by her infrequent appearance. Although she is the daughter of a young educated couple—her mother translates French for a living—her relevance to the story is minimal, and her presence is limited to Quino's last installments.

We can account for Quino's peculiar vision in part by locating it in terms of his North American forebears. In a recent compilation of his works (with a foreword by Daniel Samper Pizano, the Colombian columnist), Quino admits that his initial idea was to produce a kind of amalgam of *Blondie* and *Peanuts*, where it would prove feasible to criticize the urban milieu while making advantageous use of the unthreatening façade of a group of kids. *Blondie* was developed in 1930 by Chic Young in an attempt to ridicule the frivolous youth of the jazz era. The strip eventually evolved into a critique of marriage as a cornerstone of society; Dagwood, a hapless spendthrift, loses his inheritance at the time of his marriage to Blondie. The habitual setting for *Blondie* is domestic, which provides a foundation for the successor scenes within the closed setting of an Argentine apartment building, where the parents of Mafalda, Libertad, and Susanita struggle, just as the American suburban family does. In each strip, inner space is associated with relief from fatigue, as well as from the tension born of the interaction with neighbors.

The other comic strip, *Peanuts*, begun by Charles M. Schulz in 1950, may be a less acute stimulus for Quino's imagination, since, unlike *Mafalda* (where adults, although they do not play key roles, nevertheless have a certain importance), the world of children in *Peanuts* is a closed environment. The playground of the Peanuts gang is a microcosm of lawns and white fences that easily sugggest the suburbs of any U.S. city—and perhaps less easily the streets of Buenos Aires. *Mafalda* may be more decisively related to another American strip: *Nancy*, begun in 1940 by Ernie Bushmiller. Several critics—Steinberg, among others[11]—have correctly pointed out many common features. This is no secret; even Quino acknowledges the similarity. In strip 933, for example, Mafalda boasts of her closeness to Nancy, just as in other strips he shows that the walls of Mafalda's room are decorated with posters of Charlie Brown and Snoopy.

The crucial difference between these American strips and Quino is the presence of urban space. Because a comfortable equivalent for American suburbia does not exist in Argentina, Quino situates the children in a Buenos Aires neighborhood of the sixties, where the roving gang becomes, in effect, a group of *flâneurs*. Through the gaze of the children, the Argentine metropolis is a space filled with life, where the boundaries between the private and public spheres fall apart. Quino transforms the sidewalks, parks, and playgrounds into something new: a stage for the exercise of critical play. *Mafalda* pretends to outline a concrete terrain for the children's activities, with precise limitations of space and time. Yet, time after time, the result is only conflict of a peculiarly urban sort.

The policeman to whom Miguelito asks about happiness (835), for example, becomes someone who must not guard Miguelito's home, for, as the child states, "With what sort of face do I throw things at somebody who has guarded our house?" (1104). Incoherence abounds in the story; information is contradictory. The representation of space becomes ambiguous because the author never adopts a straightforward posture. The places he should criticize sincerely are always missing; instead, Quino's indictments seem a bit out of place. It is obvious that apartment life in a big city is troublesome, yet the conveniences of urban life are what stand out, even in the face of the shantytowns and the impoverished landscape that Mafalda once glimpses from a train window (306). Furthermore, rural utopias simply vanish—"lovely lakes surrounded by mountains and wonderful forests!" the child proclaims, when she recalls her vacation (644).

The school, the gang's second home, only further ratifies the social dictates of the established order; in one learning exercise, the children repeat: "The masses are healthy." (The original phrase, meant to be a pronunciation exercise, is "La masa es sana," with a playfulness that does not translate well into English.) Street situations, on the other hand, make economic relations more evident. Thus events regularly translate to matters of social and mercantile nature: personal relations ("Gee . . . I thought the idiots were on strike, but I now realize they've come to work," remarks Susanita [328]); the romantic ("He doesn't look like a bad husband. How much did you pay for him?" the child asks a lady passing by [1443]); and even the academic ("Well, what can I tell you? It appears I have inspired in the teacher a certain commercial sympathy," states Manolito after failing miserably [510]). However, Mafalda abstains from openly criticizing the means of production. When she describes the world of ants ("Come, Felipe, poor ants! . . . They work like slaves all their lives, and in the end, what for? To have baby ants that will in turn work like slaves all their lives" [1107]), she favors the park, never daring to associate insects there with the ants that have invaded her apartment. The same ants follow her dad to work, establishing a clear bond with his status as an employee, as well as a clear connection between the world inside and out.

In *Mafalda*, public space serves the role of a mischievous agglutinant. In strip 20, Mafalda witnesses the passing of a military officer, a worker, and a priest, distinctly stratifying the options of power. The institutions, although viewed with a critical eye, are finally upheld by their omnipresence in the strip's urban narrative. In strip 810 Mafalda persists in her account of social classes, incorporating a housewife, a student, and a pensioner; all are understood as viable alternatives for life, and there is minimal attention paid to gender or age discrimination. In strip 1437, the by-products of modernity—pollution, a faltering economy, and the growing use of synthetic materials—appear merely as so many phenomena that help to dehumanize urban life. The street becomes the ultimate site for venting all quandaries, from digressions to prohibitions. In strip 362, Felipe considers the possibility of a collapse of distances. The distressed child faints upon imagining everything at once: the Kremlin, the Lone Ranger, Jerry Lewis, Africa, the Beatles, the Berlin Wall, Disneyland, Pelé, Vietnam, Cuba. The isolationist implications of the experience are comically clear: it would be disastrous to bring the world to Argentina.

Strip 612 introduces various pedestrians anguished by unemployment, as well as problems with their automobiles and legal affairs. The strip ends by showing Miguelito tormented by an absurd conundrum: are angels able to fly backward? Conclusion: all their petty anxieties are equally worthless, negligible. Matters capable of generating significant dissent among the population are recurrently depicted as trivial. In strip 861, for example, during her walk to school, Mafalda witnesses, successively, a car accident, the rage of a man before an out-of-order pay phone, and the misery of an indigent. But the street presents all as spectacle; poverty, as a social issue, is relegated to the stature of an occasional mishap. In strip 878, spring becomes the suitable season for everything—perhaps too much, argues the child: flirting lovebirds, frivolous tabloids, and workers that play merry melodies. To equate labor with the gaiety of spring only naturalizes whatever else it could signify.

The streets of the city become the convenient site to postulate grandiose dilemmas in an unavailing fashion ("Where does one start pushing this country to move it forward?" asks a perplexed Mafalda [240]) and serve to validate the children's behavior. The group meets all kinds of adults: hippies, snobbish elders, a handful of pensioners, weeping widows.

They accumulate evidence that justifies a generational conflict ("Do not exaggerate, this is only what follows whatever you started," Mafalda reminds an elder [1262]). Yet nothing comes of it, and filial duty is continually upheld by her frequent trips to the grocery store (1217).

Similarly, the park authorizes all manner of opinions. "In my case, what I hope turns out fine is my life," claims Miguelito on a typical occasion (794), upon finding Felipe playing with a top. However, repeatedly the park actually enables the gang to impugn whoever contends with their fortunes. "Did you ever consider that the young people who suffer today because adults leave them no choice are the same who tomorrow, once they become adults, will leave us no choice?" suggests Mafalda to a horrified companion.

Quino manipulates the argumentative language of the story ostensibly to present an alternate reality. In the process, however, he acquits his audience rather like Susanita when she overwhelms her mates with all her gossip (1229): there is too much, and it all comes to the same thing. Conformist attitudes are condoned, passivity is justified, and the demise of social consciousness is excused. Whereas *Peanuts* (say) is supposed to be fun and to communicate little more than the Anglo-Saxon sense of fair play, *Mafalda* stubbornly parodies the Argentine loss of national identity.[12] But for the main character, a child of flirtatious acuteness, it finally makes no difference whether she is discussing pulmonary health or chastising the Beatles, whether she is vilifying the relation between the automobile and its passengers or questioning the good faith of advertising. *Peanuts* might be critically inert with respect to the American way of life (even if it includes among its children one who suffers from a psychoanalytic hangover, another who seeks shelter in the supposed apathy of baseball, and still another who employs a dog as alter ego). *Mafalda*, despite its seemingly more deceitful posture, ends up being equally tepid, because its varied urban space fails to complicate a more single-minded ideological design that only produces comfortable bourgeois comedy.

An Unlikely, Greasy Hero: *Boogie, el aceitoso*

Laughter has been described as the socially acceptable form of showing one's teeth. In a sociopolitical situation where people are either victims or victimizers, it is inevitable that a comic strip should take advantage of the logic whereby the victim is mocked. In Latin American modernity, this duality of victim/victimizer, or oppressed/oppressor is arguably the quintessential binarism, whose consequences reverberate throughout the entire continent. The deep-rooted relation between these poles results in the establishment of a common symbolic order that simultaneously restricts and directs the exchange of guilt between a dominant North America and a subordinate Latin America. As usual, culture is obliged to operate within established limits. *Boogie, el aceitoso,* by Roberto Fontanarrosa, is a model for this exchange—and the strip shows its teeth with a vengeance.

Mafalda, Felipe, Manolito, and Libertad are supposed to live in a neighborhood of Buenos Aires. Boogie "the Greaser" lives at the other end of the globe, in the New York metropolitan area. To make a living, he works as mercenary, bodyguard, or hit man—occupations that are emphasized in the text. The violence of his methods echoes, at least in the beginning, the excesses of the military. His physiognomy, marked by a square jaw, denotes a firm, bullet-proof personality. Boogie finds himself equally at ease in a shooting in Queens or in the Byzantine grid of Manhattan. His weapons, apart from the omnipresent uzis, Winchesters, Colts, and magnums, have to do with a dejected severity that at once reveals and indicts the prejudices and corruptions of North American civilization.

But why make a hero of a paid assassin, and why set him in New York? A simplistic reading would explain the plot as simply based on the appeal of the American gangster—a script akin to certain popular comic strips in the French publishing industry. A reading more attentive to *argentinidad* would note that, first, the paid assassin—the hoodlum, the tough guy—bears a certain affinity to a specific national type: the *compadrito* or *malevo,* the champion of the Buenos Aires underworld. *Malevaje* stories constitute a tangible portion of the mythology of the Southern Hemisphere and are, to a certain extent, the urban offspring of a legendary tradition that started with the archetype of the gaucho, Martín Fierro. The man of the margins in the nineteenth century—whom Adolfo Saldías described as "the principal force of suburbia . . . a kind of midpoint between the urban man and that of the country"[13]—has gone through the filter of the mind of Roberto Fontanarrosa and has landed as a rugged mercenary in Queens.

In *Teoría del argentino,* Arturo López Peña states that the most impressive trait of the *compadrada,* the cadre of rogues inhabiting the periphery of the city, lies in "its profound deformation of a balanced and normal individual."[14] In *Boogie*, imbalance becomes standard. Nothing fits; the world is inhabited by a pack of misfits and loonies. The norm is the individual, marked by what Borges described as the ethics of men who stand alone and expect little from anybody. Even if *Boogie*'s exacerbated individualism comes from his Anglo-Saxon upbringing, it also forms part of the creed of the *malevo*. The unabashed arrogance with which he delivers blows and beatings has much to do with the Argentine soul of the man of the margins. The dark suit, the knife, and the kerchief around the neck have given way, a century later, to the somber overcoat, the revolver, and contempt for the weak; the periphery now finds an image of its symbolic patrimony in the gloom of Queens.

There is another explanation for the displacement of one country onto another: is this not the concept with which the Latin American media often flirt—that the dreams and comforts of a foreign way of life may be the dreams and comforts of the Latin American bourgeoisie? Or that the cultural expressions of a different political context—rap, for instance—may serve as examples in domestic latitudes? Or even that the ethical dilemmas of one community may serve as a paradigm for others? One must acknowledge that Latin America, as a long-standing consumer of the symbolic goods of the developed world, has consistently relished, with ineffable delight, the fallacies of others. Hence, before such boosterism, *Boogie*'s placement in a North American context seems refreshing.

The practice of condemning the incongruities of that other order—in this case North American, although it might well be European—is exactly the game of *Boogie*. Boogie lives in New York, flaunts his prejudice against North American minority groups, infringes the law with unbelievable confidence, and ignores the order of the system—all forms of behavior that establish immediate empathy with the Latin American upper classes. *Boogie* deconstructs the grand myths of the North: he slaps feminists, riddles with bullets dissolute liberals and oppressed blacks, is rabidly anti-Semitic, and ridicules the black market, the Ku Klux Klan, gays, and the neurotic discipline and collective mind-set of Asians. He is infinitely politically incorrect amid an American culture that preaches correctness—and, what is worse, he offers no trace of remorse. Because his context and predicament are completely North American, *Boogie* confronts the Latin American public with repressed problems that nevertheless belong to their own daily routine: racism, homophobia, consumerism, disdain for life.

Boogie can be understood as a deconstruction of old evils, Latin American vices accumulated as a result of the habit of imitating foreign cultures. To point out the complacent indifference of the Latin American bourgeoisie, Fontanarrosa takes a hard line—much in contrast to Quino, who abstains, as if in fear of offending. Fontanarrosa employs both the arguments and façade of the American comic strip to bring the reading public face to face with the dark side of Latin American identity.[15] From his example, we can see how it is more practical for a broader Hispanic public to consume an expression of its own culture in American packaging, rather than in the language of an apparently more kindred nation. In turn, the aesthetic vocabulary of New York is revealed as genuinely paranational in nature, for the achievement of the comic strip demonstrates the viability of the reproduction of Anglo-Saxon graphic art in the Latin American scene.

Boogie is a remarkable specimen of Latin America's pop culture for a number of other reasons. First, the treatment of North American space can be distinguished from that of traditional strips in the Sunday paper or comic books. While the latter choose to represent an impenetrable enclosure of action, a freezing of time and space, the typical trait of the Boogiean method is its permissiveness, a characteristic that allows a freer disposition of the argument. The customary boxes confining each segment of the comic strip are often absent in *Boogie;* sometimes a partial frame, with rounded corners like that of a television screen, becomes the profile of a head or face or becomes a balloon containing dialogue.

Whether modernity is understood as the spatialization of time or the temporization of space, it is difficult to find a medium that combines these elements as gracefully as the comic strip. In the fashion of the storyboard, which film directors use for graphically planning how scenes will be framed, it is possible in the comic strip to perpetuate an instant or to collapse time infinitesimally. In *Boogie*, the verbal elements respect no boundaries, because some of the lines designating the frames blend into the art work itself, while the narrative chronology is condensed or expanded according to the artist's taste. The violent outburst of "Un Whisky" ("A Whisky," 5) barely consumes fractions of seconds, for example, even though the paper dilates the action with cinematic élan.[16] In a diametrically opposed fashion, the unadorned phrase of the main character in "Es la vida, Lennie" ("It's Life, Lenny," 5) is juxtaposed against the impassive advance of technology, thereby compressing his mourning for an old '52 Ford by formidably dense pressures. (See figure 4.1.)

There is also the matter of intertextuality. In *Boogie*, Fontanarrosa contrives a wild brew of portrayals of several types, exposing intertexts wherever he deems them handy; as a result, within this all-inclusive mode, nothing seems necessary to exclude. "Todo el horror" ("The Horror," 5), for example, flirts with Conrad and alludes to the horrid spectacle, during early

Figure 4.1 "Es la vida, Lennie" ("It's Life, Lenny"). *Boogie*: "But you have to see it." *Man:* "My old Ford 52." Reprinted by permission from Roberto Fontanarrosa, *Boogie el aceitoso*, vol. 5. Buenos Aires: Ediciones de la Flor S.R.L., 1982.

hours, of a disheveled, unkempt, foul-smelling lover. The endless parade of quotations and characters on countless other occasions includes Cassius Clay; or the ballad-loving serial killer who dreams singing "Cutting Me Softly" (in an open parody of Roberta Flack's hit); bar owners who (despite having in-laws well connected to congressmen and brothers working as SWAT lieutenants) exploit Puerto Rican dishwashers; renegade Green Berets; fear-ridden husbands trying to hide while they murder at a dis-cotheque; fatalistic Muslim bodyguards; some members of the CIA and the KGB; along with Creedence Clearwater Revival, Walt Whitman, Conrad, Buñuel, Baldwin, Philip Dick.

How to account for this diversity of the strip, except to say that it par-ticipates in more narratives than can be formally restricted to any one medium? A more extended instance: in "Una valiosa tenacidad" ("A Valu-able Tenacity," 5), José, who personifies the Latin immigrant, narrates how he entered North American territory, crossing the Gila desert, where he was abandoned by his "coyote" to suffer thirst and hunger for a period of six days. After surviving, thanks to the consumption of roots and insects, he is rescued. Once at the hospital, he desperately proposes marriage to a nymphomaniac nurse who then abuses him. After having eventually beaten her in return, he is sentenced to four years in prison. Upon comple-tion of time, and once he has become a citizen, he is drafted to fight in Viet-nam, where he loses a leg. Finally, handicapped and defeated, he returns to the sublime North American motherland. Boogie, who has stoically lis-tened to the whole account, concludes with a dry sentence: "Tenacity has its rewards, José." Fontanarrosa truncates the rosy myth of the American dream by transforming it into a hazardous voyage to hell about which very little can be concluded. (See figure 4.2.)

In "Una vieja película" ("An Old Film"),[17] Boogie shares some drinks with Dany, who narrates the following events. Once, when he is about to enjoy an old Doris Day flick, Dany hears some obnoxious music coming from the apartment next door. The noise is produced by his neighbor, a huge Haitian man. In search of solidarity for his protests ("We must not allow the subjugation of these immigrant bastards"), Dany rushes to his other neighbors. Surprisingly, he finds his building filled with foreigners: an Armenian couple who do not understand a word of English, a Pakistani

Figure 4.2 "Una valiosa tenacidad" ("A Valuable Tenacity"). *José:* At last I got out. Finally I had my citizenship. I was free from jail and from Eloíse. And I even had some money she left when she died. That was when I got drafted and sent to Vietnam. Now, I'm back. I'm fine. Sure, I lost a leg, but I'm fine. *Boogie:* "Tenacity has its rewards, José." Reprinted by permission from Roberto Fontanarrosa, *Boogie el aceitoso,* vol. 5. Buenos Aires: Ediciones de la Flor S.R.L., 1982.

family, two Hindu sisters, and, to make things worse, fourteen Puerto Ricans sharing a single apartment. Boogie remarks, sententiously: "In New York, Dany, Americans will soon feel the pressure of racism." The comment is sententious. The story virtually drowns the banality of its meaning, even though we may nonetheless feel that the maxim serves well enough for millions of Latin Americans who are consistently discriminated against in racial terms by white North Americans of European descent.

Figure 4.3 "La noche de los chicanos" ("The Night of the Chicanos"). *Chicano:* "Son of a bitch! I can't believe you're standing there. Don't you know you shouldn't be hanging out in the streets after eight? Gee, what a shame! You're getting me down, gringo . . . Oh, how annoying, so white and blond, I feel like beatin' some sense into him. He sees us all hairy and bearded, the gringo. He sees us as blacks and not as whites. He thinks we are 'sold out—fritters' or 'pachucos' . . ." Reprinted by permission from Roberto Fontanarrosa, *Boogie el aceitoso,* vol. 1. Buenos Aires: Ediciones de la Flor S.R.L., 1982.

In *Boogie,* the voice of the periphery takes hold through the steady presence of minorities, although what is spoken is neither consistently narrated or interpreted. In "La noche de los chicanos" ("The Night of the Chicanos," 5), an entire gang faces Boogie, who massacres them ruthlessly (figure 4.3). However, in "Alí El Bakhar" (5), Boogie uses Muslim fatalism mockingly to condemn xenophobic stereotypes. In "Rudolf, el reno de la nariz roja" ("Rudolph, the Red-Nosed Reindeer," 1), the racism turns out to be an expression of the black community. How to align this with "La trinchera del óvulo" ("The Trench of the Ovule," 2) where Fontanarrosa attacks the myth of militant feminism? (See figure 4.4.) In "El shuffle del niño pobre" ("The Poor Kid's Shuffle," 2), he deals with unemployment in African American communities: "Why should one bother creating sources of employment for the Blacks?" In "Ten cuidado, Pedro" ("Be Careful,

Figure 4.4 "La trinchera del óvulo" ("The Trench of the Ovule"). *Black journalist:* "Hello, super macho. You are Boogie, aren't you? I am from the women's liberation magazine *The Trench of the Ovule.*" *White journalist:* "And since we know you think of yourself as tough, as cruel with the girls, we want to write something about you. All right, sweetheart?" Reprinted by permission from Roberto Fontanarrosa, *Boogie el aceitoso,* vol. 2. Buenos Aires: Ediciones de la Flor S.R.L., 1982.

Pedro," 5), the Mexican notion of the "certified male" comes to life, to
denounce homophobia.

In *Boogie,* capitalism functions as a more stable subject for criticism;
boastful of its victory, it permeates everything. Boogie purchases weapons
in vending machines ("Las cinco monedas" ["Five Coins," 2]), and a
memento of world conflicts, the Maginot Line, becomes a line of articles for

Figure 4.5 "Black Is Black." *KKK man:* "You can't deny you would like to see a black man
burned." *Boogie:* "It doesn't have to be a black man, necessarily. I don't think hatred should be
compartmentalized. On the other hand, the last time a black man was burned, they showed it
on television." *KKK man:* "That's true. But the raffle ticket gives you a chance to win an art
work, with the money going toward producing new spectacles. We spend a lot on gasoline."
Boogie: "The government should prohibit the burning of blacks, given the gasoline crisis."
Reprinted by permission from Roberto Fontanarrosa, *Boogie el aceitoso,* vol. 2. Buenos Aires:
Ediciones de la Flor S.R.L., 1982.

personal defense ("La Línea Maginot" ["The Maginot Line," 2]). A CIA agent ceases torturing him because he respects private property as a "basis of our way of life" ("Todos los hombres del presidente" ["All the President's Men," 2]). In "Por unos dólares más" ("A Fistful of Dollars," 1), Boogie eliminates a Palestine activist, thanks to the few extra dollars offered by Bernstein, his true client. In "Pubis salvaje" ("Wild Pubis," 2), he toys with the idea of launching an album, adding Ray Conniff music to a series of illegal and clandestine recordings. In *Boogie* ("Black Is Black," 2), even the Klan is more interested in marketing policies than in threatening and persecuting blacks. (See figure 4.5.)

Fontanarrosa's difference from Quino is nowhere more evident than in how he devotes himself to the flagrant indictment of relations of production. The arms race, for example, becomes a creative contest in "Baby Kangooroo" (Fontanarrosa's spelling). In "Heredarás el fuego" ("To Inherit the Fire," 1), the heir to a bomb factory sets himself on fire to protest the end of the Vietnam War; as a result of his family's bankruptcy, he decides to imitate pacifist fanaticism. In "7 de diciembre del 1941," Boogie explains that the prohibition against manufacturing arms forced upon the Japanese industry is not caused by fear of an armed conflict but the potential loss of markets. (Figure 4.6.)

It is clear that Boogie works for a living. It is also very clear that he enjoys his work. In "¿Dónde se han ido todas las flores?" (1)—a direct allusion to the Pete Seeger song, "Where Have All the Flowers Gone?"—he complains about Joe, who kills for a hobby. To Boogie, work is good, despite whatever else it may be. The fact that his business is violence and death is a mere coincidence. Still, in "Hágalo usted mismo" ("Do It Yourself," 2), having mercilessly shot his interlocutor, he states: "The day I do this job just for the money, I will leave everything and set up a leper colony." (See figure 4.7.) Unlike Quino, who reproduces a Roman Catholic understanding of work as penance, Fontanarrosa everywhere suggests that there can be a certain pleasure in work, even if it involves murder and does not elude the question of money.

In the more recent episodes of the strip, however, the violence diminishes, at least at an explicitly graphic level, as the typical locations change. Characters now mention Fifth Avenue, Macy's, and Central Park. The brawls are repeated, but the bursts of machine-gun fire are gone; a sporadic

shot seems to suffice. Life remains, however, ultimately a bloody contest, a vision to be distinguished, above all, from those who would soften its contours and restrict its social base. In "El discreto encanto de la poesía" (2), a parody of Buñuel's title, *The Discreet Charm of the Bourgeoisie,* the upper class is equated with those who make poetry something tacky, laughable, filled with sentimentality.

Figure 4.6 "7 de diciembre del 1941" ("December 7, 1941"). *Man:* "Did you tell me you are Japanese?" *Boogie:* "Yes." *Man:* "Then come up, you alone." *Boogie:* "Why?" *Man:* "I hate the Japanese. I hate them. I cannot avoid the memories of that morning of December 7, '41. Or all we suffered to get them out of their filthy hiding places in Saipan, Iwo Jima, Tarawa, Guadalcanal." Reprinted by permission from Roberto Fontanarrosa, *Boogie el aceitoso,* vol. 5. Buenos Aires: Ediciones de la Flor S.R.L., 1982.

It is impossible not to compare Fontanarrosa with Quino, who has been unable to face the reigning injustice, racism, sexism, greed, and vacuity in Latin American cities because his vision of social and economic life takes place, finally, solely at the level of the local neighborhood. Therefore, in Quino's case, a validation of Argentine reality is more evident. His merit, unlike Fontanarrosa's, lies in his ability to materialize and express the way of life of the population, his capacity to reorganize the dominant order and

Figure 4.7 "Hágalo usted mismo" ("Do It Yourself"). *Man:* "Only one thing I ask of you. Boogie. Let me do it with my own hands. I am a stupid individualist." *Boogie:* "The day I do this job just for the money, I will leave everything and open a leper colony." Reprinted by permission from Roberto Fontanarrosa, *Boogie el aceitoso,* vol. 2. Buenos Aires: Ediciones de la Flor S.R.L., 1982.

integrate it into the context of daily events. *Mafalda* exhibits what Pierre
Bourdieu classifies as class ethnocentrism. Such a frail vision of the established order rather paradoxically becomes its greatest cultural contribution. In *Mafalda*, the essential is a routine in which the lack of open resistance to hegemony—national or international—is just its way of
inhabiting the city, of walking through parks, of watching television, of
interacting socially, and, in sum, of generating immediate identification
with its object: the petit-bourgeois universe of Buenos Aires.

From the Inner City to the Outskirts

Boogie "el aceitoso," Fontanarrosa's hired assassin, signals a subtle displacement of Latin American consciousness, from being Argentine to being
North American. The language of the comic strip becomes more productive
when it adopts the ruling form in the communications media, the English-
speaking, multicultural Babel of North America—that is, New York—
including its own versatile versions of the periphery. To emphasize once
more: it seems in this logic more practical, for the Hispanic public, to consume an expression of culture in a format similar to the North American,
than in the language of a sister nation. Thus, the idea behind this essay has
been to argue, finally, for a beneficial reading of this transition and to reveal
how this change contributes to the location of a Latin American cultural
subject.

If it is true, as Martín-Barbero assures us, that things were once far
away because a mode of social relation made them seem distant, and only
later, with technology, was it possible to contemplate and revere even the
most foreign of them, the trick now lies in communicating what is near by
adopting the semblance of what is distant. In other words, since in recent
decades the advance of the international media has familiarized the public
with the consumption of frequently elaborate and colorful information
from remote corners of the earth, the moment may have arrived for a
native practice to feed Latin American palates with the technical display
and the wizardry popularized by imported formulas.

In sum, we have two alternatives for the reproduction of social reality:
a soft, domestic approach *(Mafalda)* and a hard, internationalist one *(Boogie)*. While Quino articulates his complaint with a reiterated pretense, the

strategy of Fontanarrosa is much more direct. *Mafalda* incorporates the representation of sectors of merely relative, if not marginal, worth. *Mafalda*'s business is more exclusively that of the middle class. Only under the occasional economic crisis—a recurrent event in Latin America—do the timid voices of such people as housewives, small businessmen, and retirees come to life. The scorn and sarcasm to which Quino regularly exposes his audience serve only as endorsements for a fixed class position.

Boogie's business, on the other hand, is the often repressed discourse of the masses. A parade of misfits roams through the comic strip: prostitutes, alcoholics, delinquents, drug dealers, junkies, and Mafiosi. Fontarrosa's excess is the inherent synonym of a virtual image, incorporating a vast absent audience. In Boogie's fragmented sense of reality lies a more sincere hope for criticism; in his deformity, he gives voice to different segments of society that usually abide unheard. Mafalda's location is a subordinated culture, where the alternative to resist barely exists, Boogie's is a torn culture, with a few interstices to spare.

Following Martín-Barbero, this reading privileges mediation.[18] The medium—in this case, the printed comic strip—reproduces a particular style of life, thereby universalizing it. The population, feeling itself part of a national subject, is impelled to see itself represented. Mediation, in turn, denotes the cohesive role of the medium, through which the public recognizes and identifies itself, sharing the cognitive experience that leads to the formation of a national imaginary. As such, the representation of a comic strip plays a key role in how readers conceive of themselves and relate to their surrounding spaces. By adopting a specific focus on the urban experience, the audience manages to share constructs of class, gender, and race, and thus either validate or reject particular social paradigms. In *Mafalda* and *Boogie*, two very distinct offers are available.

Mediation describes the mechanism by which the medium manages to materialize its version and to express both the generosity and restriction of its message. In short, if the medium defines the space of communication, mediation in turn defines the space of the medium. In *Mafalda*'s case, the cultural practice has to do with how the comic strip teaches its public to behave in the city and to take hold of it. An analysis of the articulation the strip's message, though, leads one to discover the loss of an urban center. A city once comprised of domestic neighborhoods is now nonexistent. Hence, if Quino remains valid at all, it is because his readers embrace a considerable amount of nostalgia; the centers that they recall avidly are now surfacing elsewhere—in the urban sprawl from places as far away as the New York of *Boogie*.

Parallel to this circumstance, a new dimension of power begins to forge itself in the periphery. After the chaotic growth of the last decades, the Latin American city has now abandoned any pretension to unipolarity; its geometry has been altered, incorporating new spaces of development. The population, eager to obtain material goods, gains hold of suburbia. The metropolitan layout dissolves into many pieces, merging the suburbs into a latticework of social disarray, while the inner city becomes a place of calamity. In this way, graphic urban representation is no longer feasible through some sort of integral configuration. The totalization instituted by modernity is useless. On the contrary, a fragmentation more proper to postmodernity marks the unavoidable outcome. That is why, from *Mafalda* to *Boogie*, we proceed from the inner city to the outskirts, where one country now recreates itself in the form of another.

III

Nation as Idea

5/ Framing the Peruvian *Cholo*

Popular Art by Unpopular People

MILAGROS ZAPATA SWERDLOW *and*
DAVID SWERDLOW

IN THE 1980S A NEW WAVE OF "FOLK ART," FEATURING likenesses of the peasant class, made a place for itself on the shelves and walls of Lima's upscale art boutiques and souvenir shops. In Peru, this work can now be found in posh hotels, in attorneys' and doctors' inner offices, and in many other settings where collectors wish to display their attention to high fashion. Outside Peru, this highly marketable work can be found in the homes of those who receive catalogues or on-line advertisements from enterprises that market international products with folk art appeal.[1] To appropriate what David Rockefeller (with the public naivete that only the very rich can afford) says of contemporary African art, a contemporary Peruvian production "would be appealing to use in a home or an office; . . . it goes well with contemporary architecture."[2] How, then, should we assess the fact that these works are created by members of an oppressed group of men and women known as *cholos* often living in remote, technologically primitive areas in the northern department of Piura? Clearly, this commodified popular art, in both ceramic and painted forms, should be addressed in terms of its social significance. Doing so, we believe, yields an insight into Peru's complex social web that has been under perilous reconstruction since Francisco Pizzarro's arrival on the continent in 1532, and which includes the construction of racial differentiation in Peru.

After an extended discussion of the term *cholo,* we shall describe the popular art in question. As these works are produced and consumed by a wide variety of people, we consider them as they are seen by artists, Peruvian consumers, and international collectors, respectively. Finally, we consider the implications of how this art is produced and consumed. Hans Robert Jauss argues that a "past text cannot, of its own accord, across the ages, ask us or later generations a question that the interpreter would not first have to uncover or reformulate for us."[3] Similarly, a consideration of the figure of the *cholo* reveals that the text of the *other* from a racial or national perspective crosses the boundary of cultural difference only as art whose national and ethnic origins must be effaced.

In Terms of Being *Cholo*

First we should define the term *cholo*.[4] This racially motivated designation is understood and used by both the folk art's producers and consumers, and it both begs for and resists definition. The term is somewhat different from *mestizo*. A *cholo* is a person perceived to be more Indian than white, while a *mestizo* is perceived to be more white than Indian. Magnus Mörner writes that "the usually derogatory term of *cholo* is often heard but proves hard to define. Yet it probably emerged as an expression of the suspicion that an individual claiming Mestizo status was merely an Indian trying to escape his own oppressed condition."[5] Howard Handelman describes the *cholo* as "a person of Indian origin who lives among *mestizos* and has been partially integrated into the white Spanish-speaking culture of the highlands.[6]

Ximena Bunster and Elsa Chaney identify the term as a pejorative term used to describe Amerindians, unless it is "used as a technical term in anthropology."[7] And finally, consider Mario Vargas Llosa's take on the term, from his autobiography, *El pez en el agua,* and the "ambiguous margin" it identifies:

> En la variopinta sociedad peruana, y acaso en todas las que tienen muchas razas y astronómicas desigualdades, blanco y cholo son términos que quieren decir más cosas que raza o etnía: ellos sitúan a la persona social y económicamente, y estos factores son muchas veces los determinantes de la clasificación. Esta es flexible y cambiante, supeditada a las circunstancias y a los vaivenes de los destinos particulares. Siempre se es blanco o cholo de alguien, porque siem-

pre se está mejor o peor situado que otros, o se es más o menos pobre o impor-
tane, o de rasgos más o menos occidentales o mestizos o indios o africanos o
asiáticos que otros, y toda esta selvática nomenclatura que decide buena parte
de los destinos individuales se mantiene gracias a una efervescente construc-
ción de prejuicios.

(In particolored Peruvian society and perhaps in all societies which have many
races and extreme inequalities, *blanco* [white] and *cholo* are terms that refer to
other things besides race and ethnic group; they situate a person socially and
economically, and many times these factors are the ones that determine his or
her classification. This latter is flexible and can change, depending on circumstances and the vicissitudes of individual destinies. One is always someone
blanco or *cholo* in relation to someone else, because one is always better or
worse situated than others, or one is more or less poor or important, or possessed of more or less occidental or *mestizo* or Indian or African or Asiatic features than others, and all this crude nomenclature that decides a good part of
one person's fate is maintained by virtue of an effervescent structure of prejudice.)[8]

These various understandings of the term *cholo* and its ramifications all
point to the notion of social mobility as it is predicated upon an individual's
race and culture. Even though Vargas Llosa claims that *blanco* and *cholo* are
terms that express more than race and ethnicity, he does not disclaim the
terms' racial motivations. More poignantly than Mörner and Handelman,
he is also interested in the phenomenon of mobility itself. Fluid socioeco-
nomic and cultural factors push Peru's biological factors into motion so
that race itself becomes indeterminate, a floating signifier, a concept on the
move.

The *cholos'* transitional situation is evidence of this phenomenon. *Cholos* are in constant transit because they are of a social class conceptually
based on an individual's or family's supposed movement from or between
racial categories, rather than membership in one category. Undeniably, the
cholos' transitional status lends support to Appiah's argument that biological race is indeed a fiction, since "at the margins there is always the
exchange of genes."[9] Thus, Vargas Llosa's "ambiguous margin" becomes
the operative metaphor for the blur of racial categories. With that knowl-

edge, Appiah warns, "talk of 'race' is particularly distressing for those of us who take culture seriously. For, where race works—in places where 'gross differences' of morphology are correlated with 'subtle differences' of temperament, belief, and intention—it works as an attempt at metonym for culture, and it does so only at the price of biologizing what is culture, ideology."[10] It is precisely this "biologizing" of culture that marks the difficulty experienced by Peruvians as they make, sell, and buy the art of the *cholo*.

To return to Mörner's and Handelman's definitions: Mörner claims that the term *cholo* "emerged as an expression of the *suspicion* that an individual *claiming* Mestizo status was *merely an Indian* trying to escape his own oppressed condition."[11] The obvious bias here, one assumes, reflects Peru's cultural disposition more than latent racism on Mörner's part. In any case, we must notice the "hegemonic impulse"[12] to see *cholos* as suspicious individuals who make bogus claims, while Indians are somehow degraded by being "merely" themselves.

Handelman writes, more objectively, "The term is often used disparagingly by whites or *mestizos* to suggest that the *cholo* is pushy or overly brusque."[13] In daily affairs, for example, the *cholo* who follows a *mestizo* and asks for money or a quick job may be described as pushy. In a more general sense, however, *cholos* are pushing the boundaries of race. They are attempting to push themselves into the space and class inhabited by the *mestizo*. Seeing the *cholo* as brusque—(*rudo, estúpido, sin educación, feo*— rude, stupid, without manners, ugly)—*mestizos* and elites may be attempting to connect the *cholo* more firmly to a perceived Indian identity which from their elitist gaze becomes an unrefined being with no role in the narrative of Peruvian progress. Understandably, one goal of the *cholo* artists may be to change that perception.

Cholos in the Artists' Gaze

The Artists

Much of the art featuring and/or created by *cholos* comes from the northern coastal region, especially the department of Piura.[14] Within the context of this discussion, it is important to ascertain whether these artists are considered, by themselves or by others, to be *cholos*, especially if we are to interpret an artist's gaze in terms of race. Not surprisingly, few artists talk about their racial background. Also, becoming a successful artist or entrepreneur may reclassify or declassify an individual as to race.[15] Thus, unless the artist has given some indication about his or her background, or has been otherwise identified, we have left the designation open.

In the first half of the 1980s, many of these painters from northern Peru began to gain recognition.[16] Like the well-known Andean works of folk art that have traditionally focused on Cuzco's stone streets and the Indians that inhabit them, paintings from the north celebrate the region's landscape, working people, and customs in the *costumbrista* style. Unlike the Andean works, however, Piura's painters began to deviate slightly from traditional *costumbrista* techniques. Cubism and symbolism, most notably, entered modestly into these artists' visual vocabularies.

Although paintings by some of these artists have achieved popular and critical acclaim, the ceramic art from Chulucanas has taken center stage in this drama. A ceramic figure by "master potter and artist" Gerasimo Sosa can be seen, for example, smiling from the glossy cover of *Arts and Crafts of South America,* printed in 1995.[17] Exhibitions of Sosa's and other Chulucanas artists' works have been mounted around the globe. Sosa's home and place of work, however, lie on a dirt road in a town where many bathe and wash their clothes in a reservoir. Like Sosa and his wife, Juana, several other important artists from this area live and work in premodern conditions.[18] In total, about twenty families from Chulucanas are involved in what amounts to mass production of ceramic pieces.

According to Davies and Fini, the ceramicists of Chulucanas began in the mid-1960s to explore the forms that two decades later would gain national and international attention. In the sixties, tomb robbers in the area had discovered pottery from the ancient Vicus and Tallan cultures (circa 400 B.C.). Shortly after, in Chulucanas, Quechua pottery specialists called the Sanoc Camoyac group began to research and experiment so that they might imitate and work with the techniques and forms used by the Vicus people. Of particular interest was the "negative painting" of these pre-Columbian works.[19] A bilingual brochure from Lima's El Artesano gallery describes how, in order to avoid stains from salty water, "artisans use rain water fresh from Andean creeks to mix the materials" and that "the traditional furnace which has been used generation after generation since the pre-Inca times" is wood-fired.[20]

As much as the marketing efforts of El Artesano and other similar concerns try to keep the art produced by the Chulucanas as "Indian" as possible, the artists have been able to see themselves apart from that constraint. Davies and Fini write in the brochure,

> At first the potters imitated the forms of the Vicus pieces, but gradually developed a freer expression, using stylized figures from their own environment. The most popular form to emerge is the *chichera*—a fat lady who makes and sells *chicha*, fermented corn beer. Some of the potters in Chulucanas are artists rather than artisans, producing unique and highly prized pieces. Each piece is signed, and the majority are sold in galleries and shops in Lima and abroad.
>
> While for many years the value of pre-Hispanic art forms and traditions was little regarded in Peru, the "indigenist" school of thought of the 1960s resurrected many of the earlier styles by bringing folk ceramics to the attention of the *mestizo* and white people in Lima—people as distant from the indigenous inhabitants of their country as someone living in Europe might be.[21]

While Davies and Fini see these artists as innovative, free thinkers, like the retailers who wish to retain the naive "Indian" flavor of these productions, they too stress the "indigenous" quality of the Chulucanas people and their work. These people are never referred to directly as Indians—which they are not. Of course, neither are they referred to as belonging to the white or *mestizo* elite to whom they sell their works. In other words, the discursive space is cleared for the unspoken designation: *cholo*.

Art

When artists of any origin or designation choose a subject, Heidegger suggests, they work from a conception of what constitutes art, as well as what art constitutes. In Piura, the most recognizable component of local art is the "robust woman" (for example, the *chichera*), who would be referred to as a *chola*. And, as an art critic writes in Piura's chief newspaper, figures of these "robust women" are very common in his region's art, for they "give the work a lyric expression that exalts work and the goodness of nature."[22] While other subjects are also prominent, the robust woman is the most repeated image. She is seen working in cotton fields, selling flowers, doing household chores, tending to children, and simply looking out from the glassless windows of her adobe and straw home. Mauricio's painting sees her on the coast, carrying fish home or to market. (See figure 5.1.)

What, it must be asked, do these repeated images have to say about the *cholo*, about how this group of people see themselves in the world? The most obvious intention may be to see and ennoble the *cholos'* existence, to reveal their beauty. Could the underlying motivation, however, be the desire to gaze back and interrogate, if not incriminate, the *mestizo* consumer?[23] These particular questions lead us to a general question about the issue of social class in all artistic production.

Not unlike the Peruvian art critic quoted earlier, Heidegger offers, in his

Figure 5.1 Untitled oil painting by Mauricio, 13″ x 9″. Photo by L. Gwen Christopher. Private collection of Milagros Zapata Swerdlow and David Swerdlow.

discussion of Van Gogh's "A Pair of Boots," a romanticized vision of the
boots themselves and, by extension, the relationship between art and its
working-class subject:

> On the leather lie the dampness and richness of the soil. Under the soles slides
> the loneliness of the field-path as evening falls. . . . The equipment is pervaded
> by uncomplaining anxiety as to the certainty of bread, the wordless joy of hav-
> ing once more withstood want. . . . This equipment belongs to the *earth*, and it
> is protected in the *world* of the peasant woman. From out of this protected
> belonging the equipment itself rises to its resting-within-itself.[24]

From Heidegger's perspective, Van Gogh has endowed a class of people,
who might otherwise recede into the background, with positive value. Still,
we must ask, what is that value? Or, more appropriately, whose value is it?
To whose *world* does that value "belong," and in what *world* is it "protected"? The peasants'? Van Gogh's? Heidegger's?

Heidegger's position on the origin of art, according to Fredric Jameson,
sees art as that which "emerges within the gap between Earth and World or
. . . [between] the meaningless materiality of the body and nature and the
meaning endowment of history and of the social."[25] Thus, with Van Gogh's
and Heidegger's interpretations before us, the most credible assertion may
be that, on historical and social grounds, it is they, much like the Peruvián
critic, who need to believe in an essentially satisfied peasantry who see the
trials of poverty and hard work to be part of a necessary and beautiful suffering that "exalts work and the goodness of nature." These elitist values
are then inscribed in the art that pulls its subject from the unframed earth
toward (and perhaps into) its frame or world view.

Unlike Van Gogh and Heidegger, the artists who represent *cholos* seem
to be of the earth that is being pulled into the frame of their art's world.
Since art is popularly viewed as a noble pursuit, the framer and the framed
may be pulled into that world of nobility. This inscription takes the form of
two components: art's presumption of permanence and art's designation of
beauty.

First, since classical times art has acquired—or has aspired to create—
an aura of timelessness, of permanence. Whatever stands outside of time is

somehow above and beyond the oppressive strategies of any moment in a particular society's history. One asks, therefore, where does *cholo* art figure in this conceptualization? In one respect, since they know themselves to be subject to the vicissitudes of time and place, *cholos* exist as pliable figures in the national imagination. The possibility of granting *cholos* concrete viability and permanence through art, then, could be an especially powerful influence on the artist's vision. The logic here is that being a definitive something is better than being an indefinite anything. Therefore, artistic permanence assists, at least in theory, to defeat racial and social transience.

The second component, art's designation of beauty, may be comprehended as enabling even more positively a sense of collective self-esteem. Notions of femininity, in this effort, are particularly crucial. In the Roman Catholic, European tradition, women are frequently symbols of physical and (especially from the Latin American perspective) spiritual beauty— from Petrarch's Laura to Hollywood's Marilyn Monroe, from Michelangelo's *Pietà* to India's Mother Teresa. What then is the concept of beauty as represented in the form of the *chola*? How do artists convert the *mestizo*'s frequent designation *cholo feo* (ugly *cholo*) into *chola bella* (beautiful *chola*)?

First, consider the "robust" nature of these women. To some extent, this representation challenges the classical form of Western feminine beauty insofar as *chola* women tend to be full-figured and large-boned. In both ceramic figures and paintings, their gently curving forms are emphasized through the use of line and composition. Hence, in this context, these curves seem to address the play between soft and hard, delicate and robust. The use of warm, earthy, or glowing colors over and against minimalistically represented facial features adds substantially to the suggestion of an interior beauty that can be recuperated by representing women who lead lives of hard physical work. Also, the emphasis on child care and the matronly figure aligns the *chola* with the biblical Mary who occupies such an important position in the Latin American Christian's religious imagination, as well as Mama Ocllo, the Incas' mythical earth mother of creation.

Of course, *cholos* do not normally see and buy these art works. With what some might call postmodern savvy, these artists seem to know how far they can push the *mestizo* and elite white consumers into accepting a beautiful representation of the *cholo*. While the art may propose a new aesthetic that could contribute to a renewed construction of social order, the artists know that "oppositionality" (in Appiah's terms) can be "saleable" only when "its commodification guarantees for the consumer that it is no substantial threat."[26] Thus, the represented *cholas* still seem to project a deferential or subservient attitude, for example, in their lowered heads or minimized or erased facial expressions. As the more oppressed sex of an oppressed racial class, woman thus becomes for the *cholo* the symbol of both beauty and oppression. It is ironic, to say the least, that these beauti-

Figure 5.2 "Amor de Cholo," ceramic by Juana Sosa, 9″. Photo by L. Gwen Christopher. Private collection of Milagros Zapata Swerdlow and David Swerdlow.

ful representations may coexist, in the homes of wealthy whites and *mesti-zos*, with the real *cholas* who work there as maids.

Works

For many reasons, including concerns about gender, Juana Sosa's work titled *Amor de Cholo* (figure 5.2) is remarkable. The image is not entirely uncommon. In fact, a less than stylish on-line, mail-order gift operation out of Miami[27] advertises an eighty-dollar incarnation of the image as comparable to Rodin's *The Kiss* in that it captures "every bit of the same sweet feelings." Juana Sosa's particular piece, however, compels our attention because the actual words "Amor de Cholo" are inscribed on the figure itself. When *mestizos* or whites use this phrase, they evoke a less than favorable image. Generally, they are referring to their vision of a *cholo* and *chola* engaged in a public, violent, and/or unrefined display of sexual urgency.[28] Sosa's piece, while public, could not be described as violent or unrefined. To the contrary, *Amor de Cholo* displays tenderness. The inscription seems to put the *mestizo* and white world on notice. Sosa proposes that *cholos* are beings capable of beautiful lovemaking. Also, the work emphasizes that the *chola* is not only a mother and caregiver, but also a sexual being who is the equal of her lover, not below him. As these two people look at one another without deferring to or even recognizing the *mestizo* and white gaze, Sosa posits an independent world apart from the racial categories that surround it. Her inscription marks that claim.

Also remarkable for its claims is a well-known but less popular ceramic image created by the Max Inga, also of Chulucanas (figure 5.3). In this image, a *cholo* occupies the position of Christ on the cross. Instead of plain wood, the cross is constructed of a shovel and a machete, and the shoeless, dark-skinned *cholo* is dressed in the *campesino's* typical ragged work clothes and hat. It may be the threatening nature of this powerful image that accounts for its relative obscurity. Far from insinuating that the *cholo* is a godly figure, this image situates him as someone who has been sacrificed. Like Christ in relation to the Roman Empire, he is the victim of an oppressive force that ridicules him and attempts to rob him of his sense of self. Hence, the image also reclaims Christ as a figure in touch with the plight of the oppressed. Finally, one is encouraged to ask, for whose sins is this *cholo* dying?

The act of interrogation seems to be even more explicit in Mauricio's large painting of a young woman (figure 5.4). In comparison to his smaller treatment of the two fishmongers (figure 5.1), this piece reaches far beyond the traditions and confines of *costumbrista* depictions of working life. Most notable is the young woman's ambiguous gaze compared with the nonexistent gaze of the fishmongers. The faceless fishmongers cannot see; they

Figure 5.3 Max Inge, untitled ceramic, 12″. Photo by L. Gwen Christopher. Private collection of Milagros Zapata Swerdlow and David Swerdlow.

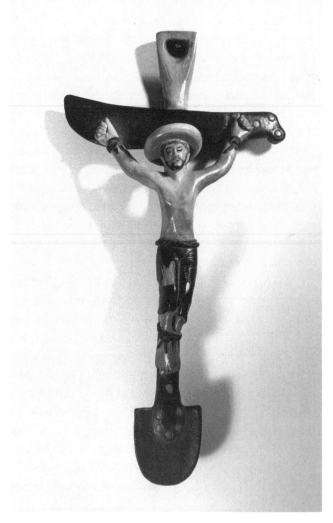

can only be seen as a group. They work for others. They are celebrated for their forms and for the work they perform, and as individuals. In contrast, the young woman under the moon has no apparent work to perform. As the full moon hovers above her, casting a rectangular shaft of light onto a stone whose presence seems more than incidental, her context can only be described as symbolic, far from the realism of the fishmongers' coastline. The painting is clearly about her, as an individual in a world of forces. She looks both inward and outward, questioning herself and those who view her. Her eyes and arms seem to be in search of a place in which she may come to rest.

She is *of the moment* in the same sense that John Berger uses to describe Hélène Fourment as she is rendered in Rubens's painting: "Clearly she will not remain as she is for more than a second. In a superficial sense, her image is as instantaneous as a photograph's. But, in a more profound sense, the painting 'contains' time and its experience."[29] As such, Hélène and the

Figure 5.4 Untitled oil painting by Mauricio, 25″ x 24″. Photo by L. Gwen Christopher. Private collection of Milagros Zapata Swerdlow and David Swerdlow.

young woman are in control of what can be seen of them. Unlike many of their peers, they may be said to control their image and, in that sense, themselves.

Another interesting and possibly alarming feature of this painting is the young woman's light complexion. Is the young woman a *chola* on the way to being a *mestiza*? Compared with the fishmonger and the women in many other of Mauricio's paintings, she is much "whiter." Does this suggest that the whiter you are, the more control you have over your destiny? If so, is this painting an indictment of racism, an expression of latent desire, or merely recognition of a social fact? The question lingers on her face, as if in the viewer's eye.

Precisely who is the intended viewer for this painting? With whom does the image of this woman hope to be in relation? We cannot know. To try to represent what artists try to say would mean to speak for them and their intentions. We do know, however, that the pieces have an impact at their point of reception, the *mestizo* and white world. Nothing is more lost in this impact than the possibility of an aspiration or desire of the *cholo* that is not dependent on any racial category. In effect, this desire is unrepresentable because, quite simply, it would be unacceptable at the point of reception by *mestizo* and white Peruvian society. This absence may indicate that the *cholo*, as Juana Sosa projects, may yearn for a stable, collective identity that is not dependent on any other racial category. Or more pessimistically, it may indicate that the *cholo* would not dare consider him or herself in relation to the *mestizo* or white. Mauricio's painting occupies the ground between these two positions; his subject reaches through the "ambiguous margin."

Cholos in the *Mestizo* Gaze

Many *mestizos* and whites feel it is in their interest to make it difficult to pass through the racial border area or the "ambiguous margin," as Vargas Llosa conceives it. And, just as artists may see their work as liberating the *cholo* to be proud of his or her *cholo*-ness, the elite consumer retains this same work as a way of enslaving the *cholo* in a lower, subservient social rank. Just as the visual arts wish to convey a sense of permanence or timelessness, they also trap their subjects within their frames. Only a few escape.

When one purchases an image of the *cholo*, one also purchases, at some level, the person represented by the image. Hung on the wall or sitting in the display cabinet, the image serves its owner. It is decor. It brings pleasure. It moves only at the owner's command. It looks down in deference, or it works in the owner's fields. As an added attraction, these *cholos* are made to look beautiful, perhaps suggesting to the viewer that they enjoy their subservience. Few if any *mestizos* or whites might admit to such motivations or pleasure. Their reason for buying this art is likely to be the one typically given by any buyer of art: it is beautiful. Much like a ride in the country, these works reveal the simple pleasures of rural life. The stressful chaos of modern life is relieved by the unmolested beauty of premodern tradition. The colors are soothing. The composition is graceful. Time pauses.

Yet, the pause of time is framed by their pre-Columbian heritage. Looking into the tender eyes of the maternal *chola* (figure 5.5), made from Peru's own clay and detailed in the indigenous tradition, presents a way of appreciating, if not claiming, an Indian history. Of course, most Peruvian *mestizos* and whites are very proud of their nation's Inca heritage, as long as it remains embedded in the distance of history, or located in the beautiful ruins and artifacts of Machu Picchu or Sipán—that is, as long as it remains frozen in art. Once that history is set into motion and begins to impinge on the personal present, however, it becomes threatening. History reappears as memory, which is no longer controllable. The *cholo*, in person, reminds the *mestizo* of his or her own mixed heritage.

Part of that heritage is, of course, Spanish, and that heritage elevates the *mestizo* to a position of authority and, at some level, responsibility. In "Questions of Conquest," Vargas Llosa considers that heritage and responsibility:

> Immense opportunities brought by the civilization that discovered and conquered America have been beneficial only to a minority, sometimes a very small one; whereas the great majority managed to have only the negative share of the conquest—that is, contributing in their serfdom and sacrifice, in their misery and neglect, to the prosperity and refinement of the westernized elites. One of our worst defects, our best fictions, is to believe that our miseries have been

imposed on us from abroad, that others, for example, the conquistadores, have
always been responsible for our problems. . . . Did they really do it? We did it; we
are the conquistadores.[30]

As much as Vargas Llosa identifies and interrogates the underlying guilt of
the *mestizo* class, he also suggests the continuing tendency of Western elites
to override that guilt and exploit the underclass. Owning and marketing art
featuring and/or created by *cholos* may be aptly described as a capitalistic

Figure 5.5 Untitled
ceramic by Juana Sosa,
9″. Photo by L. Gwen
Christopher. Private
collection of Milagros
Zapata Swerdlow and
David Swerdlow.

conquest. One of the more interesting aspects of this exploitation should be discussed in terms of its international component.

Cholos in the Foreign Gaze

The fact that Peruvians have made this kind of art popular, and have even begun to export it, is an important development in the entire culture's self-conception. When the art work is marketed, it gains a kind of credibility that is no longer controlled by its producer or by its seller. How these commodified forms are received abroad, principally in the United States and Europe, begins to affect how Peru is perceived abroad and, eventually, how that message is returned to Peru.

Most of the foreign consumers of both the ceramics and the paintings have little knowledge of Peru's current status. Perhaps they have heard of the Shining Path's terrorist activities, have considered the novelty of an "Asian" president (Alberto Fujimori) in a Latin American country, or have even shaken their heads over Peru's part in the production of cocaine. Beyond that, Peru is the land of the Incas—locked forever in the period before the seventeenth century.

The face of the *cholo* is not marketed or recognized as an image of conflicted modernity, but of the purely primitive. This mystification is hard to overlook in the following language from an on-line gift catalogue:

> Five hundred years before the birth of Christ, the Peruvian potters of Chulucanas became widely acclaimed. In the 1920s descendants of these potters returned to the soil of their past, studied archeological and historical information about their forefathers and dedicated themselves to recreate their ancient art. They succeeded. Chulucanas pottery is now among the finest in all of South America.[31]

While the catalogue credits the potters of Chulucanas with the sophistication necessary to study archeology and history, it also buries that information as much as possible within a frame of the primitive. Since the first sentence casts the potters back five hundred years, it is difficult to know whether it is speaking of the Vicus, pre-Columbian culture, or of the makers of the art being sold in the catalogue. The mistaken date in the second

sentence should also be considered. The people of Chulucanas began this
work in the 1960s, not the 1920s. The error may be yet another attempt to
keep the work as premodern as possible. Finally, when the potters are said
to "recreate *their* ancient art," the consumer is led to believe that the people
making this art align themselves with the ancient, not the contemporary.
Clearly, the advertisers have a sense of what the consumers desire: an
image that reflects their conception of Peru's people—that is to say, the face
of the Inca, who stands for all pre-Columbian people of Peru, if not Latin
America.

When, we might ask, has any other image of Peru been consistently
exported? When has there ever been an internationally released documentary about contemporary life in *mestizo* Peru? In contrast, the number of
documentaries about Peru's pre-Columbian history, as well as contemporary life in the premodern regions of the Andes, seems monumental. In a
manner not unlike the way *mestizos* wish to own and control the image of
the *cholo*, the international market wishes to own and control the mistaken
image of Peru as a Third World nation whose commodified face is entirely
Indian.

The artists themselves may be working against this mystification. Every
ceramic piece made by the Chulucanas, for example, has its creator's name
inscribed in its base. Most often, these names announce a Spanish, rather
than Indian heritage. Some artists and artisans even put their addresses
under their names. Clearly, they want their identities and their localities to
be recognized—even if only for the sake of garnering future business.

Unfortunately, as Appiah argues in regard to an analogous situation in
the production of contemporary Yoruba art, "The sculptor of the bicycle,
by contrast, will not be known by those who buy this object; his individual
life will make no difference to its future history."[32] In an attempt to recuperate the culture along with the art form, Appiah argues that "nevertheless, there is something about the object that serves to establish it for the
market: the availability of the Yoruba culture and of stories about Yoruba
culture to surround the object and distinguish it from 'folk art' from elsewhere."[33] Certainly, culture and surrounding stories distinguish the folk art
of northern Peru as well. Those stories and traditions, however, rarely cross
the border with the commodified art. As the *mestizo* and white elites of Peru

frame the *cholos* and deny their departure from the premodern world, the international consumer economy frames Peru and denies its entry into modernity.

Conclusion

The art representing *cholos* exists as another floating signifier used to ennoble, devalue, mystify, or enshrine their situation. From one perspective, this work, as art, solidifies the *cholos'* position by using the force of tradition to give them an identifiable, desirable place in the world. Another perspective receives these works not as art but as serviceable decor that keeps the *cholos* in their place. Finally, as "folk art," this work may be received as nothing more than a representation of the primitive in its generalized, stereotypical form.

Like the subjects they represent, these works resist and beg for classification. They are yet another product of Peru's ongoing racial identity crises most notably situated in the nation's contradictory obsessions with history and progress. *Cholos* and the work that represents them occupy the space, the "ambiguous margin" where these obsessions conflict. Outside of Peru, there is no conflict: Peru is only history—material for defining the progress of the consumer nations that it services with its folk art. Consequently, the European and North American gaze reinstates Peru's indigenous complexion.

A synopsis of Jose Antonio del Busto Duthurburu's argument in his work *El Mestizaje en El Peru* offers the most idealistic resolution of the racial difficulties revealed in the popular art by and about *cholos*: "El día que los peruanos sintamos orgullo de ser mestizos, el día que nos digan cholo y reaccionemos como si nos llamaran hombre o peruano, habremos alcanzado el equilibrio" ("The day that Peruvians feel proud to be *mestizos*, the day that we are called *cholos* and react as if we were being called a man or a Peruvian, we will have reached equilibrium").[34] These sentiments may have also been the message that inspired and derailed Vargas Llosa's internationally supported presidential bid in 1990. That surprising failure, along with the continual problems the nation experiences whenever it confronts its racial divides, suggests how deeply embedded racism is in Peru.

At one point Fredric Jameson poses the following dilemma: "What we must now ask ourselves is whether it is not precisely this semiautonomy of the cultural sphere which has been destroyed by the logic of late capitalism."[35] The situation of the figure of the *cholo* in Peruvian art provides an unusually compelling example of how the same factors that make the culture so divided also enable it to appear as a unified subject for the international market. Of course, we can also argue that only when a work is authentically seen within the seam, margin, or rift of its own origin does it become art that engages the interpreter on something resembling its own terms. The question nonetheless remains: who is the interpreter, from where, and for what reasons? With respect to the *cholo*, the reasons—popular or unpopular—cannot ever be totally recuperated.

6/You're All Guilty

Lo Cubano in the Confession

JAMES J. PANCRAZIO

> The truest confession is the one that avers that
> all confessions are false, that being is the
> telling of false tales about being.
>
> **González Echevarría,** *The Pilgrim at Home*

IN JULY 1996, THE CUBAN MOVIE STAR ROSITA FORNÉS WAS scheduled to make several appearances in Miami.¹ This was a rare opportunity for the most famous of the so-called vedettes to perform in South Florida. Promoters booked theaters in South Miami Beach and at El Centro Vasco on the famous Calle Ocho. As the dates approached, many questions arose regarding Fornés's politics. After all, she still lived in Cuba and had not publicly broken with Fidel Castro's government. When it became known that she had no intention of breaking with Castro and in fact planned to return to Cuba after her performances, the most reactionary sectors of the exile community organized protests. Spanish-language radio stations refused to broadcast paid advertisements, anti-Castro groups organized a boycott, and on July 11 a Molotov cocktail was thrown through the window of the Centro Vasco. After facing intimidation, terrorism, death threats, and a potential boycott, the owners of the Centro Vasco felt obligated to cancel the performances.²

What Rosita Fornés was asked to do was to stage a public confession. Such insistence is not an isolated incident. For instance, when Cuban songstress Albita Rodríguez defected to Miami several years ago, she was placed in a similar situation. Nevertheless, she refused demands on Cuban radio to "repent" for growing up communist.[3] Roberto González Echevarría has documented the public confession in Cuba as a cultural trend that followed in the wake of the revolution.[4] He holds that the radical transformation of the island provoked a profound meditation about the role of the individual in history. While the official discourse of the revolution promoted a sense of rupture with the past, the confessional autobiography appeared as one of the ways in which intellectuals could publicly vindicate their class and make amends for never having been authentic revolutionaries.[5] Just so, in postrevolutionary Cuba,[6] arguing the case against the apolitical Latin American intellectual, Ernesto "Che" Guevara wrote, "La culpabilidad de muchos de nuestros intelectuales y artistas reside en su pecado original; no son auténticamente revolucionarios" ("The guilt of many of our intellectuals and artists resides in their original sin; they are not authentic revolutionaries").[7]

Since the early days of the revolution, artists and intellectuals have walked a narrow line between confession and self-justification, only to insinuate that if they are guilty it is because everyone else is guilty. One such example is Heberto Padilla's famous public confession of 1971. In a rereading of one of the most dramatic moments of recent Cuban history, César Leante demonstrates that the confession contains a "lenguaje doble" ("double language") that undermines its sincerity. He argues that Padilla sought to "transmit" an underlying message that would indicate that his confession was a sham. One such example is his use of the word *desconocer* (to deny, to not know, to disavow). When Padilla refers to the group of foreign writers that have supported him, he says, "Desconocen, muchos de ellos, el hecho de que yo hubiera tenido esas actividades, de que yo hubiese llevado a cabo tales posiciones" ("Many of them *do not know/deny* that I would have had those activities, that I would have carried out those positions").[8] Here, both Padilla's inverted syntax ("activities" and "positions") and the word *desconocer* read as "to disavow," suggest that the confession should be read as twisted and deformed. Further, Padilla's refusal to speak about the role of the state security forces in his detention only alludes to their active participation. He says, "Los compañeros de Seguridad me han pedido que no hable de ellos" (The comrades from Security have asked me not to talk about them). Aware of the presence of the international media,

Padilla appropriates the conventions of self-criticism to accuse the state of greater moral and ethical violations. Leante refers to Padilla's "confession" as a mockery. It can be argued, instead, that it was a theatrical coup d'état, a performance of a confession that brought international scrutiny to his case. His so-called acceptance of guilt is only a pretext to reframe individual responsibility in terms of society at large.

One usually considers the confession as a sign of an individual's betrayal of the moral community, and Cuban history provides ample examples of betrayal, transgressions, and violations of national and international trust. The list is seemingly endless: José Martí's suicide/martydom, Antonio Maceo's assassination, U.S. intervention in the Cuban War of Independence, Eddy Chibás's confession/suicide, General Ochoa's trial and execution, Fidel Castro's so-called betrayal of the revolution, and the border crossings by Cuban Americans.[9] The general assumption is that when the individual performs a public confession, not only does that person capitulate and accept the position of power, but, as Paul de Man observes, the purpose is to "overcome guilt and shame in the name of truth."[10] To rejoin society, the accused must perform an act of self-effacement in order to accept and reaffirm ideological orthodoxy. However, does self-criticism necessarily imply an acceptance of the dominant ideology? When Guevara accuses artists and intellecuals of the "original sin" of not being real revolutionaries, is he suggesting that these artists and intellectuals have an internal consciousness of wrongdoing? Or is he arguing that Latin American intellectuals are deserving of blame or censure? It is my contention that, while Cuban confessional discourse emerges from within a framework of an accusation by a moral authority, at no time does it imply conversion, contrition, or repentance. Much too often, the postrevolutionary confession is considered a servile act of deference to the revolutionary authorities in order to obtain advantages and social position, rather than a means of illuminating the problematics of hegemony and the illusory sense of social continuity in both Havana and Miami.[11]

First I will concentrate on the example provided by a popular recent Cuban film in which the depiction of the confession is further vexed by gender issues. I will then demonstrate how the confessional strategies of displacement and substitution permeate Cuba's more elevated cultural discourse by examining the works by novelists Alejo Carpentier and Guillermo

Cabrera Infante. To conclude, the same confessional strategies can be seen being played out in Miami's exile community.

My purpose is not to decry the intolerance habitually demonstrated by hard-liners on both sides on the Straits of Florida; rather, I intend to show how the rhetoric of confession has been ritualized by many artists and intellectuals in ways that illuminate the whole of Cuban culture. While the *autocrítica* and the confession have become quite common in postrevolutionary culture, what makes them particulary Cuban is the presence of an alternative discourse, a *choteo*, that undermines the sincerity of act of confession and reframes blame as collective.[12] Indeed, to confess is simply part of being Cuban—with one enormous distinction: to confess is not to confess oneself, but to confess others. This account does not dispute the historical roots of the practice of the confession in Cuban history since its inception. Instead, it will explore the means through which these specifically Cuban confessions become not simply a reflection of how individuals perform in the culture, but how the culture itself performs in individuals. Cuban culture is confessional culture without individual guilt. And confessional culture authorizes what it is to be Cuban.

Strawberry and Chocolate

An intriguing example of the inversions of the guiltless confession is provided by the popular film *Strawberry and Chocolate*. Based on the award-winning short story, "El lobo, el bosque y el hombre nuevo" ("The Wolf, the Woods, and the New Man") by Senel Paz, the film was quickly heralded as one of the best recent Latin American films, winning first place at the Havana Film Festival in 1992. While the filmmakers said that their only intention was to make a film that was "moving, full of humor and emotion," they eventually collected more than twenty awards in international film festivals and even an Oscar nomination.[13] On the international market, *Strawberry and Chocolate* was also a sensation. It brought in over $4 million in Spain and almost $270,000 in the first three weeks, showing in only twenty-four theaters in the United States. It has been credited with establishing an opening that has brought gay culture out of the closet in Cuba.[14]

Strawberry and Chocolate has also been seen as a provocative film that exposes the dark stain of homosexual repression in revolutionary Cuba.

The film provides a sympathetic look at Diego (Jorge Perugorría), a gay man who strives to promote Cuban culture, and a naive university student named David (Vladimir Cruz). Although their relationship initially begins by their mutual attempts to disgrace each other, they manage to become close friends. The film becomes a love story that takes place during a time of intolerance when conformity to the system is a real temptation. But before we dry our eyes, we must be aware that the film is just as much an example of the filmmakers's political savvy as a cultural product of the revolution. As Dennis West observes, "Gutiérrez Alea is a committed revolutionary."[15] There are no doubts about the director's politics. West adds, "As an ideological project, [the film] appears to represent a belated attempt to recuperate the gay community for the Cuban revolutionary project. The film's message of tolerance can be read as a call for revolutionary solidarity in the face of the current economic debacle and an increasingly cloudy political future."[16] Although the film is critical of the revolution's errors, it certainly maintains itself within the framework of Cuban cultural production.

While the film may appear to be an acceptance of guilt and shame, the director's use of the comic *enredo* or embroilment is not so much to poke fun at society's contradictions, but to purge its guilt. The film uses comedy to heighten the perception of social corruption in a fallen society, as well as to mediate the guilt and responsibility inherent in self-criticism.[17] In this sense, *Strawberry and Chocolate* reframes individual responsibility as collective (as if to express, "No sense in feeling guilty, we all have to act this way to survive").[18] *Strawberry and Chocolate* reframes oppression with the notion of intolerance, a problem in which everyone plays a part. In effect, the film collapses into an exercise of confessions in which everyone confesseses everyone else. Homophobic oppression, in other words, is not the only wrongdoing portrayed in the film, but instead constitutes the material for renewed confessions of various kinds, which begin with Cuba's metaphorical dishonoring at the beginning. When Diego realizes he cannot seduce David, he substitutes for the actual seduction the appearance of seduction. He "accidentally" spills a cup of coffee on David's shirt to simulate the "stain." Diego waves the soiled shirt outside his apartment window like a flag announcing his victory to the world. As the *enredos* accumulate, David risks losing the main benefit that the revolution has brought him, his education. With the twists and turns of the *enredo*, David, who had conspired to put Diego behind bars, becomes instead the victim. *Strawberry and Chocolate* is eventually transformed into the story of a Cuban homosexual's confession for attempting to tarnish the reputation of a young patriotic revolutionary. Diego, like Heberto Padilla, is pressured into making a public confession. While he refuses to sign any document, he does in fact make a private confession for his wrongdoing.

But what is the status of this confession? Paul Julian Smith observes that the film's evenhandedness—conveying the message that even the victims of oppression can be oppressors too—is false symmetry. He adds, "When the deck is stacked so overwhelmingly against one partner (when gays have been invisible in Cuban cinema for so long), any such balance serves only as ostentatious negation, an attempt to wish away the massive repression that has taken place."[19]

Traces of the repression of Cuban gays that characterized the postrevolutionary period are nonetheless apparent in the film through the overt "sanitization" of the gay characters so that they can, in a sense, share their guilt with all of the audience. If they were too different from their viewers, that could prevent the necessary empathy that is so important in this context of Cuban confession. This sanitization is further accomplished by the careful choice of actors. According to members of the gay community in Cuba, the roles were actually reversed.[20] The character of the gay intellectual was played by the straight Jorge Perugorría,[21] whereas the character of the young communist militant is played by Vladimir Cruz, a gay actor.[22] Not only is sanitized commentary substituted for social criticism, but also homosexual seduction is likewise replaced by the two main characters' attempts to persuade the other to think differently. The seduction of a body becomes the seduction of the mind. At this point, sexuality gives way to instruction and understanding based on the common ground that unites all "real" (read: revolutionary) Cubans: self-determination and anti-imperialism. It is at this point that the characters' voices blend into a single perspective. Rather than exposing the notion that an unshakable faith in any ideal (religious or political) is an inescapable route to repression, the film's characters vindicate the ideal by stating, "Los errores de la revolución son aparte de la revolución" ("The errors of the revolution are not a part of the revolution").

After viewing a film like *Strawberry and Chocolate*, one could well ask the following question: does self-criticism (or criticism of revolutionary excesses) imply repentance? While the film appears to be a denunciation of homosexual repression, critics have been quick to observe that it is easy for directors like Gutiérrez Alea and Tabío to denounce events that occurred almost twenty years ago. In his review of the film, entitled "Rotten Strawberries and Bitter Chocolate," Cuban refugee Albert Jimper writes that although the director Tomás Gutiérrez Alea is very talented, "his biggest skill is not making movies. It's surviving at any cost. Alea was one of the artists who watched his gay friends be carried away, while he took a female companion, denounced gay behavior as subversive and immoral, and hid under the protective wing of the director of the Cuban film institute."[23] What is most ironic about the film *Strawberry and Chocolate* is not so much that it reframes the oppression of Cuban homosexuals as a family squabble, a misunderstanding among revolutionaries, each eager to confess. In fact, the confessional dynamic of the film spills over onto the critics of the film, each confessing the other's guilt. Therefore, any attempt to have a group of people concerned with the future of their country ignores the dynamics of confession of the film while questioning whether any group can have the responsibility for the destiny of the country. The idea of their country is overcome by the energies of confession.

The Harp and the Shadow

The substitution and displacement strategies in *Strawberry and Chocolate* can be comprehended more fully as a restaging of the dilemma of how Cuban intellectuals brought themselves in line with revolutionary ideology in the 1960s and 1970s. Most particularly, if we consider the case of Alejo Carpentier we understand anew the totality of the need to confess in Cuban culture. Carpentier's late fiction is particularly representative of how postrevolutionary discourse redirects responsibility and blame from the individual to society as a whole. Critics often register this redirection by basing their readings on the question of Carpentier's commitment to the Cuban revolution. Although Carpentier's final novel, *El arpa y la sombra* (*The Harp and the Shadow*, 1980), chronicles the fictional confession of Christopher Columbus, critics have largely agreed that the author is actually criticizing himself. The novelist is confessing the "original sin" of not being an authentic revolutionary, as well as simultaneously dramatizing his selling out.

Unable to decipher Carpentier's motives in terms of Marxist ideology, critics have attempted to plumb the author's psyche. For example, in "Framing Carpentier," a title that unknowingly evokes both "contextual readings" and "false accusations," Eduardo González characterizes the novelist as constantly demonstrating bitter self-contempt.[24] Furthermore, there is a general consensus that Carpentier's work is always at the border of self-parody, self-deception, and biting self-censure.[25] It is not without reason that critics have read the narrator as a mask for the author. But if Columbus is Carpentier, then the Inquisitionlike Vatican must be a mask for Cuba's hard-line, politico-cultural elite, the same bureaucracy that makes Diego's life impossible in *Strawberry and Chocolate*. In short, one could argue that Carpentier uses the image of Columbus to simulate a confession and simultaneously thumb his nose at his accusers by reminding them that guilt is collective.

The displacement and substitution that plays out in the novel depends on a clear division between an authentic inner self and a false social self. While the dying narrator is awaiting the arrival of the priest to administer his last rites, he reflects on the social mask he created to acquire power. The narrator accuses himself of self-invention and "falsity of self" for having promoted his project. He actually addresses himself, "Cristóbal, Cristobalillo, tú que te inventaste, durante el viaje, el nombre de *Christo-phoros*, pasador de Cristo, cargador de Cristo ("Christopher, Cristobalillo, during the voyage you invented the name *Christo-phoros* for yourself, the one who brings Christ, the bearer of Christ").[26] He admits to reading himself into the Bible and using biblical imagery to acquire power. However, as with the toothless critiques of revolutionary excesses in *Strawberry and Chocolate*, self-accusation is hardly a sign of repentance. Bakhtin writes that in this type of confession there is a constant "refusal to accept a possible judgment . . . and as a result tones of resentment, distrust, cynicism, irony, defiance appear."[27] About this confessional self-accounting "turned inside out," he adds that the "worst kind of invective is the just invective, which expresses in tones of malice and mockery what the other himself could say about himself in penitential-petitionary tones.[28]

The social mask, or the *I-for-the-other*, is always a body: consider only the fact of Diego's exaggerated effeminacy in *Strawberry and Chocolate*. In Carpentier's writing, this is most evident when Columbus meets Queen Isabel in Granada. The narrator relates how he used his physical appearance to give himself the qualities of the traditional Roman conqueror. Nevertheless, he characterizes misrepresentation or misreading the social mask as a defect "en nosotros" ("in ourselves").[29] The use of the collective pronoun displaces guilt and reframes it as part of the human condition. In this sense, the confessional discourse constantly fluctuates between guilt and blame; the narrator balances self-deprecation with accusations. Carpentier uses parenthetical phrases, contradictory predicates, intertextual citations, and shifts in perspective to establish the norms of social conduct.[30] Thus, self-criticism always places the narrator in a social context where everyone acts as he does. With few exceptions, Columbus characterizes all as so many usurpers, actors, whores, and knaves. His crew consists of a group of rogues fleeing justice, recently baptized Jews and Muslims, *pícaros* and adventurers.[31] When Columbus admits that he has lied, cheated, or stolen, he does so to implicate his accomplices and competitors. Even Queen Isabel is an opportunist, more interested in having sex with Columbus than granting him ships and provisions. As she says, her only reason for continuing the colonization of the New World is "por joder a Portugal" ("to fuck Portugal").[32] Thus, while Columbus is actively accusing himself of lies and deceit, he implicates the queen and her bedroom politics.

Carpentier's narrator emerges as both self and other, accused and accuser, sinner and penitent man, actor and author.[33] Although the narrator can never be the man that he was, there is a certain continuity between the two. At the end of the novel, the narrator announces that the confession he is rehearsing to himself is one that he will never make. He demonstrates that repentance, contrition, and guilt are little more than yet another social mask that, given a lack of other resources, he wears when it is convenient.[34] In light of the behavior of the queen, the crew, and Spanish society, Columbus decides that he is no worse than anyone else and absolves himself. In *El arpa y la sombra* the narrator thereby rejects individual responsibility and reframes guilt as blame. Alejo Carpentier's fictionalized confession creates a society that rationalizes lies, falsity, manipulation, betrayal, and deceit. In sum, Columbus absolves himself of the need to confess by condemning everyone else.

Mea Cu(lp)ba

The strategies of displacement and substitution in the confession are so embedded in postrevolutionary culture that they frequently appear in exile writing. *Mea Cuba* (1992), Guillermo Cabrera Infante's collection of auto-biographical essays, is another reflection on how responsibility, guilt, and blame are intertwined. The title of the work involves the obvious play on words alluding to the act of penitence. He writes, "Cuba es, por supuesto, *mea maxima culpa*. Pero, ¿Qué culpa?" ("Of course, Cuba is *mea maxima culpa*. But, what guilt?").[35] If we read the confession as a public discourse in which the accused confronts the charges of accusers, we find that Cabrera Infante directs his confession to the Cuban exile community. He states that his reasons for writing the book are not his own. Although his friends have requested him to write, it is his enemies who have forced him to make a book of the "obsessive" articles that have appeared in the press.[36] Forced into writing a confession, he begins by stating what his enemies know only too well: he was a communist who fled from communism. Furthermore, he admits that his parents were among the founders of the Cuban Communist Party. He even recalls Joseph Stalin's picture hanging in the kitchen next that of Jesus Christ. Because his authority to speak for and about Cuba is in such a precarious position, he adopts a seemingly intimate discourse of the confession. But Cabrera Infante not only admits his responsibility for Cuba's cultural revolution; he must also show that he is one of the victims. Therefore he expiates his own guilt while at the same time joining the ranks of the accusers denouncing the revolution.

At several points in *Mea Cuba*, Cabrera Infante refers to his own state of exile as a veritable paralysis, an invisibility and a social nonexistence. When newspapers like *El País* claim that no writers of "escala intelectual" ("intellectual stature") like Juan Marinello, Fernando Ortiz, Alejo Carpentier and José Lezama Lima have abandoned Cuba, he argues that their "being" in Cuba is a direct result of their "being" dead.[37] The notions of being and death have a curious relationship in *Mea Cuba*. When Cabrera Infante returns to Cuba from his unofficial exile to attend his mother's funeral, the death of a maternal figure corresponds to the death of life in Cuba. The mother (*mater*, maternity, matrix) is the place of new beginnings and growth. However, the metaphorical death of Mother Cuba plunges life itself on the island into a living death that the author compares to being a "zom-

bie."[38] In effect, the author effaces himself to blend into a chorus of the
voiceless dead that have shared his precarious political position. He accomplishes this primarily through gossip, unpublished documents, and what
Paul de Man calls "prosopopeia" *(pros pon,* face, mask, dramatic character
[*pros-* + *opon,* face,] + *poiein,* to make), literally to create a mask for a voice
that does not exist, a voice from beyond the grave.[39] Cabrera Infante creates
an entire chorus of the dead who affirm that they too were victims of the
revolution. This haunting chorus is comprised of ex-revolutionaries, writers who escaped during the Mariel boatlift, and even Nicolás Guillén and
Alejo Carpentier. All of these voices merge with Cabrera's to denounce the
social circumstance of which they were all very much a part.

Between anti-Castro diatribes, meditations on suicide, and nostalgia for
Havana, Cabrera Infante confesses his "original sins." His first, as director
of the literary journal *Lunes de Revolución,* were his attacks on the poet José
Lezama Lima.[40] His second was his making Virgilio Piñera the "escritor de
la casa" ("house writer") and the third was having brought together too
many talented people.[41] The author also writes Lezama Lima's unofficial
biography. In terms of his self-absolution, the poet is a key figure. Not only
must Cabrera Infante resurrect him and then ritually kill him again, but
also he needs Lezama to absolve him for having killed him off in the first
place. Ironically, the author must engage in the same character assassination that made the poet's life literally (and literarily) impossible in Cuba. The
biography does not focus on Lezama's intellectual contribution to Cuban
culture; it does, however, discuss his homosexuality at length. While admit-
ting responsibility for the personal attacks against Lezama, the author also
implicates the members of his staff at *Lunes de Revolución.* In the end he
confesses, "Lo que hicimos en realidad fue tratar de asesinar la reputación
de Lezama" ("In reality, what we did was try to assassinate Lezama's reputation").[42] But a confession of collective guilt only serves to hide individual
responsibility. Just as Padilla into his captors and Carpentier into Columbus,
Cabrera Infante disappears into a collective *we.*

Throughout *Mea Cuba,* the author constantly writes and rewrites the
same incidents. Most pertinent to his absolution is the episode where the
revolutionary government censors and sequesters the film entitled *P.M.*
When the editors of *Lunes de Revolución* protested, the new government
scheduled a meeting to decide its fate. It was at this meeting that Fidel Castro announced the new direction of Cuban cultural politics, "Con la Rev-

olución todo, contra la Revolución nada" ("Everything with the Revolution, nothing against the Revolution"). This event appears twice in *Mea Cuba*. Early in the book, Cabrera Infante focuses on the history of the cultural revolution in Cuba and, two hundred pages later, emphasizes José Lezama Lima's intervention in the discussion. The poet not only defended the film, but also defended the magazine that had so viciously attacked his youthful excesses.[43] Lezama, from beyond the grave, absolves Cabrera's peccadillos and thus legitimizes the author's perspective.

We're All Guilty!

While focusing principally on writers and artists who have had direct contact with the revolution, I want to emphasize that the confession as a cultural practice does not exclude Cuban writers in exile. For many journalists and radio personalities in Miami, explaining, justifying, and condemning is a full-time job.[44] One of the best examples of how the confession permeates Cuban cultural production is Guillermo de Zéndegui's essay "Todos somos culpables" ("We're All Guilty"). He argues that the revolution was made possible because the majority of Cubans lack self-consciousness. He refers to the Cuban idiosyncrasies of individualism, ambition, envy, and intransigence as the inherited defects of Spanish imperialism. He contends that all Cubans must submit to the ritual of confession as preventive medicine against the temptation of social revolution.[45] Was it not precisely the refusal to participate in this ritual confession that so infuriated Cubans in exile when Rosita Fornés and Albita Rodríguez first came to South Florida? Their refusal to confess became, in each case, a confession of refusal. Of course, this refusal can also be seen as yet another manifestation of national identity.

My purpose is not to show that Cubans in Miami—any less than in Havana—are intolerant of difference; instead, it is to demonstrate how the rhetoric of confession is deployed as resistance to guilt and shame. The confession in postrevolutionary Cuban culture has been exacerbated in an atmosphere where large numbers of people are encouraged to repent and make radical ideological changes overnight. It might appear to signify a ritualized rupture with the past in a society that is predisposed to guiltless repentance. However, this rupture is in fact a reconstitution of the individual "confesser" as *culture within the culture*. In this sense, not only are guilt, blame, and responsibility politically charged issues that urge the populations in Havana and Miami to self-defense and resistance, but also those same issues justify their own excesses.

Ruth Behar narrates a failed attempt to establish a dialogue with the island's government when Miami attorney Magda Montiel Davis was filmed kissing Fidel Castro. Behar, also a member of the group, but who didn't attend the meeting with the Cuban president, confesses how easily she could have fallen into the same role "unconsciously being flirtatious in an effort to catch Father Fidel's attention." But, as we have seen, self-reflection is a precursor to generalizing about Cuban society in general. Turning the confession outward, she writes, "For no matter how strong and conflicted our emotions about Fidel may be, there is an erotics to his domination. Women deny it at their peril. Men, too, but in a different way, not daring to admit they could be seduced by a more macho man."[46]

Confession ranges across the whole cultural spectrum. As we have seen, *Strawberry and Chocolate*, *El arpa y la sombra*, and *Mea Cuba* operate in terms of the same strategies of displacement and substitution. Similar to what Paul de Man documents in Jean-Jacques Rousseau's *Confessions*, the multiple excuses and accusations in the Cuban confessions exculpate the confessors, thus rendering the confession redundant in terms of its origin. De Man quotes Rousseau in his magisterial reading of the *Confessions*, "Qui s'accuse s'excuse" ("He who accuses himself excuses himself").[47] The confessional discourse in postrevolutionary Cuba is consciously self-destructive; it serves to ritually efface the self, to dismantle individual responsibility, and to place guilt just beyond the vanishing point. The whole vocabulary of confession proves to be an enduring and unifying characteristic of Cuban culture across time, political allegiances, and the Florida Straits.

7/ The *Cueca* of the Last Judgment

Politics of Chilean Resistance in *Tres Marías y una Rosa*

OSCAR LEPELEY

S INCE ITS INCEPTION IN THE FIRST YEARS OF THE REPUBLIC, Chilean theater has had the intention to reflect upon the national reality in its various phases, crises, and transformations. This tendency was already clear when, on September 10, 1812, during the struggle for independence, the patriot Fray Camilo Henríquez wrote in the newspaper *Aurora de Chile*, "I consider the theater as a public school, and therefore the dramatic muse is a great tool for politics." Fray Henríquez championed theater as an essential part of the struggle for emancipation from colonial oppression. The theater, as the pedagogic hand of the builders of the nation, "should fill the stage with the sublime majesty of Melpúmene, breathe the noblest feelings, inspire hatred against tyranny, and unfold all the republican dignity." At the end, Henríquez prophetically says that the tears wept in the theater would not be sterile, because "their fruit will be the hatred of tyrants and their works."

Indeed, during the independence wars of the nineteenth century, theater figured not only as political commentary, but also as a forum for debates about a number of issues: the republican system, separation of church and state, parliamentary excesses, and the horrors of oligarchic regimes. At the beginning of the twentieth century, the Chilean theater testified to the rise of new social classes, as well as to the cultural manifestations of the humblest parts of the population. In the 1940s, however, the theater went through a profound renovation with the creation of the Teatro

Experimental de la Universidad de Chile (Experimental Theater of the University of Chile) in 1941, and the Teatro de Ensayo de la Universidad Católica (Essay Theater of the Catholic University) in 1943. Both promoted the presentation of plays that reflected the problems of the day.

In the 1950s, when the contradictions in Chilean society became even more acute, once again the theater became a privileged forum for their denunciation and discussion. A new generation of playwrights, which included Egon Wolff, Isidora Aguirre, Sergio Vodanovic, Luis Heiremans, María Asunción Requena, and Alejandro Sieveking, wrote of a Chile poised on the threshold of modernity. The enormous changes and the social turmoil of the 1960s, as well as the beginning of the socialist government of Salvador Allende, were assembled and transformed into theatrical material by a number of theater companies that endorsed a system of collective creation.

For some one hundred fifty years, Chile had been one of the most stable democracies in Latin America until the coup d'état of September 11, 1973, when President Allende was deposed. The military, now in power, took control of the nation and started a generalized repression against all democratic entities. The dictatorship lasted seventeen years, during which time freedom of expression was forbidden, all political activity and criticism of the government was persecuted, and any person considered an enemy of the regime was detained, tortured, or executed.[1]

Despite repression and censorship, the Chilean theater was able to articulate a critical protest against the military government during the dictatorship. Between 1976 and 1981, thirty-one plays critical of the government were written and staged in Chile.[2] The play *Tres Marías y una Rosa* is one of the most representative works in this corpus, not only because of its position as a pioneer, but also because of its extensive use of a form of popular culture in Chile—the *arpillera*—as the vehicle for criticism. The play was the result of the extensive research done by members of the Taller de Investigación Teatral (Workshop for Theater Research), a group that broke off from the Theater of the Catholic University of Santiago in a search for an alternative way to produce theater under the Pinochet dictatorship.[3] *Tres Marías y una Rosa* opened in Santiago in July 1979.

Research for *Tres Marías y una Rosa* was conducted in a poor neighborhood of Santiago in a workshop of *arpilleristas,* poor women whose hus-

bands were unemployed as a consequence of the crisis precipitated by economic measures imposed by the dictatorship. *Arpilleras* are hand-sewn
tapestries fabricated from scraps of cloth appliquéd to rustic panels made of
burlap or canvas bags—like those used for carrying potatoes, flour, or
sugar—on which miniature dolls are displayed against landscapes of tiny
houses, animals, neat rows of vegetables, and fruit trees.[4] The background
usually includes the sun and mountains. Of course, in one respect, the art
of making *arpilleras* belongs to a universal feminine tradition of needlework. In Chile, more particularly, the origin of the *arpilleras* can be traced to
the embroidery of the folklorist Violeta Parra in the 1960s.[5] Parra's art was
followed by the embroiderers of Isla Negra, whose pieces were exhibited in
the Louvre in Paris.[6] During the Pinochet dictatorship, Chilean *arpilleras*
became a voice for the denunciation of human rights violations and an
expression of the everyday difficulties of life under the repressive regime.

The action of *Tres Marías y una Rosa* takes place in the courtyard of a
modest home in a marginal neighborhood in Santiago; it is the house of
Maruja, chief of the *arpillera* workshop. The other three characters are
María Ester, María Luisa, and Rosa. When the story starts, Rosa, who is
pregnant, has just asked to be admitted into the workshop. The product of
the women's work will be taken to a central store, which exports it for sale
abroad. With the money earned from their work, the women can buy basic
necessities for their families, since their husbands are unemployed. Rosa's
husband is a special case, however. He is employed at the beginning of the
story, but the form of payment he receives—a practice that became fairly
common in Chile at the time of the dictatorship—does not enable him to
support his family. Instead of money, he receives the equivalent in goods
produced at the factory.

The lives of these four women, three Marías and one Rosa, become a
site where the incongruities of the regime are clearly and carefully
depicted. At the same time, the play provides a forum for reflecting on the
nature of art and on the role of these women as artists and political beings.
They speak the popular language of the Chilean poor, especially those sectors that are silenced and subjugated by the official discourse. The reproduction of popular dialects in the play evokes the people from several parts
of Chile. Thus, the play can be seen as a free space that has been won in

spite of fear of repression. The use of dialect provokes contestatory, sarcastic laughter against submission to the official discourse. The fact that the characters of the play are *arpilleristas*, victims of the economic experimentation currently going on in Chile, also forces the audience to confront the reality of the life of the poor, officially idealized as contented with their lot in life and supporting the economic reforms imposed by the military regime. Ultimately, the play poses *arpillerismo* as the answer to the modernizing pretensions of those indifferent to the social cost of a forced authoritarian utopia. Moreover, by privileging the women's needlework as something born out of the experiences of the poor, the play also suggests that other oppressed groups can make their voices and their protests heard, that their sufferings, joys, and hopes can be represented.

I wish to discuss *Tres Marías y una Rosa* not just as a theatrical event at a difficult moment in Chilean history, but more especially as a rich text wherein history is depicted in the human faces of four women, perhaps the humblest victims of the repression that devastated Chile during the military dictatorship. This discussion of *Tres Marías y una Rosa* will demonstrate how popular art, specifically the art of making *arpilleras*, can become a powerful means of commentary and a vehicle for resistance.

The Poetics of the *Arpilleras:* Murals of Life

It is part of the tradition of *arpillera* making that the *arpillerista* should capture her vision of the world at the historical moment she is living in. This tradition can be formulated in the two tendencies of the *arpilleristas'* art. The first is a realist-naturalist poetics that trusts it can show a reality sufficiently illustrative on its own terms. In the play, this aesthetics is articulated by María Ester in Rosita's second lesson about the art of making *arpilleras*. As the scene begins, Maruja explains to the novice, Rosita, that the theme of an *arpillera* is the daily experience of life:

MARUJA: Yes, this work is very beautiful, Rosita.
ROSITA: Yes, that is true.
MARUJA: The theme has to be related to things that happened in your life, do you understand? Because we are interested in our own things, Rosita. Some-

times we think we don't care, but we do care.

ROSITA: I am not sure I can do this.

MARUJA: You have to look back and remember something that has happened in your own history, do you understand?[7]

Later, one of the experienced *arpilleristas*, María Ester, reaffirms the documental-testimonial poetics that the Taller de Investigación Teatral (TIT) proposed at its inception; the aesthetic postures counterpoised against one another constitute a metacommentary about the aesthetics of the play itself.[8] Later, María Ester summarizes the aesthetics of the realist documentary:

MARIA ESTER: . . . Open the window, look outside. What do you see? Tell me!

ROSITA: Gee . . . I don't know!

MARIA ESTER: The people! This is what you see out the window: *the reality of life.* That is, the theme of people's lives: houses, children, buckets of water, dogs, flies . . . (209, emphasis added)

As it seems clear, this is a call for Rosita to picture the miserable conditions endured by most of the Chilean poor. María Ester's intention is to unveil to the audience a reality that they probably do not know. Of course, the gesture is also a way to attain what Brecht defines as arousing by the repudiation of desire as a way of changing what is clearly perceived as unjust. María Ester wants to stress the idea of denouncing misery when she indicates to Rosa that when she looks out the window she can see the lamppost. "This is very important! How do you get electricity in your house?" (209), she asks. Rosita answers, "I am connected to my sister-in-law's electricity, and she gets hers from the street" (209). That is to say, misery has led these persons to connect to each other clandestinely to obtain the electricity they need for their homes.

The second notion of poetics proposed by the play is represented by María Luisa. Instead of searching for inspiration in reality, María Luisa proposes that the source of the *arpillera* art lies in introspection. She advises Rosa to close her eyes and to look inside herself, into her conscience, for the impressions that life has left in her; thus, she maintains, Rosa will set free her "artistic imagination":

MARIA LUISA: The first thing you have to do is to put a cloth around your eyes, very tight. Because when you do an *arpillera you have to look inside, not anywhere else*. Then with your eyes covered you start going inside, inside, inside, until suddenly, *zas!* there is something *like a fountain that begins to flow*. With this flow you draw the *arpillera*. Do you understand? (212–13, emphasis added)

In this way, María Luisa says, when one looks inside and sees one's own experiences, inspiration is born: "Now I just say what I have inside and I paint a big mural of life" (213). It is clear that the *arpilleristas'* recommendations to Rosita revolve around the issues that were being debated by the Chilean theater at the time. Should it become realist-naturalist theater or not? *Tres Marías y una Rosa* is precisely an aesthetic synthesis born of this dilemma.

However, on one subject all Rosita's art "teachers" agree: the work must be an expression of *Chilenidad*—Chilean spirit—that must define the Chilean soul at that particular historical moment. This is expressed primarily through the representation of the Andes, a telluric site, extending the length of Chile from north to south, which becomes such a symbol that it seems impossible to imagine the national landscape without the mountains' ubiquitous, solemn presence. The first thing Rosita sees in Maruja's *arpillera* is "a snowy mountain" (206). María Ester makes her explanation very explicit: "The first thing you have to do is put the mountain in." When Rosita asks if a mountain range she sees in an *arpillera* is the Andes, María Ester answers that it cannot be the range along the Chilean coast, which it is not very high or snowy. It must be the Andes, because representing the Andes is the only way to let those in foreign countries know that this is Chile. By anchoring their "murals of life" firmly in Chilean soil, these tapestries seek to reveal specifically Chilean problems and thus to denounce abroad the conditions of life to which the military regime has reduced the poorer segments of the population.

As her learning progresses, Rosita is ready to start embroidering. She announces that she will start her first *arpillera* "with the Andes range on a background of sixty by forty" (209), the typical dimensions of the *arpillera*. If the idea of the mountain, in the symbolic field, is "associated with the idea of meditation, spiritual elevation, and communion with the saints,"[9] its use is no less meaningful when applied by these simple women who think about the misfortunes of their lives and their country as they struggle to improve their material and spiritual conditions for themselves and for their families.

Tres Marías y una Rosa, with its latent subversive message, pictures a moment in Chilean history when *arpillerismo* itself, because of its potential for illustrating themes that could be considered subversive, evoked the ire of the military regime. Authorities tried to stunt its development by supporting instead an official *arpillerismo* to replace the private workshops. Themes displayed in officially sanctioned *arpilleristas* either exalted the armed forces or represented an innocuous urban folklore. Rosita reports a discussion she had with Carmen, a member of another workshop, who delivered her *arpilleras* to the official, state-sponsored workshops in charge of selling them:

> ROSITA: Yes. She has a workshop here in the neighborhood. My sister-in-law works for her making *arpilleras* depicting military parades, folkloric dances, so . . .
> MARIA LUISA: That's true. And Carmen gets thirty dollars for each *arpillera* in the *butic* of Providencia. (214)

Whereas products of the official *arpillera* workshops commanded high prices in dollars at stores in the rich parts of town, the dissident *arpilleristas* in the play are having problems selling their work, for both economic and aesthetic reasons. In the first act of the play, we learn that the stores have rejected María Luisa's *arpillera* about the Last Judgment because it was not easily understood. Maruja tells her: "They found your Judgment confusing" (216). That is to say, María Luisa's fertile imagination has forced her to explain her work in words. Because she has opted for a poetics in which she alters reality according to her own inspiration, she now must pay the price for her audacity. The dialogue continues:

> MARIA LUISA: I don't see how they cannot understand that here there are two paths: one leads to glory, the other to hell. It's that simple.
> ROSITA: Yeah, if we can understand it here, how can they not understand it there, I ask.

MARUJA: The ones who go down are not dressed like dogs; they are people wearing fur coats who go to hell, as I explained to René Pérez.

MARIA LUISA: And what did he say?

MARUJA: He said that they looked like Saint Bernard dogs.

ROSITA: But that's absurd! How can they confuse a lady with a Saint Bernard, I ask!

MARUJA: And where is God? René asked me. Any one of these angels here can be God, I told him.

MARIA LUISA: That's when you messed it up! Can't you see that God is this one here coming down in a UFO?

ROSITA: I think it is because of this UFO that they don't understand your *arpillera* in the central store.

MARIA LUISA: The fact is that for me God is from another galaxy. That's why he travels in a flying saucer to judge the rich and to forgive the poor. (216)

In spite of the commercial failure of this *arpillera*, finally it is María Luisa's poetics that imposes itself. The first act ends dramatically with the news that delivery of *arpilleras* to the central store has been suspended because it has an excess of stock it cannot sell. The women then face the disappearance of their only source of income. María Ester and María Luisa decide to leave the workshop and go to work in the official workshop run by Carmen. Rosita decides to continue working with Maruja, who insists along with her colleagues that they should try to find a collective solution to the problem.

When María Luisa takes her *arpillera* about the Last Judgment to the official store in Providencia, the piece is censored and then rejected for political reasons; the owner tells her that in an *arpillera* "there cannot be either rich or poor . . . because now we are all equal. Now there are no differences" (225). This repeats a demagogic slogan that the repressive political regime adopted to deny class differences and even the existence of classes altogether.

After they see what work in the official workshop entails, María Luisa and María Ester ask to be accepted back in Maruja's workshop. She permits their return because the local priest has commissioned a giant *arpillera* to be placed in a new chapel soon to be opened. This *arpillera* will be equivalent to sixty normal *arpilleras* in size. María Luisa is happy with the new dimensions, since her ideas "do not fit into a sixty-by-forty rectangle" (227). The theme of the *arpillera* will be the Last Judgment.

The Last Judgment: Hell and the Cross-Eyed God

The feverish activity demanded by the new task of making the giant *arpillera* corresponds to the carnivalesque representation of what is supposed to be a solemn sacred theme. The backdrop for last act of the play is the half-finished gigantic *arpillera*. One figure represents the conventional Christian God, with a long beard and a "bastante enojado" ("very angry") look on his face, his finger pointing at something (240). Behind God of course is the inescapable snowy mountain range, from which two paths originate; one leads to glory and the other to hell. To add to the carnivalesque effect, those who are supposed to be in heaven are represented as extremely bored: "In heaven there are some clouds and some very bored people sitting on the clouds" (241). On the other hand, hell is represented as a modern commercial building called a "caracol" ("snail"). Such buildings were very common in Chile at the time. The consumerist fever that the building represents reflects the desire of the military regime to change the habits of the population from austerity to boundless consumption. The *arpillera* denounces such schemes and proposes a resistance by condemning consumerism to hell.

However, the *arpillera* shows that the devils "lo están pasando fantástico" ("are having a great time," 241). Even fire, traditionally seen as a punishment for those condemned to hell, is represented as enabling an element of pleasure, since it is used to prepare barbecues. This is the carnivalized image of a joyful hell where the bad have fun while the good languish in heaven. Of course, this carnivalized view of the Last Judgment cannot help provoking laughter, in spite of what the *arpillera* reveals about Chilean life. In Bakhtin's words, "In the act of carnival laughter, death and rebirth, negation (ridicule) and affirmation (joyful laughter) are combined. This is profoundly ideological and universal laughter."[10] The *arpilleristas'* intention is to unmask the economic model that enables a few to enjoy their capacity for consumption while the majority observe the excesses of the rich. If personal success is measured by buying power, this theatrical discourse contests the official discourse, questioning and trying to weaken it in order to incite change.

A carnivalesque tone pervades this scene with its systematic profanations; just so, the figure of God that the *arpilleristas* have created is cross-eyed. One woman notices the problem and remarks, "We've got to do something. God cannot be left with one eye looking in one direction and the other one another direction, because this way he is cross-eyed" (241). The episode suggests that God appears in the process of being created by these humble women; because he is a God-in-process, he is incomplete. María Luisa tells Maruja, "You were in charge of making God; now you've got to finish him" (241). These are carnivalesque commentaries that seem to call to the deity to intervene in the problems that burden the poorest parts of the population; otherwise, God will correctly be seen as a cross-eyed deity who cannot see clearly the difficulties that the authoritarian regime has brought to Chile. Besides, if he does nothing to correct the situation, God is incomplete, and only the *arpilleristas* will be able to finish making him with both their labor and their suffering.

A *Carabinero* God

But the position of God is also a subject of discussion among the *arpilleristas*. María Luisa expresses the idea that God is above all worldly powers. No matter what position one occupies in society, inevitably one has to submit to his final judgment—nobody can evade it.

> MARIA LUISA: These people cannot escape because God has powers to take all of them to prison!
> ROSITA: How can he take people prisoners if he is not a policeman?
> MARIA LUISA: He is not a policeman, but everybody has to pay attention to his judgment. (242)

The women reproduce here the experience that the authorities have made a fact of daily life; a strong authoritarian presence represented by the uniformed police. The Chilean police retained absolute power to arrest whoever they wanted, without consideration for personal rights—which of course were limited in any case under the permanent state of emergency. This total power perceived in the police is carnivalesquely transposed to the figure of a *carabinero* God. In this way, the play also expresses the idea that the authority of the dictatorship is not untouchable and that it will one day have to take responsibility for its acts of violence and account for its sins before the highest authority. And, by extension, it also suggests that the dictatorship will have to settle accounts with the popular authority that will be reconstituted once democracy returns to the country.

As the women discuss their representation of God in the *arpillera*, there is a systematic lowering of the divinity of the several kinds of authority he stands for. At this point, the play resembles the parodic treatment of sacred texts that was permitted and quite common in the Middle Ages, when not just the texts but also the sacred rites were parodied, "under the cover of the legitimized freedom of laughter."[11]

The Popular Counterculture of Florcita Motuda

The desacralized tone of the play actually appears from the very beginning, with the song "Pobrecito mortal" ("Poor Mortal Man") played very loud. Both the first and second acts start with this song. The play has two acts, divided into six scenes. The song was composed and originally performed by Raúl Alarcón, nicknamed Florcita Motuda, a singer who entered Chilean artistic life in 1977 with "Brevemente gente" ("Briefly People") at the Festival de la Canción of Viña del Mar. This annual festival, telecast throughout the country (as well as elsewhere in Latin America and in Miami), had become an effective propaganda tool for the military regime, which managed to keep the people distracted by such entertainments. Alarcón, however, surprised the organizers of the festival by challenging the requirement that artists should appear in approved costumes. Florcita Motuda appeared on stage in carnival dress. As the official magazine *Ercilla* described him, he had on "his yellow plastic coat, his motorcyclist sunglasses, and his enormous cowboy boots [that] almost caused his elimination from the event." The article added that some of the organizers judged him "a little bit crazy."[12] This provocative figure also challenged the established musical and artistic canon with songs that invited reflection about solidarity among human beings—for instance, "Brevemente gente."

Including a song by Florcita Motuda and noting the _arpilleristas'_ admiration for him immediately suggests that _Tres Marías y una Rosa_ intends to desacralize, and indeed to contest, the hegemonic discourse about the country. Rosita expresses her admiration at the beginning of the second act: "I like this Florcita Motuda! I find him so charming . . ." (222). From this point on, her admiration leads quite naturally to her suggestion that Florcita Motuda can please even God, and that he too should appear in the _arpillera_ of the Last Judgment:

> ROSITA: So! The little angel goes playing the cueca with a cornet like Florcita Motuda plays!
> MARIA LUISA: That is why God is happy, because Florcita Motuda is in the group!

Therefore, this carnivalesque Florcita Motuda, about whom the polemic writer Enrique Lafourcade states, "He is Groucho Marx, and he is Picabia, and he is Tzara, and he is Dalí, and he is Arrabal . . . [he is] fantastic!"[13] represents the vehement desire for change underlying this carnivalesque representation of the world. From the first scene of the first act, when the stage set shows a courtyard of "a modest house in a marginal neighborhood" (196), with some clothes drying in the sun, it is clear that the play will try to represent the reality of the poor. As the stage fills with the lyrics of Florcita Motuda's song, the play declares its intention to contest the official discourse whose aim is to keep the people silent.

When Rosita poses as a model for the angel who will announce the Last Judgment, she appears dressed as a winged angel, "rouge on her cheeks and a birthday cornet in her mouth" (241). María Ester goes beyond Rosita's interpretation of the angel and suggests a further identification with the singer: "There is something else needed for your angel to look like Florcita Motuda. Here, put on my sunglasses!" (243). Rosita puts them on; the angel in the Last Judgment ends up with sunglasses.

The Sad _Cueca_ of the Last Judgment

Despite all the work the women put into the gigantic _arpillera_, the general impression of the piece is one of sadness. When the priest sees it, he does not say anything. Rosita, on the other hand, expresses her opinion openly: "For me, this Judgment is way too sad!" (242), and suggests how to make it better. The angel, for instance, "has to appear dancing the *cueca*! That will make him look more modern too!" (242). The idea of the angel of the Last Judgment dancing the *cueca*—the national Chilean dance—is hard for Maruja to accept. But the idea is not so crazy, since the priest, when he finally admits that he finds the *arpillera* too sad, asks the women to arrange for a performance of folkloric music and dance at the ceremony opening the chapel where the *arpillera* will be placed. Besides, according to María Ester, the priest finds the *arpillera* not only sad, but also "not very Chilean." Maruja cannot understand the priest's objections, since the piece has the usual Andes range in the background. But it seems that this time the Andes alone cannot do the work of representing Chile, so Maruja asks María Ester to bring a guitar and to sing folkloric songs at the opening ceremony. No matter how much they try to adjust the *arpillera*, there comes a moment when the *arpilleristas* have to face their work and perform their self-criticism. Rosita takes the initiative and proposes drastic changes:

ROSITA: You know what I'd do with this Judgment, Luchita?
MARIA LUISA: No!
ROSITA: I would make it a lot happier.
MARIA LUISA: But the Judgment cannot be happy!
ROSITA: But see, the problem is that here the devils of hell are having much more fun than the saints in heaven, and this is not right, because then everybody is going to want to go to hell!
MARIA LUISA: But this is the way I saw it in the film!
MARUJA: Which film?
MARIA LUISA: The film with the story of Master Michelangelo when he was lying on some scaffolds to paint the Last Judgment!
ROSITA: Was this film in color?
MARIA ESTER: It was a film with Charlton Heston. What a stud!
MARIA LUISA: How about the pope! You should see how he forced the Master to work . . .
MARIA ESTER: Just like Maruja does to us.
MARIA LUISA: He was sick and still he had to work every day until the Judg-

ment was ready. And was this Judgment happy? No, of course it was not happy! (244)

Rosita still does not like the idea of a happy hell: it is inconceivable that people who have done evil in life, who have made other people suffer, who have not helped others and have instead subjugated and tortured them, could be happy enjoying eternal life in hell. For Rosita, this is not exemplary punishment at all. In the above dialogue, María Luisa reveals her source of inspiration, the film *The Agony and the Ecstasy,* which is then used for some carnivalesque comparisons. The *arpilleristas* take the role of the master Michelangelo feverishly working in the Sistine Chapel under the pressure and vigilance of the pope—a situation in the play represented by Maruja's constant pressure to hasten the work on the *arpillera.* Obviously, the impression the final product of the *arpillera* piece gives is not happy; yet, as María Luisa says, Michelangelo's *Last Judgment* was not happy either, since his working conditions were unhappy. Rosita insists in making the Judgment a little happier and suggests some drastic changes:

ROSITA: With all due respect, the first thing I'd do would be to change God's face.
MARUJA: And what kind of face would you give him?
ROSITA: A more modern face, because this one is too angry.
MARIA LUISA: But God has to look angry because God cannot go around having fun with modern things; besides, the Last Judgment is not modern stuff.

But Rosita insists that God must be happy because "what he is saying is 'the good ones follow me.'" This is a reference to another form of entertainment, because these words were the slogan of the antihero of the Mexican TV show, "El Chapulín Colorado," very popular in Chile at the time. Not content with just giving God a happier face, Rosita also suggests making heaven happier with the incorporation of the idea of a patriotic celebration: "In one side of heaven I would put some very nice *fondas* with lots of little colorful flags. . . . And many people together, playing the guitar, dancing and eating."[14] Rosita's suggestion leads the women to a discussion of the consumption of alcohol in heaven. María Ester believes it is not allowed:

"Booze must be forbidden in heaven!" (245). But María Luísa closes the discussion when she reminds her colleagues of the stories in the Bible: "Alcohol cannot be forbidden in heaven because in the wedding party at Cana Jesus transformed water into wine! He must have had his reasons, no?" (246). Maruja also finds approval for holding a party in a biblical passage: "Because our Lord told us very clearly that heaven is a banquet to which we are all invited" (246). The issues are resolved through democratic discussion, and the "Judgment is approved by majority of votes!" (246). The carnivalization of the Last Judgment is completed by music; to make the Judgment happier, the women finally agree to put in a *cueca*:

> ROSITA: The matter will be resolved if we make these people dance the *cueca*. That's simple.
> MARIA ESTER: The *cueca* of the Last Judgment!
> MARIA LUISA: That's what we should call the piece: "The Cueca of the Last Judgment." (246)

This is the point at which the angel of the Judgment becomes Florcita Motuda, and he is pictured playing a cornet to please God. Of course, María Ester wants to go even farther in this carnival and suggests including her idol John Travolta in the piece, but the others reject the idea because this is a Chilean mural supposed to reflect the problems of the marginalized Chilean people. "This is not a discotheque," Rosita reminds her. If this is a popular Chilean party, it has to have *fondas*, and for María Luisa, if the *arpillera* has *fondas* "it must have some beef barbecue, and even some barbecued pork ribs" (246). Her suggestion is approved, and all the women decide that hell should help with this celebration:

> ROSITA: Let's use some of these little flames from hell; they're pretty good for the barbecue.
> MARIA LUISA: Good idea! Help me here with the fire, Miss Maruja.
> *(They transfer some of the fire from hell to heaven).* (246)

This way, the fire from hell is carnivalized, becoming an element for the enjoyment of life and for the happiness of the poor people, quite apart from their economic capacities. The idea is further developed when María Luisa says that she is sure that money is not worth anything in heaven; they should put a sign reading: "Everything is free in heaven!" (246). Rosita, in turn, wants to appropriate the utopia for earth right now; she wants to add to the sign: "As well as in earth."

Elements of Epic Theater

Since its inception, the Taller de Investigación Teatral has proposed to make a theater to document Chilean reality and has adopted the point of view of the oppressed. The dramatic action of *Tres Marías y una Rosa* is clearly based on the contradictions in Chilean society of the 1970s caused by confrontations among economic, social, and political forces. Yet the TIT members wanted to encourage an empathy with the characters and to historicize the dramatic action, thus provoking in the spectators a critical attitude toward what they observed. This process, they believed, would lead the spectators to a richer understanding and knowledge of material reality and consequently inspire them to seek change. The Brechtian concept of epic theater was one of the tools used by the dissident Chilean theater during the dictatorship, because it proposed, as Brecht prescribed, to transform the spectator "into an observer . . . [to] awaken his intellectual activity."[15]

It is not surprising, therefore, that at the end of *Tres Marías y una Rosa* the conflict is not resolved; rather, the fundamental contradiction of an armed authoritarian minority oppressing a defenseless majority is even more apparent. For this reason, the final *cueca* is sad. The stage directions read: "They start to sing the *cueca* of the Last Judgment, but it comes out very downhearted" (248). The singing is so sad that Rosita comments, "Once again this song sounds like a funeral, eh?" (248). And, when the final *cueca* starts playing, Maruja starts dancing beside the finished *arpillera*; she dances alone—an allusion to the drama lived by thousands of women whose husbands, sons, or other relatives had been "disappeared," victims of federal agents. The *cueca sola* (literally, the solitary *cueca*) became an act of protest that had a great emotional impact, since it was practiced by the victimized women. The reaction of whoever observed the scene was the typical reaction sought by epic theater: identification with what spectators see on stage and a consequent understanding that something has to be done in the exterior world.

Distancing Effects and Nonidealized Characters

The characters in *Tres Marías y una Rosa* are not idealized. The women constantly argue and nag one another, and thus the play produces the "distancing effect" that epic theater strives to obtain in order to avoid identification with the characters.[16] Brecht says that theater "must renounce everything that represents a tendency to hypnotize" the spectator.[17] Compare the moment when Maruja faces María Luisa and they discuss whether to accept Rosita in the workshop; in front of the others, Maruja accuses María Luisa of having another source of income because she takes in washing. María Ester at first opposes Rosita's admission to the workshop; she feels betrayed when she learns that Maruja has already accepted Rosita and demands: "There must be a vote! You cannot go on making alliances with people on our back! This is a trick!" (207). Maruja replies: "I don't play tricks! And listen, don't you dare to disrespect me in my own house!" (207).

Rosita is at first characterized as a little silly, slightly naive; she does not understand instructions and her ideas are very childish. When María Luisa teaches her the introspective method and asks Rosita to suggest ideas for an *arpillera* with extraterrestrial themes, Rosita can only think of Disney characters:

ROSITA: The first thing we have to put in the *arpillera* is the Andes mountain range.
MARIA LUISA: That is to say, the UFOs start landing on the Andes when, suddenly, they see . . .
ROSITA: *(Again with her eyes covered.)* Mickey Mouse!
MARIA LUISA: Then Mickey Mouse was getting off the UFO when suddenly he meets . . .
ROSITA: *(Uncovering her eyes.)* Donald Duck!

When the central store decides not to accept any more *arpilleras*, a crisis breaks out in Maruja's workshop and the women argue sharply about her leadership. Maruja insists on a democratic resolution: "We have to find a solution together, all of us in the workshop" (220). Her words provoke a heated exchange with María Luisa, revealing how the official discourse has penetrated the poor people's way of thinking. María Luisa upholds a hier-

archical arrangement and charges Maruja to find a solution without both-
ering the others.

> MARIA LUISA: We're not going to get involved in this problem. Here you are
> the only one responsible for these solutions.
> MARUJA: By golly, what are you talking about, María Luisa!
> MARIA LUISA: That's why we elected you the boss, for you to solve the prob-
> lems. And don't tell me you don't like to be the boss!

The first act ends with the breakup and division of the workshop; Rosita
stays with Maruja; María Ester and María Luisa decide to work for the official workshop in Providencia, where their *arpilleras* are rejected as subversive. When they ask for readmission, Maruja accepts them on certain conditions: "No more fights," and "María Luisa must work more and chat less"
(226).

Characterization, besides distancing the actors from the spectators,
also obeys another precept of epic theater: the dramatic action will not
arise from character flaws but the faults of the society in which the story
takes place.

Dramatic Ruptures

Toward the end of the play there is a curious rupture of the dramatic
illusion when the action—the women are working quickly to finish the
arpillera—accelerates artificially "as if in a fast camera." The stage directions explain that the characters must move "back and forth very quickly,
so that the piece is finished off in seconds" (247). This adaptation of cinema
technique, which contrasts with the rhythm of the scene (which has hitherto corresponded to real time) follows the Brechtian precept to avoid illu-
sionary theater in order to provoke reflection about the issues.

The play ends by breaking the fourth wall—the imaginary wall that
separates the spectator from the dramatic action. All the women except
Maruja leave the stage and carry the *arpillera* through the aisles of the theater. Alone on stage, Maruja closes the window to her house in a gesture
that indicates that the audience has had an opportunity to participate in
the life of this modest house and in the lives of these poor women. The ges-

ture also signals that it is time to take some action to change the conditions that the play exposes. The reflexive tone of the work is reinforced when Maruja slowly surveys the audience, then descends from the stage and moves toward the entrance hall, just as the spectators will do in an instant.

The Spectator as Creator of Meaning

The text of *Tres Marías y una Rosa* is meant to open up a space for the spectator to fill in with his or her own information about the real problems of life under the dictatorship. In those more or less ambiguous moments— "spots of indeterminacy," those "gaps" in the text[18]—the viewers can decodify the play according to their own "horizon of expectations"[19] that appears in the coded dialogue between the dramatic fiction and the ideas brought from reality.

One of the first allusions to contingent reality is a comic episode described by María Luisa about thieving cats; it evokes the climate of terror to which the forces of the dictatorship have submitted the poorer sectors of the population. One day María Luisa arrives at the workshop with scratches on her arms and face. She explains that the previous night a group of cats had invaded her kitchen and were stealing food; María Luisa and her children had to fight to put them out of the house. She also tells her colleagues that her first reaction when she got up was to grab her identification booklet, "because we got used to sleeping with the booklet by our side" (198). The audience can recognize here the military's forceful entry into people's houses in the poorer neigborhoods late at night, after the curfew. Soldiers would arrest all males above fourteen years of age, herd them into stadiums, and keep them there for hours until they were identified. The primary purpose of these raids was to keep the population in poor neighborhoods always afraid, insecure. This is the reason María Luisa sleeps with her identification booklet in her hands. The episode also serves to denounce another threat of violence that the military authorities regularly directed against the poor: the low-flying helicopters that buzzed the houses of the poor to remind them of oppressive vigilance. When María Luisa describes her fight with the cats, she says that she grabbed one by the tail "and started to turn it around like a helicopter. Do you remember the helicopters that flew over the neighborhood at night? I did just the same with the cat" (199).

María Luisa refers to couples who have been separated when the husband has to leave in search of work in other places and, in her case, outside the country. The family thus has to suffer the indefinite absence of the father and husband, and the woman has to cover the roles of both mother and father. When María Luisa was awakened by the noises in her kitchen, her first impulse was to call her husband, but "suddenly I remembered that Mario is in Argentina looking for a job!" (199). She had to face alone with her children the potential danger that invaded her house in the middle of the night.

Rosita also refers to a real condition that contemporary spectators could recognize. She is first presented as living in desperate poverty. When María Luisa asks that Rosa be accepted in the workshop, she says to Maruja: "Just imagine, this morning she wanted to throw herself in the Mapocho" (200), alluding to the desperate action taken by some during the dictatorship of drowning themselves in the river that crosses Santiago. This is also a macabre reference to the practice of throwing into the Mapocho the bodies of dissidents after they had been tortured and executed. Some Chileans and foreigners were horrified witnesses, and the spectators presumably knew about the practice.[20]

María Luisa also says that Rosita, who has two children and is again pregnant, lives in such misery that there is no food in her house: "She has nothing to eat! I have to keep giving her little cups of rice, little cups of sugar, because the poor thing has nothing to put in the pan" (201). María Ester, who at first is against the admission of another member to the *taller*, states, "We all have problems." But Rosita's situation is very complicated; her husband has a job, and so technically she cannot be accepted in the workshop, which is meant to employ only those women whose husbands are unemployed. Her situation reveals the unscrupulous practice of those who took advantage of the economic situation by not paying their employees in cash. Rosita explains how the system works:

ROSITA: Well, yes, my husband is working, but he does not get paid.
MARIA ESTER: What do you mean they don't pay him? Isn't he working?
ROSITA: Well, he works in a toy factory, but the owner said that he cannot pay

his employees with money, so he pays them with merchandize. He pays my husband with toys. *(She then opens a bag and shows some horrible plastic toys.)* Donald Duck, Mickey Mouse, Pluto . . . (202)

At the same time, the scene denounces injustice against Chilean workers by suggesting that Chilean industry was very ill-prepared to face the new policies of a free market in which imported articles would surpass national products in price and quality. María Luisa explains, "Who is going to buy these ugly, poorly made things, when the stores are full of imported toys?" (202). Therefore, although her husband has a job, Rosita concludes that "it is the same as if he was unemployed if they pay him with merchandize nobody buys." To make things worse, her husband forces her to go into the streets to try to sell the ugly toys.

It is not coincidental that the play presents this tension between a marginal craft such as the *arpillera* and the plastic toy, one of the icons of the consumerist society. The crisis in the country is so acute, however, that a plastic toy loses even its appeal as a symbol of a richer world. On the other hand, the marginal, folkloric *arpillera* acquires a modest status because it interests buyers from other countries, and enables its makers to make a modest living by their craft.

The fact that the *arpillera* craft is eminently feminine can also be seen as the expression of another tension within the patriarchal Chilean society. Now, due to the economic disaster the country is going through, men lose their jobs and have to accept the fact that their wives support the family. The men's humiliation over their loss of the role of breadwinner is expressed in the following exchange between Rosita and Maruja:

MARUJA: Have you spoken to your husband about [getting a job here]?
ROSITA: No. I haven't said anything to him.
MARUJA: You should speak to him first; otherwise he will get angry later.
ROSITA: He can't say anything! If he has no money, he cannot say anything!
MARUJA: Listen, Rosita. Men get all upset because they are not the ones bringing the money in. (203)

These exchanges also serve as a vehicle for denunciation of the domestic violence they suffer, the faithlessness they have to endure, and finally the drunkenness they have to witness. Rosita's plight seems even more painful because she is pregnant, young, and innocent. Her situation also serves to show another social phenomenon that became widespread during the crisis, the eviction of people from their homes. In order not to become homeless, Rosita, her husband, and her children are forced to move in with her sister-in-law. This situation is reflected in discussions about the themes for the *arpilleras*:

> ROSITA: . . . In the last days, when we were still holding on to our house, the only food we had was cooked cabbage. We boiled it with salt and ate it slowly.
> MARUJA: This is a theme of extreme poverty, Rosita.
> ROSITA: It is the exploitation of the worker, Maruja. (207)

But Rosita's situation is not new. When María Ester asks Rosita to describe where she lived when she was first married, the play inventories the precarious conditions in which the poorest workers lived. Rosita says that it was a one-room frame house. The furniture was a bed, two chairs, a small table, a defective stove, some kitchen utensils, and nothing else. This miserable house "didn't even have a window" (210).

The text also opens up a space for the *arpilleristas* to refer to the tortures committed by the military against dissidents. El Negro, Maruja's husband, had been an important union leader. He was detained and submitted to torture, like many union leaders in Chile. María Luisa passes this information to Rosita as she teaches her how to make an *arpillera*:

> MARIA LUISA: Yes, El Negro was a union leader, an important one. People say
> that *inside there* . . . (*And then she speaks directly in Rosita's ear.*)
> ROSITA: No! . . .
> MARIA LUISA: That is why he is kind of strange. Poor Maruquita has suffered
> a lot because of him. (212)

The "inside there," emphasized in the text, is of course the political prison commonly known to exist, and the words María Luisa speaks in Rosita's ear (which the audience does not hear) become virtual: they are meant to be filled in by what the spectators themselves know about the abuses of the military. The gesture of saying something that the spectators cannot hear, paradoxically, is worth many words, because it is heavy with meaning. It was difficult for government censors to make accusations against a play that did not enunciate the atrocities committed against the people. The only thing they might do would be to accuse the spectators of mentally filling in the blanks with subversive messages.

Another important aspect of this scene is the insinuation that El Negro is working actively in the clandestine resistance to the dictatorship. His departures from the house after hours, as well as his unexplainable tardiness, make Maruja complain, "I wonder where that man is . . ." (217). This image of active resistance is reinforced when we learn that Maruja and El Negro have a son living in California and that the family had the opportunity to move to the United States. But El Negro did not want to abandon Chile. Maruja explains, "El Negro didn't want to leave. He said that our son, since he is young, can go if he wants. We'll stay right here" (222). The opposition to the dictatorship had instructed their militants not to leave the country unless their personal safety was in imminent danger. All indications in the text point to El Negro as an active member of the clandestine resistance.

By using these techniques, the play gives the spectators clues to an enormous quantity of information about the current situation in Chile. Their horizon of expectations—their denunciation of the intolerable conditions of daily life under the dictatorship—are made manifest. The signifying potential of the theatrical text sets these expectations in such way that they refer to themes such as repression, invasion of homes in the middle of the night, relentless harassment of those in poor neighborhoods, forced separation of couples, the population's extreme poverty, precarious housing, torture of political dissidents, and even the possibility of an active resistance to the dictatorial regime. Although the censors could hardly stand to have such play produced, they could do nothing because the play did not say anything explicitly. Finally, it was up to the spectators to utter the final word and decide whether they wanted to become accomplices in the play.

The World Vision in *Tres Marías y una Rosa*

Lucien Goldmann writes that all human behavior is meaningful and functional, tending to modify an unbalanced situation: "Human acts constitute both the answers from an individual or collective subject and attempt to modify a situation given in a favorable sense to the aspirations of this subject."[21] The dramatic text in *Tres Marías y una Rosa* identifies the world vision of that sector of the Chilean population who suffered most from the social, economic, and political measures adopted by the dictatorship that took power in 1973. This collective subject of unemployed men and women, who fought desperately for survival and for better living conditions, gives meaning to the world vision presented in the text.

The antagonist in this play is the unnamed, unpersonified force that has invaded daily life and caused pain and misery to those who can least afford to resist and defend themselves. Even though unnamed, those who control and dictate Chile's repressive politics are condemned in *Tres Marías y una Rosa*. In her observations about the *arpillera* of the Last Judgment, María Luisa makes it clear that those who promote evil are those with economic power; she had already condemned them and put them in hell: "It is the people who wear fur coats who go to hell" (216). Thus, her version of God "travels in a flying saucer to judge the rich and to forgive the poor" (216), who, if they have any faults, should be forgiven, since they have not been able to develop themselves totally. María Luisa explains her system thus: "All the poor go to heaven without judgment because they haven't had the opportunity to be people" (218).

David Benavente and members of the TIT sponsor the "lucid voices" of the social body whose vision of the world is reflected in *Tres Marías y una Rosa*; Benavente and the others have, as Goldmann says, "lived intensively, and for a long time endured a series of problems, and have made an extraordinary effort to give them a meaningful solution."[22] It comes as no surprise, therefore, that the play's potential for denouncing the evils of the military regime was realized with such power that even the military intelligence agents recognized in a secret memorandum, "This play has good theatrical quality. Of all the plays presented until today it is the one with more political content and the one that makes [the most] direct and clear allusions."[23]

A week after the play opened, the company received a citation to appear at the Ministry of Defense, where a high intelligence official interrogated them about a news item in the conservative Santiago newspaper *La Segunda* on July 31, 1979. The article says, among other things, that the play's only purpose is to "unleash hatred among social classes and to throw the workers against the public." It goes on to say that the characters, "four women from an imaginary place, with husbands who are looking for jobs in Argentina . . . accuse a neighbor of being a 'traitor to the working class' because she is selling *arpilleras* displaying scenes of September 18."[24] Members of the company who went to the Ministry of Defense showed the censor the text of the play. Evidently the text contained none of the lines mentioned in the newspaper article, nor any others that could be considered subversive. It is quite possible that the person charged with examining the play only looked for sentences that openly accused the military of abuses against the people; since these do not exist in the play, it was impossible to forbid the continuation of its performance. After a long discussion, the problem was clarified and the imminent closing of the play avoided.

With *Tres Marías y una Rosa*, the dissident Chilean theater became a manifest fact in the political arena. In fact, not only did the play run for several years in Chile, but also it was successfully staged in Europe and the United States. Its subsequent effect is equally undeniable: more than thirty plays of the same nature appeared from 1976 to 1981. The tenets for the theater that Fray Camilo Henríquez outlined still appear valid more than a century and a half later. Recalling Henríquez, the tears shed by the audience for *Tres Marías y una Rosa* have not been sterile.

8/ Tango, Buenos Aires, Borges
Cultural Production and Urban Sexual Regulation

DAVID WILLIAM FOSTER

Por que el tango es macho.
Popular saying

IF ANYTHING IS KNOWN ABOUT BUENOS AIRES, IT IS THIS: Buenos Aires is the home of the tango. Although most people know the tango only as dance—dance accompanied by music, to be sure, but one that records the tradition of the tango as poetry before it was ever orchestrated and choreographed—it is impossible to consult a respectable guidebook about Buenos Aires without observing that the tango is one of the great tourist attractions of the city.[1] While one may quibble with this characterization of the tango because it is thought to appeal to a universalized international tourist audience, there can be little question that it is an icon for the city as much as beef or the putative European base of Porteño culture. Popular characterizations tend to homogenize these three icons, failing to separate out the distinct cultural bases of each one (respectively, rural creole culture in the case of beef production; urban immigrant culture, typically but not exclusively Italian, in the case of the tango; and ultramarine French and English culture, the basis of the European flavor). Similarly, each enforces the other as somehow quintessentially Argentine.[2]

The tango is correlated with the city in such touristic—and semiofficial images—as a juxtaposition of dancers posed against the backdrop of the cityscape, either viewed panoramically (Avenida Corrientes) or in specific

167

localities (such as the Caminito district, with its multicolored mosaic of wooden houses). Somehow the tango synthesizes the driving (masculine?) energy of the "city that never sleeps"; beyond the Porteño facade of sophistication, the hard-edged (masculine?) brutality of the tango represents the "real" essence of Buenos Aires.[3] Such propositions assume that the much-maligned, massive lower-class group of Italian immigrants of a hundred years ago has somehow given the city a defining cultural stamp that is universally accepted. Alternately, such correlations imply the proposition that while one will not find wildly dancing tango couples in the streets, in the plazas, and on strategic corners in the shadows of famous monuments, the entire city is nonetheless imbued with the tango. Synecdoches and metonymies of it can profitably be sought in the commerce of everyday urban life. After all, one way of describing the allegedly Argentine tendency to give darkly melodramatic interpretations of sociopolitical events is to speak of "el tango nacional."

Such highly generalized, superficial interpretations of cultural phenomena always carry an element of truth, and they are often important pedagogical tools, especially when so little is known about the cultural practices of a society. However, they may have little to do with a theoretically grounded attempt at deep cultural interpretation, even if it has little immediately to do with something like the tango. That is, some form of cultural theorizing, with a specific application to Buenos Aires, may find the tango to be irrelevant or marginal, at best; phenomena not usually featured in tourist guides are in fact more useful. This is certainly the case if the tango has become essentially a fossilized cultural form, preserved for reasons of romantic nostalgia or promoting tourism but little adhered to in primary or emerging cultural practices. All societies have a reserve of such fossilized forms. Concomitantly, however, there remains an imaginary Buenos Aires that defines itself in terms of the tango: the tango is Buenos Aires, and Buenos Aires is the tango, such that certain tangos have become the city's theme songs.

I do not wish to imply that the tango has no current meanings for Porteños and other Argentines, nor that the tango is so much bad-faith pap to amuse naive tourists. What should be questioned is the extent to which tourist guides and semiofficial images grant the tango a privileged status as a dance and overinvest it with transparent meanings regarding the national essence whereby the city mirrors the tango and the tango models the city in return. The image of juxtaposed mirrors is not likely to render much that is useful for a principled discussion of the interaction between urban space and cultural production because it is based too reflexively on two things: the assumption that products of a culture automatically reflect that culture—for example, "The brassy music of a Sousa march captures perfectly the brash nature of turn-of-the-century American ruthless capitalism"—and the mechanistic notion that certain societies will inevitably generate certain generic types—"The violent nature of Argentine social history accounts for the bleak pessimism of so much of Argentine literature."

Another way of examining the relationship between cultural production and urban space is to investigate how cultural production proposes a specific interpretation of urban life. It is not important if an image does not match dominant or prevailing views of the city. Quite the contrary, such an interpretation may end up creating a particular view of the city that, while unique and unacceptable at first, may come to constitute a prevailing understanding, much like Dickens's portraits of London back-street life or Twain's regional backwaters. Dickens's city is now considered to be quintessential London; where would American cultural shibboleths be without Twain's Hannibal?

A reading of tango lyrics, far from providing an easy interpretation of what becomes an obvious social truth (the artist comes along and sees for us what our limited, untrained vision was not able to see, but what we can now see with the clarity of art), creates, conditions, and imposes problematical meanings every bit as vexed as the social or historical circumstances they pretend to elucidate. Culture, after all, is a socially symbolic act.

Many of the fabrications concerning Buenos Aires either do not match patented interpretations or have been suppressed by them because they would not survive the challenge of problematic or dangerous counter evidence. This seems to be especially true regarding sadomasochistic humiliation—based on classicism, sexism, and homophobia—of forms of interpersonal behavior in public or semipublic spaces. Consider the lyrics of a tango written by Alfredo Le Pera: "Con una mueca de mujer vencida / me dijo `¡Es la vida!' Y no la vi más'" ("With the pained face of a defeated woman / she said: 'Such is life!' And I never saw her again").[4]

I propose to analyse the urban dimensions of tango not so much as a concrete evocation of Buenos Aires as an expression of its dominant socio-sexual ideologies. In its insistent enactment of dramas of erotic love, the tango expresses the way in which the city is a witness to that love. The spectator, acting as a witness (a role played over and over by the audience in the performance of the tango, whether as song, instrumental music, dance, or combinations of the three) is invited to enforce the dominant sociosexual ideology of the city. Later I will argue that the most interesting way to understand the images of Buenos Aires in the work of the premier twenti-eth-century Argentine writer, Jorge Luis Borges, is to trace the same ideo-logical resonances, whether the city is evoked in general, in the form of cer-tain *barrios,* or as a figure of history.

1

Few Argentine tangos actually evoke urban public spaces. Indeed, if the mainstay of the tango is the melodramatic recollection of betrayal in love (typically, of a male narrator by a perfidious woman)[5] and if the tone is essentially confessional (directed toward the audience, another male inter-locutor, the woman herself, or a combination of these possibilities through direct and indirect quotation), then private spaces would seem to be most at issue. However, personal dramas, particularly romantic entanglements, usually end by involving the public sector in significant ways.

Furthermore, the tango is resolutely heterosexist: although, curiously, the tango may have been originally danced by men awaiting turns with prostitutes in turn-of-the-century riverfront brothels in Montevideo, Buenos Aires, and other cities along the Río de la Plata network, there is no trace of homoeroticism in the canon. The heterosexism of the tango has two principal implications for its narrative rights. First, it insistently explores the dynamics of sexual relationships. Like compulsory heterosex-ism in general, such an exploration is underlaid less by the privilege of romantic love than by the imperative for it: romantic love is not a choice, but an obligation, whether as part of an ideology based on the need to per-petuate the species or as part of a need to affirm sexual allegiance. Tango lyrics rarely speak of children: it would seem that love goes awry before the reproductive imperative can take place.[6]

Thus, the jilted lover's lament has the primary, generalized effect of demonstrating the authenticity of his male identity: the repeated pursuit of women, whether or not specifically the Don Juan syndrome, demonstrates the appropriate quality of a man's sexual needs, even if fate and women themselves make it impossible for him to hold a partner. To perform appropriately as a heterosexual is part of a public/publicized demand, and the public domain is filled with confirmations of the exclusive legitimacy of heterosexuality, beginning with the insistent repetition in advertising, which began during the heyday of the tango, of the fundamental social conjunction of man and woman, or of the family produced by that conjunction.

The second implication of the tango's heterosexism is that the demonstration of proper heterosexual urges takes place—must take place—in the public domain. Certainly, the tango itself is often performed in public. Although it may be enjoyed in private—on recordings, or in singing and dancing at a private party—the tango is most often associated with large-scale public display: Gardel's movies, concerts, and exhibitions, radio and television broadcasts, café, cabaret, and plaza performances. One could argue that the public display of the tango is not the same as the sense of public display conveyed in the events described by tango lyrics or their enactment in dance—an observation that reveals how displayed culture is essentially voyeuristic, since it is typically based on the open performance of the private lives of individuals.[7]

The public spaces represented internally by the tango are, first and foremost, stages for the life of the immigrant laborers it sings about: streets, dance halls, brothels, cabarets, and bars, hospitals and asylums, boarding houses, police stations, and detention centers. These are all forums where the identity of the individual is enacted, whether it be the identity of another that is sung about or, typically in the first-person lyrics of the tango, the drama of one's own sexual entanglements. The staging of the tango imagines the rest of society as assembled in these spaces listening to or overhearing the personal story being told. This circumstance is most vividly revealed in films, when the thin thread of the drama stops while the star sings: everyone else stands around and listens, as though there were nothing else in the world to do but to hang on to every word of what is being sung.

However, the audience is not passive, whether literal or imagined. Rather, the function of the audience, beyond simply justifying the singing as an act of social communication, is to serve as a gauge for the legitimacy of what is heard. On some occasions, while the song is sung in a work framed by characters other than the singer-narrator, another character steps forward and comments on the song, saying something like "Che, hermano, compartimos tu pena" ("Gee, brother, we share your pain"). But an explicit reaction is not necessary. The very act of singing, of explicitly articulating one's personal drama, is to solicit support from those who are imagined to hear it, and if that articulation takes place in a public space, where the audience is likely to be partially or wholly made up of strangers, then the approval sought is in terms of the overall ideological structures of the society the audience represents.

What I envision here, then, is how tango lyrics, quite aside from specific references to urban public space, are constructed to have meaning in that space, to the extent that they seek to engage both the understanding and the acquiescence of the audience to legitimate what the singer is narrating. Specifically, since the most common theme of the tango lyrics is love gone astray, the lyrics appeal to various facets of hegemonic heterosexuality, both in the sense of privileged man-woman love, but also the particular quality of the relationship between man and woman, especially the subordination of the latter, given the attendant presumption that, as a daughter of Eve, she will likely end up betraying a man.

Woman's putative capacity for betrayal helps to explain the way in which tangos naturalize betrayal as the other side of romantic love: consider "Percanta que me amuraste [mujer que me abandonaste]" ("Woman Who Abandoned Me") by Pablo Contursi and Samuel Castiosta. This leads to the obvious contradiction inherent in heterosexist romantic love: on the one hand, it is presumed to be the only legitimate form of human love, as recognized by religion, law, and accumulated social practice, while on the other hand, it is assumed that, at least in dominant forms of cultural production that include the tango, romantic love will end in failure. It is precisely this failure that gives the tango and other cultural forms something to talk about.

Of course, one might argue that romantic love is not what the tango is about, but special cases of sexual attraction that veer close to sadomasochism. Indeed, one wonders if the tango is bound to see straight love as always leading to forms of sadomasochistic experience, given the enormous suffering its lyrics express. The tango does not enact the version of joyful man-woman union endorsed by certain versions of patriarchy, particularly public rituals centered on church weddings and accompanying manifestations. Instead, the tango presupposes the public recognition of the necessity of heterosexist coupling and its subsequent betrayal, and it further demands public approval of the masculinity of the narrative voice and the legitimacy of his lament.

How this is carried out in a typically urban tango may be seen in "Bailemos" ("Let's Dance") by Reinaldo Yiso and Pascual Mammone, a text that makes overt reference to the tango as danced enactment of an interpersonal relationship; significantly, the dance takes place in public, and again significantly, there is an explicit appeal to the reaction of observers. Moreover, the masculine narrative voice is clearly exercising explicit censorship on the already silenced voice of his female partner, with the implication that her discourse would exceed the bounds of public display: "No llores, no, muchacha, la gente está mirando / bailemos este tango, el tango del adiós" ("Don't cry, girl, because people are staring / let's dance this tango, the farewell tango"). The tango is both the enactment of their failed affair and, therefore, a sign of its closure, "el tango del adiós." To complete the tango is to complete the affair once and for all. It is this double finality that is performed before the world at large: "El tango ya termina . . . salgamos a llorar" ("The tango is over . . . let's go away and cry"). Crying is a different language of expression from either singing or dancing: one is performed before the people, while presumably the meaning of "salgamos" is that crying will be done in private and, one assumes, alone.

No matter how trite and kitschy, pathetic fallacy establishes a range of easily identifiable paradigms for the public nature of the tango. Homero Manzi's and Aníbal Troilo's "Barrio de tango" is only one among many texts that assemble such rhetorical clusters, beginning with the proposition that the tango and the neighborhood are interchangeable: the entire lived collective space exudes the tango:

> Un pedazo de barrio allá en Pompeya
> durmiéndose al costado del terraplén,
> un farol balanceado en la barrera
> y el misterio de adiós que siembra el tren.

Un ladrido de perros a la luna
y el amor escondido en un portón,
los sapos redoblando en la laguna,
y, a lo lejos, la voz del bandoneón.

Barrio de tango, luna y misterio,
calles lejanas ¿cómo estarán?
Viejos amigos que hoy ni recuerdo
¿qué se habrán hecho, dónde andarán?

Barrio de tango, ¿qué fué de aquella
Juana, la rubia que tanto amé?
¿Sabrá que sufro pensando en ella
desde la tarde en que la dejé?
Barrio de tango, luna y misterio
desde el recuerdo te vuelvo a ver.

Un coro de silbidos allá en la esquina,
el codillo llenando el almacén
y el dramón de la pálida vecina
que ya nunca salió a mirar el tren.

Así evoco tus noches, barrio de tango,
con las chatas entrando al corralón.
Y la luna chapoteando sobre el fango,
y, a lo lejos, la voz del bandoneón.

Barrio de tango, luna y misterio,
desde el recuerdo te vuelvo a ver . . .

(A piece of a neighborhood in Pompeya
Sleeping on the slopes of the embankment
A street lamp swinging in the barrier
And the farewell mystery that the train sows.

Dogs barking at the moon
And love hidden in a gate,
Toads croaking in the lagoon,
And, far away, the voice of the *bandoneón.*

Neighborhood of tango, moon and mystery
Faraway streets, how are you now?
Old friends I can no longer remember
What have they done, where could they be?

Neighborhood of tango, what happened to
Juana, the blonde I loved so much?
Does she know I suffer remembering her
Since the afternoon I left her?
Neighborhood of tango, moon and mystery
From my memory I can see you again.

A choir of whistles in the corner,
The crowd filling up the store
And the melodrama of the pale neighbor
Who never went out to look at the train.

This way I evoke your nights, neighborhood of tango,
As the carts enter the *corralón.*
And the moon splashing in the mud,
And, far away, the voice of the *bandoneón.*

Neighborhood of tango, moon and mystery,
From my memory I can see you again . . .)[8]

The dominant motif is to identify the narrative voice with a specific neighborhood. The initial rhetorical move is to situate the speaker as "see-ing/hearing" the *barrio* in memory and to confirm the accuracy of that memory through physical details (doorways, hanging lanterns, mud pud-dles) and impressions (the sound of a *bandoneón,* the mystery of moon-washed streets, the sad drama sensed in the pallidness of a woman). The physical commonplaces are in turn associated with individuals who provided the speaker with a sense of belonging to a community: "viejos amigos" ("old friends"), Juana (such neighborhood girlfriends are always recalled in tangos as first loves), and the crowd hanging out at the corner grocery store.

Such physical features and individuals provide the sense of a community—not necessarily one he has lost, but one that the twists and turns of life have separated him from. The nostalgia of his evocation leads one to assume that he is the worse for it, which of course justifies his melancholic return to the community in his mind. Such a topos of the lost Garden of Eden or the innocence of youth, correlated with the old neighborhood, is unquestionably one of the sentimental pulls of the tango, as much as it is a veritable narrative of the culture of Buenos Aires, the city of "one hundred neighborhoods."

But there is an interesting internal duplication in "Barrio de tango" that brings us back to how the neighborhood—attested to in later years by the mind's eye—is itself a collective hypostatized witness to the life of its members. This is the case of the comment on what is assumed to be the tragic story of the "pálida vecina" ("pale neighbor") but, more significantly, it is the case of the reference to "el amor escondido en un portón" ("love hidden beneath a portal"). Such love trysts, which presumably involved the narrator and "aquella / Juana," are a game featuring both public display and the public commentary the lovers evoke. The desire for privacy on the part of the lovers hiding in the shadows of the specifically eroticized space of the doorway is counterbalanced by the need for such trysts to take place in public spaces like doorways in the first place. Society provides a guarantee of relative (and always precarious) privacy; members of the proletariat are the ones to feel the repression of social convention. Thus, there is no alternative but to make a public spectacle of love, which likely also means intercourse, since the tango also speaks frequently of women who are seduced, abandoned, and often left pregnant (perhaps, in fact, the case of the "pálida vecina").

One way of reading this reference in the poem is as referring to the narrator's own meetings with Juana: in evoking the *barrio*, he also sees himself and Juana exchanging kisses and intimacies in a doorway. In this way,

"Barrio de tango" brings us back to the way in which the personal stories of individuals always end up correlated with the scrutinizing gaze of society, because, unlike other types of ballads with sentimental narratives (for example, the Mexican *canción ranchera*, which rarely has a geographically specific anchor), the tango is insistently involved with Buenos Aires in general and with certain specific locations associated with the social classes of the tango.[9]

The tango is filled with precise references to districts of Buenos Aires, to streets and intersections, to bars, cafés, and cabarets, and to other notable landmarks. One could construct a geographic inventory of Buenos Aires on the basis of tango lyrics. However, my interest here is to demonstrate that the urban society of the tango, and most definitely its social classes (to which upscale audiences accede through the interesting dimension of the "slumming" they provide), are the legitimating force of what is being sung about. Certainly all cultural production, whether or not it speaks of direct social correlations, depends on the legitimation provided by some version of the hegemonic ideology. By consequence, then, cultural production anchored with sociogeographic specificity is only making explicit (with or without irony) its grounding in a specific ideological legitimation.

Therefore, when the tango speaks of the social formation of the narrator—that is, when the lyrics recall the process of his coming of age in a specific social group—it may do so by making reference to specific settings, such as "un pedazo de barrio allá de Pompeya" ("a part of a neighborhood in Pompeya" in "Barrio de tango") or to specific institutions, as in the case of "Cafetín de Buenos Aires" ("Café of Buenos Aires") by Enrique Santos Discépolo and Mariano Mores:

> De chiquilín, lo miraba de afuera
> como a esas cosas que nunca se alcanzan . . .
> la ñata contra el vidrio,
> en un azul de frío . . .
> que sólo fué después viviendo
> igual al mío . . .
> Como una escuela de todas las cosas,
> ya de muchacho me diste entre asombros

el cigarrillo . . .
. . . la fe en mis sueños
y una esperanza de amor . . .

¿Cómo olvidarte en esta queja,
cafetín de Buenos Aires?
Si sos lo único en la vida
que se pareció a mi vieja . . .
En tu mezcla milagrosa
de sabihondos y suicidas
yo aprendí filosofía . . . dados . . . timba
y la poesía cruel
de no pensar más en mí . . .

Me diste en oro un puñado de amigos
que son los mismos que alientan mis horas;
José, el de la quimera . . .
Marcial—que aun cree y espera—
Y el flaco Abel—que se nos fué—
pero aun me guía . . .
Sobre tus mesas que nunca preguntan
lloré una tarde el primer desengaño,
Nací a las penas . . .
bebí mis años . . .
y me entregué sin luchar.

(As a tiny child, I looked at it from the outside
As one looks at things one can never reach . . .
The nose against the glass,
In a blue cold . . .
That only later I could live
Just like mine . . .
Like a school of all things,
As a kid, among frights you gave me
The cigarette . . .

. . . And the faith in my dreams
And a hope for love . . .

How can I forget you in this lament
Cafetín of Buenos Aires?
If you are the only one in life
That looked like my old mother . . .
In your miraculous mixture
Of wise men and suicides
I learned philosophy . . . information . . . gambling
And the cruel poetry
Of no longer thinking about myself . . .

You gave me a bunch of golden friends
The same that still inspire my days;
José, the fanciful . . .
Marcial—who still believes and waits—
And the thin Abel—who left us—
But still guides me . . .
On your tables that never ask questions
One afternoon I wept over the first heartbreak,
I first felt pain . . .
I drank my years
I surrendered without struggle.)[10]

Although there is one (probably unintentional) irony in this text—if the *cafetín* taught the speaker to no longer think of himself, then why is he engaging in the solipsistic nostalgia of the tango?—the text offers a straightforward enumeration of the details of social formation. Specifically, it is the masculinity of the speaker—his transition from being a little boy to being a fully defined man who has the right to enter a privileged masculine space such as the café. Once more, we note the involvement of the tango with a cult of masculinity constantly under seige, continually threatened by often futile efforts to maintain its integrity.

The cult has often been criticized as perpetuating, through the intense romantic monumentalization of the tango in Argentine society, a myth of masculinity: women and homosexuals are threats to male integrity, and, apart from moments of rage, men must maintain an overarching aloofness from life's everyday affairs.[11] While the tango, like much of Western culture, may assume the naturalness of masculine identity and masculine privilege, as something that is, has been, and will always be, "Cafetín de Buenos Aires" echoes, *avant la lettre,* current theoretical proposals[12] regarding the complex process involved in inscribing a subjectivity as masculine and the enormous project involved in maintaining masculine identity through constant acts of assertion, confirmation, and defense.

From such a theoretical point of view, since masculinity is an assumed identity, it must be remorselessly exercised in order not to fall away, and no challenge to it can go unanswered, since to do so would be to open a fatal breach in the male facade. Even more than femininity (which is, of course, also a closely guarded facade), masculinity must be constantly affirmed in a masculinist society. Since power is in the hands of masculine subjects, who compete mightily for its benefits, an imperfection in one's inscription into the codes of masculinity weakens his right to compete and endangers his success in competing by moving him closer to those social constituencies (for example, "women" or feminized males) that are excluded from competition. Lyrics such as those of "Cafetín de Buenos Aires" help to explain the *machismo* conveyed by the tango, because they make it clear that what they are really doing, aside from expressing the nostalgic *topos* of the café as a paradigmatic neighborhood institution, is detailing how that institution is at once a factor and a site in the creation of masculinity.

The foregoing would explain the construction of the text around an axis of outside/inside. The little boy, not yet a fully constituted masculine subject, stands outside the café, in the cold, pressing his nose against the glass of the window; later, as a man, he is ensconced within the warm cocoon of the café's smoke and coffee vapor–filled interior. At the outset, the café represents a world the narrator thinks that he will never attain, the world of men and the social symbolism of the patriarchy they exemplify. At this point, now as a man, he is ready, as in the final line of the tango, to give himself up to its world, which is clearly the world of male identity and masculine privilege. The *cafetín* is both a paradigm and a microcosm. As one of the most important places where men gather, it is also a place from which non-men are excluded: children, women (except for indecent women, who are allowed to partake of masculine privilege), and gays.[13] The all-male world of the café is also a homogeneous world, because entering it means turning oneself without a struggle over to its codes and practices. Thus, the individual is constantly measured in terms of the degree to which he abides by those codes and practices—that is, the degree to which he fits in. To deviate from custom, to fail to abide by the rules, is to be cast back out into the street, reduced to standing in the cold and pressing one's nose against the window. Few men would run the risk of such banishment, and the economy of the café depends on the virtually absolute compliance of its members.[14]

The café is a microcosm. Although it is a public space within a public space—one accedes to the latter by birth, but to the former only through initiation and confirmation—it becomes the stage for enacting the dramas of masculinity. Stages always have audiences whose members are there either to legitimate or to repudiate what is performed onstage. Performers certainly implore their audiences for legitimation, and in this case it is the legitimation of what one has learned in order to be a man (his "filosofía") and what he does with that knowledge—to always act like a man. The tables of the café may well never question him, but his fellows do, if only with the glacial aloofness of their manner, for which the only emotion allowed (other than masculine rage) is expressed by the tears of deceit; to be jilted by a woman is potentially one of the most serious threats to masculine integrity. Tears trigger the revenge to which men are entitled, even if it is no more than verbal aggression.

In this way, the urban institution of the neighborhood café institutionalizes masculinity and provides first and foremost a locus both for its inscription and its careful maintenance. Moreover, the café provides a stage for enacting the dramas of masculinity and confirming the appropriateness of one's conduct as a man. The tango insistently confirms the rectitude of macho behavior, and, just as there are scant references to incomplete masculine subjects, there are equally scant references to the failure of the man to perform properly in the face of his peers. The much-changed urban cafés of Buenos Aires continue to prosper, although many have been taken over by all sorts of individuals whom the traditional culture of the tango would consider inadequate masculine subjects, including gays and lesbians. The cafés remain sites both for the witnessing of social drama and the quest for ideological legitimation, and thus they still function both as major paradigms and microcosms of Porteño society.

The tango may no longer have a universal allure in Argentina; understandably, many sectors of musical culture in the country prefer rock, which played an important part in resistance to the military and in the process of redemocratization following the withdrawal of the military from governance in 1983.[15] But enjoyment of the tango cuts across social classes, across gender boundaries and sexual identities, and it is cherished by many Argentines who are quite uninvolved in its uses as a form of tourist attraction. One can never generalize in any useful way about the involvement of complex social subjects with complex forms of cultural production, and we still have only a primitive understanding of how individuals interact with their culture, even with respect to something so apparently simple as the "identification" between spectator and spectacle.

What I have been emphasizing is not how an individual can find in the tango a heightened version of either personal tragedy or erotic suffering but rather how tango affords the opportunity to play sexual monitor. We see both the force and the ubiquity of this opportunity if we turn to Jorge Luis Borges, whose works neither refuse the hererosexist ideology of the tango nor refute its masculine privilege. One reason the role of interpellated sexual monitor remains so strong to this day is that the cultural text for tango continues as if in defiance of the vanished social circumstances that gave it rise. The subject of Buenos Aires in Borges's work is in part a meditation upon the relationship between urban space and machismo as mediated through the insistent presence of the tango.

2

Mario Pauletti claims that the only music Borges ever listened to was that of the tango as song.[16] From the publication of his first book of poetry, *Fervor de Buenos Aires* (1923), the city of Buenos Aires is a constant presence in Borges's poetry.[17] While he quickly abandoned his attempt to depict the essence of the city through *ultraísta* metaphors, Borges continued to use the city as the backdrop for an extensive inventory of his texts over the next seventy-five years. They may speak of Buenos Aires for immediate biographical reasons (*Fervor de Buenos Aires*, "Arrabal"; *Cuaderno de San*

Martín, "Elegía de los portones"; *Elogio de la sombra,* "Buenos Aires"). A detail of daily life in Buenos Aires may evoke for Borges some crucial aspect of human experience (*El Aleph,* "El Zahir"; *Fervor de Buenos Aires,* "El Truco"). A historical icon, like the *compadrito,* may signify for Borges some highly pertinent feature of social experience (*Historia universal de la infamia,* "Hombre de la esquina rosada"; *Ficciones,* "El sur"; *El informe de Brodie,* "Juan Muraña"). Some aspect of the culture of Buenos Aires may allude to questions concerning the nature of the cultural enterprise (*Cuadernos de San Martín,* "Barrio norte"; *El otro el mismo,* "El tango"; *Elogio de la sombra,* "Buenos Aires"); or some apparently inconsequential trace of urban life may be viewed *sub specie aeternitatis* as the trigger for one of the writer's particularly droll meditations on the vagaries of human life (*El otro, el mismo,* "Buenos Aires"; *Ficciones,* "El sur").

There would be little point in constructing an inventory of images of Buenos Aires in Borges's work. Borges, especially after he abandoned the concerns of groups such as those associated with reviews like *Martín Fierro,* had little interest in a folkloristic or local-color depiction of the city, and he always made it clear that the city was of neither God nor man, but of his own personal mythology. To say that Borges's writing is imbricated with the sociohistorical reality of Argentina does not mean, however, that one can discover much in attempting to discern material significance in his references to the city. Unlike the rather transparent metaphors of Eduardo Mallea or the dirty realism of Enrique Medina, Borges's Buenos Aires is not quite about any specific urban habitat by that name.

How, then, can one undertake to examine the lexeme "Buenos Aires" and its subsets that appear in Borges's texts? It would be facile to say that Borges creates metaphors or allegories of Buenos Aires, since that is what all literature does and indeed what all language does. It would be equally facile to insist—on a more specific level that would take the foregoing into account—that Borges's texts, in some metapoetic way, are conscious of and, in fact, thematize their metaphoric/allegorical renditions of Buenos Aires.[18] While his immense affection for many icons of the city and his sensitivity toward what they signified in terms of cultural experience cannot be doubted, the city—like Argentina itself—is highly problematic for Borges. If he was primarily interested in the processes by which human culture is forged and how it has meanings for individuals and societies—meanings in

a universe in which the only meanings are those created by mankind—
there is no reason to suppose that he held Argentine culture in less esteem
than international culture.

Borges certainly views Argentine culture with dismay (if one may
place under Derridean erasure a term Borges uses). For example, one of the
constants in his work is machismo and the cult of violence,[19] a topic that
has received recent attention with respect to issues of gender and sexual
identity in Borges's writing.[20] Although he at times seems to have an almost
morbid fascination with the myths of masculinity in their Argentine versions, he is often appalled by these myths and their recurring, historical
projections in Argentine social history. The same may be said about images
relating to the modern city—and yet there is always a certain immaterial-
ity about Borges's treatments of Buenos Aires, not because of his falsely
vaunted "philosophical" stance, but because of his resolute shunning of
local color.[21]

Although references to the city abound in canonical texts like "El
aleph" and the earlier "La muerte y la brújula" (where, in typical Borgean
irony, the actual geometric layout of Buenos Aires does not match the coor-
dinates given in the story, the common assumption to the contrary),
Borges's most often anthologized reference to Buenos Aires is "Fundación
mítica de Buenos Aires," the opening poem in the 1929 *Cuaderno San
Martín,* published in Madrid. There is no question that the specific quadrant
of the city Borges's refers to in the poem is the block where his childhood
home stood, a block now inhabited by elegant apartment buildings in
Palermo. The Palermo of Borges's youth, rather than the prized upper middle-class district it is today, was a suburb of modest dwellings and a principal point of settlement for thousands of southern Italian immigrants, as
indicated by its name. Today the sons and grandsons of many of these
immigrants, now prosperous businessmen, professionals, and high-level
bureaucrats, inhabit apartment buildings that stand where their ancestors
may have lived in tenements or other modest lodgings. Interestingly, until
his death Borges occupied an apartment off Paraguay Street, one of the
streets of the quarter evoked by his poem.

The basic semiotic practice of the poem is to "suppose" what might
have been the circumstances not just of the material founding of Buenos

Aires, which are expressed in terms of key preterites like *vinieron, arribaron, prendieron . . . empezó* (they came, they returned, they caught, he/she started—verbs indicating a completed past action), but of the establishment of a set of acts that are the basis for present-day social knowledge and behavior. Borges engages in a sort of retroprojection, imagining what might have been the circumstances in the remote foundation of Buenos Aires that explain some of the human landscape of contemporary life in Buenos Aires. "Fundación" is one of Borges's many texts that refer specifically to the *compadrito,* a term that, aside from its implications with respect to the political system (in which *compadritos* were used as enforcers, messengers, and factotums), is generally understood to refer to a lower-class macho type whose attitude is intended to communicate his disdainful, incipiently violent masculine privilege toward whatever falls outside the scope of what he understands to be properly masculine.[22]

Compadrito is the diminutive of *compadre* (companion/buddy), a term that evokes the homosocialism of the society of these men, in the sense that the spheres of social control, from the highest levels of government down to neighborhood institutitons, are based on a relationship of bonding and interdependence among men. Indeed, *compadre,* much more than *compañero* (the direct cognate of companion), is based on the key term of the patriarchy, *padre,* and refers to those who share the same child through baptism. When the child is admitted into the Christian community—mostly Catholic, in Latin America—the ceremony requires the presence of a father and of a co-father (as well as of a mother and of a co-mother). Here, the relationship is not one of consanguinity, but rather of shared social obligations toward the child, and, ultimately for the co-fathers *(compadres),* the relationship confirms their descent from the same symbolic Father. If the genetic father dies, the child will be raised by the *padriño,* who will make sure his godchild will be instructed according to what the genetic father established. A child can never be left without a father. It is this ideology that defines maleness, manhood, and masculinity, and it is the social violence that derives from the exercise of authority of the patriarchy and, more significantly, from the processes of internal regulation of among the members of the homosocial realm that so fascinates Borges from "El hombre de la esquina rosada" (1935) on.[23] Indeed, the common thread of all of the text

in *Historia universal de la infamia* is machismo, and it is the perception of
Borges's abiding interest in constructions of masculinity and images of
manhood in Argentina that has begun to make him of interest to gender
studies.

In "Fundación mítica," these images are not just historical harbingers,
but rather, as the title of the poem indicates, foundational myths, sources of
social and cultural institutions. The following stanza anticipates "Historia
de la esquina rosada," both in theme and in the iconic importance of the
color *rosado,* as will subsequently be confirmed as the distinctive color of
Government House (*rosado* in Argentina suggests "old rose," not to be con-
fused with the brighter or louder color *rosa,* "pink"; this is an important distinction, given the contemporary sexual connotation of the latter):

> Un almacén rosado como revés de naipe
> brilló y en la trastienda conversaron un truco;
> el almacén rosado floreció en un compadre
> ya patrón de la esquina, ya resentido y duro.

> (A roseate store resembling the back of a playing card
> Gleamed and on the balcony they talked for a while;
> The roseate store bloomed in a *compadre,*
> Already boss of the corner, already resentful and harsh.)[24]

If, as the closing couplet affirms, Buenos Aires is "tan eterna como el agua
y el aire" ("as eternal as water and air"), the social primes identified by the
poem and that provide the basic horizons of social experience and, more
important, social meaning, are also as eternal as the elements. "Naturalization" means the process by which the cultural—that which has been
created by human society as part of its social evolution—is made to appear
to be natural, outside of human history and therefore unavailable to critical analysis.

To question and to deconstruct the process of naturalization is an
important task of cultural studies, which only echoes what critical and
contestatorial writing (that is, cultural production in general) has always
done. Borges, by positing the historical origins of the foundation, by showing the mythic to have been historical rather than eternal—which is what

he does by showing that the process of human industry was involved in the establishment of the city—demonstrates that "eternal" really means "abiding" in some trimphant or categorical way.

Borges actualizes the foundational practice by referring to contemporary political events; Hipólito Yrigoyen, the first populist president of Argentina, was in his second term at the time Borges published the poem, although in the following year, 1930, he was overthrown by the country's first military coup d'état:

> El primer organito salvaba el horizonte
> con su achacoso porte, su habanera y su gringo.
> El corralón seguro ya opinaba YRIGOYEN,
> algún piano mandaba tangos de Saborido.
>
> (The first little organ saluted the horizon
> With his ailing demeanor, his hat and his gringo.
> The [people in the] *corralón* of course opined YRIGOYEN,
> Some piano played tangos of Saborido.)[25]

In this way, Borges establishes a concatenation of cultural instances whereby the sites of contemporary Buenos Aires culture, synecdochized by the *corralón* and populated by important cultural icons of the period (especially the quintessential tango), are the continuing actualizations of the founding primes.

Borges's personalization, which he accomplishes by referring to the actual city block where he was raised, of the founding and its contemporary instances, is noteworthy because it confirms his critical stance toward the patriarchal traces in the historical as well as the current instances he cites. It is important to remember that only in cases of a nightmarish delirium, as in "El sur," where the coma inspired by a household accident provides the stage on which Borges the character lives out—and dies as a consequence of—an incident of macho aggression, does Borges figure himself as a participant in the dramas of masculinity that he describes so effectively.

The foregoing characterization of "Fundación mítica de Buenos Aires" seeks to demonstrate that the images of Buenos Aires in Borges are not important in how they may describe, realistically or fantastically, the concrete reality of the city, although specific features of the city appear in Borges's writing. Rather, the interest of his texts lies in how Borges sees through urban phenomena—a city block; the remains of past features, institutions, and activities; personal recollections and projections of what might have taken place there—to suggest an interpretation of a significant element of the city's social text. In this case, it is the masculine dominance that goes back to the historical fact that Argentina, like most of Latin America, was initially colonized by men alone, by virtue of a distinctly masculine privilege that continues to prevail in the modern city.

Indeed, many other poems, essays, and stories scattered throughout Borges's oeuvre provide an intersection of urban (or semi-urban) culture, the *compadrito* and his allies, and the codes of masculinity. "El tango," from *El otro, el mismo* (1964) is from the same period as the aforementioned compositions on the *milonga*. Since one of Borges's so-called philosophical preoccupations is with time, as in the case of "Fundación mítica de Buenos Aires," he is also interested here in the link between past cultural phenomena and their reflections in the present:

> ¿Dónde estarán? pregunta la elegía
> De quienes ya no son, como si hubiera
> Una región en que el Ayer pudiera
> Ser el Hoy, el Aún y el Todavía.

> (Where can they be? The elegy asks
> Whose are they no longer, as if there was
> A region in which Yesterday could
> Be the Today, the Still and the Not Yet.)[26]

However, here, by contrast, the poetic voice makes it clear that there is no culture *sub speciae eternitatis:* cultural nationalism to the contrary, the tango is not eternal. The use of pretentious capital letters with the temporal adverbs is an ironic subversion of any eternal permance attached to what stretches in an unbroken chain of permanence from Yesterday to Today, from Ever to Always.

Borges borrows the hoary medieval rhetorical figure, the ubi sunt, to inquire into where the tango and, more significantly, where its human voices have all gone. This figure allows Borges to create an inventory of elements of the tango—or at least, of those associated paradigmatically with the tango in its most consecrated form within Argentine cultural nationalism. He identifies the tango as

> Una mitología de puñales
> lentamente se anula en el olvido;
> Una canción de gesta se ha perdido
> En sórdidas noticias policiales.

> (A mythology of daggers
> Slowly dissolves itself in oblivion;
> A song about feats has been lost
> In the sordid police news.)[27]

What is interesting about this characterization is that any allusion to the tango as a cultural product centered on heterosexual love and/or on erotic enactment is skimmed over with respect to how the tango stages acts of violence that replace the song (the specifically artistic) with a police report (a routine administrative document of the social text). Once again, Borges ends up focusing on the dynamics of the homosocial component of the masculine code. It is not stated whether the questions of *puñales* are the consequence of jealousy between men or acts of revenge by a man against an unfaithful woman; women usually do not have enough agency in the tango to avenge wrongs done by unfaithful men. But this does not matter, since the homosocial imperative always prevails: if it is not a duel between men over a woman, violence against a woman is always about another man and his own threat to the masculinity of the avenger. And the violence recorded by the police is equally a matter between men, since even if the citizen who comes to the attention of the police is a woman, it is likely because she has been involved in a violation of the code of masculinity.[28]

Borges does not deny the contemporary existence of the tango. Rather, the tango has become a repository of the past. The participants in a specific Argentine social text, that of the acute heterosexist masculinity of the turn of the century, are today to be found as characters in a cultural text that continues to give them validity because, precisely, if the tango makes any

interpretational sense, it has to do with the dynamic it evokes, still active in
the contemporary social text, even if no longer enacted by the *malevaje*
(underworld) of a hundred years ago:

> Hoy, más allá del tiempo y de la aciaga
> Muerte, esos muertos viven en el tango.
> En la música están, en el cordaje
> De la terca guitarra trabajosa,
> Que trama en la milonga venturosa
> La fiesta y la inocencia del coraje.

> (Today, beyond time and the fateful
> Death, these dead live in the tango.
> They exist in the music and in the chord
> Of the working, plaintive guitar
> Which announces in the happy *milonga*
> The feast and the innocence of courage.)[29]

Note, as in the stanza just cited, the tendency to merge *milonga* and
tango, despite Borges's avowed preference for the former. But one will also
note the assertion that the *milonga*/tango concerns "la fiesta y la inocencia
del coraje."[30] Thus, it is surprising to learn that, all of a sudden, the violence
of the tango can be reduced to an innocent celebration. Perhaps the innocence derives from the specific versions of violence in the social text of the
past evoked by the cultural text of the present as no longer occurring. More
likely, Borges refers to how the cultural text makes the social text seem innocent. Were we to witness one of the acts of violence it describes, we would
be horrified, just as we would be appalled if we learned about it from a news
report. In both cases, the violence would be "real" in a way in which it is not
when it appears in a cultural text. In this way, the cultural text "sanitizes"
the violence of actual lived experience. While on the one hand cultural
texts may be effective challenges to the ideological sleights of hand that take
place in the social text, on the other, they can come across as "innocent,"
not really blood-spattered, because of the artistic transformation of the cultural text.

Thus, the tango translates the social text, which in a sense is what allows for the sustained contemplation of actual social circumstances the artistic text demands of its reader/viewer. Yet at the same time, by underscoring how violence becomes innocent, the poem brings the reader back to how it is really a declaration of actual forms of violence—the evocation (however the tango may appear to be nostalgically unreal) of actual circumstances of life in the urban space:

> Esa ráfaga, el tango, esa diablura,
> Los atareados años desafía;
> Hecho de polvo y tiempo, el hombre dura
> Menos que la liviana melodía,
> Que sólo es tiempo. El tango crea un turbio
> Pasado irreal que de algún modo es cierto,
> El recuerdo imposible de haber muerto
> Peleando, en una esquina del suburbio.

> (This flash, the tango, this prank,
> Challenges the years of work;
> Made of dust and time, man endures
> Less than the slight melody,
> That is only time. Tango creates a cloudy
> Unreal past which is somehow right,
> The impossible memory of having died
> Fighting, in a corner of the suburb.)[31]

Borges is drawing a fine line here, claiming that the tango is both a cultural phenomenon that turns social reality into an innocent celebration of manhood and the neighborhood scenarios of its display. But at the same time he maintains that "de algún modo es cierto" ("somehow it is right") that the social reality it conjures up is more than innocent panache. Borges focuses so much on the tango in this and other texts because of its extremely problematic role in Argentine culture. It is a mainstay of cultural nationalism (not to mention of the tourist trade), as it was of Buenos Aires urban life during the period of mass European immigration. Moreover, it is both a highly complex conjunction of music, poetry, and dance while being at the same time a not particularly subtle enactment of masculinist violence that in recent years has been a target of feminist attacks on male rage and privilege.

Ironically, given its importance to Peronist populism, the tango appeals to men from a social class ready for access to political and symbolic power. Yet by the same token, their masculinity is closely monitored in the tango because it dramatizes a way of aspiring to the same power. In other words, the tango represents, in a purified form, the male dominance that must be strategically attenuated if not ideologically concealed in the sectors of bourgeois decency that do in fact wield political and symbolic power. Of course, by the time Borges wrote "El tango," the social reality that was the original base of the tango had disappeared. This is exactly the force of the ubi sunt figures; the symbolic power of the tango is no longer that of the lived social text as such. Hence, the point of Borges's poem, which is to show how the tango, having made the transition from social text to cultural production, nevertheless still has meaning for the social text through the symbolic power it exercises.

IV

Beyond Nation

9/ Myth, Modernity, and Postmodern Tragedy in Walter Lima's *The Dolphin*

JERROLD VAN HOEG

BRAZILIAN DIRECTOR WALTER LIMA'S *THE DOLPHIN* (*Ele, o Boto*, 1987) offers one variant of the widespread folktales, told from the rain forests of the Andean countries to the Caribbean basin, about the metamorphosis of dolphins into human beings. Although there are as many renderings of these stories as there are storytellers, most of these accounts share several common elements, among them the enchanted dolphin or *encantado*'s proclivity for attending regional *festas* dressed in stylish white suits in order to seduce local women and thereby to father half-human children. Indeed, these are precisely the features of the myth that Lima's interpretation takes as its point of departure.

The Dolphin is, at one level, the story of a love affair between Tereza Amaro (played by Brazilian soap star Cássia Kiss) and an *encantado* or dolphin-man (portrayed by Carlos Alberto Riccelli). Tereza is seduced by the *encantado* and gives birth to a half-human, half-*boto* son, who is released into the sea the very night of his birth. Soon thereafter, Tereza's Aunt María and her cousin Luciano arrive unexpectedly to live with the family and share their humble life as poor fisherfolk on Brazil's poverty-stricken northeast coast.

After the death of her father Zé Amaro, Tereza agrees, in part forced by financial exigency, to marry a member of the local gentry, a well-to-do businessman named Rufino Bare. Significantly, she marries him not for love but for protection, presumably from the *boto* and all he represents. At the festival of Sãn João, the *encantado* reappears to seduce local young women, nearly enchanting Tereza again and eventually claiming her younger sister Corina. Later, he appears at the wedding of Tereza and Rufino to destroy the wedding party by magically creating a hugely powerful but mysteriously localized wind, "a passionate wind that only Tereza understood." In this instance, and throughout the film, the *boto* is clearly linked to the elemental forces of nature and desire, man's irrational animal side of emotion and sexuality, and so the other of civilization against which helpless (and possibly complicit) women must be protected and regulated in order to maintain the civic order.

During the festival of Sãn João, Tereza flees to Rufino's side for protection when she spots the bacchanalian *boto*, and the men of the village band together to cudgel a stranger thought to be—incorrectly, as it turns out—a *boto*. In another instance of the social order versus the *boto*/nature, the men unite in an attempt to drive the *botos* from their fishing grounds, blaming them for chasing the fish from the area.[1] Finally, much as the Greeks assembled to rescue Helen from Paris, the men come together to hunt down the *boto* after he lures Tereza from Rufino Bare's home. This time it is at the insistence of Rufino, and the chorus of fishermen would have us believe that many are participating more for the free gasoline Rufino is providing than out of civic duty. This third instance of social cooperation, of uniting against the common enemy to protect Rufino's "property," is a more cynical one, showing as it does the pragmatic self-interest that lies beneath the appearance of selfless communal sacrifice and collaboration.

Throughout the film, the phallic symbolism of the *boto* is aligned with Dionysian desire, passion, and libidinal instinct, while the village men represent Apollonian reason, civilization, and repressed desire. Indeed, the *boto* figure has much in common with that of Dionysus. It should be remembered that in Greek folktales and literature Dionysus represents the dissolution of established polarities. He is an Olympian god who appears in the bestial forms of bull, snake, or lion. He is a male god, but he has a sensuality and emotionality associated with women. He is a Greek, but he comes from barbaric Asia, and he is neither child nor man, but rather a sort of eternal adolescent. In short, he is the *other* who represents all that is threatening to the stable order of the *polis*, all that confuses the basic antinomies that demarcate the human, rational, and civilized world from the alien, chaotic, uncontrollable, and bestial realm of nature—a predicament superbly illustrated in Euripides' *Bacchae.*

Dionysus also represents the *other* within that must be repressed, the unconscious desires, emotions, and instincts that must be controlled lest they tear apart the fragile fabric of civilization. For many, and epitomized by Nietzsche in *The Birth of Tragedy,* this Dionysiac melody is the hidden locution of tragedy. Charles Segal writes, "The Dionysiac myth of the *Bacchae* and the Dionysiac form of tragedy here work together to enable this 'anti-culture' to come forth from unconscious to conscious knowledge."[2] On this view, these tales are a manifestation of deeper human truths, the eternal return of repressed desires and fears that threaten to collapse the hierarchical structure of social difference.

In the course of the film, the *boto* surfaces yet again in order to make friends with Tereza's husband Rufino. This time the *boto* appears in the guise of a rich gringo investor whose plans to build a lavish tourist hotel on the Bare property promise to make Rufino a rich man. Rufino's cupidity leads him to invite the *boto* into his home, where Tereza is very nearly seduced again. Indeed, shortly thereafter the *boto* entices Rufino from the home and subsequently eludes him in order to lure Tereza to the beach and ultimately accomplish his task, leading to the *boto* hunt alluded to above. Finally, Tereza's cousin Luciano (who, it turns out, is really her half-human/half-*boto* son) kills the *boto*—his father—but in the process becomes a *boto* himself. These two sacrificial offerings, the patricide and Luciano's subsequent metamorphosis or sacrifice of his human half, propitiate nature (and the culture that constructs nature) and so enable Luciano to lead the other *botos* from the area, simultaneously protecting the women and allowing the fish to return, assuring the continued existence of the village and its way of life. In this manner, Luciano fills the messianic role of sacrificial victim or scapegoat that René Girard speaks of in *Violence and the Sacred.* Transgression of the social order must be paid in blood, and the sacrificial victim is necessarily the *other,* be it woman, foreigner, or beast, the *pharmakos* onto whom the violence that would normally erupt within society may be displaced.[3]

In addition to the Dionysiac elements just mentioned, there are obviously Oedipal components in this family tale of love and patricide. Incestuous overtones do indeed pervade the relation between Tereza and her cousin/son Luciano, who in one scene professes his love for her and attempts to consummate it, although (unlike Jocasta) she manages to thwart the attempt. Here it should be noted that Oedipus too, like Dionysus and the *boto*, represents the dissolution of established polarities. Oedipus is both father and brother, husband and son, seer and blind man, poison and remedy. These three figures represent a mimetic doubling that is of course the essence of the Oedipal structure, the doubling from father to son of desire, especially the desire for what the other desires. As is well known, various versions of the triangle of desire and its repression (see Freud, Lévi-Strauss, Jacques Lacan, Flieger) have been extrapolated or doubled from the familial level to the social, and this is clearly the case in Lima's film as well.

In addition to the relation between Luciano and Tereza, a love affair also unfolds between Luciano and his aunt, Tereza's sister Corina (read: mimetic double), who is eventually seduced not by Luciano but by a proxy *boto*. This transgression precipitates her suicide but, like the sacrifice of Iphigenia in Aulis, enables the *polis* to endure.[4] Her suicide is atonement for the crime of transgressing the civic order, and it also prompts Luciano to kill his father and so lose his own humanity, yet in so doing to drive the bestial from the civic realm.

The use of the Oedipal family as a leitmotif in the film, along with two surreal dream scenes involving *botos*, points directly to Freud's scientific analysis of myth, dreams, parapraxes, and so on. According to Freud, these representations or signs either reveal or create an entity known as the unconscious—depending on whether one believes that it was there all along or that it is constituted by virtue of representation. Freud's analysis of Greek myth, especially his reading of the Oedipal tales in *The Interpretation of Dreams*, is the paradigmatic example of the privileged status accorded to Western scientific discourse vis-à-vis popular discourses, of the view that scientific knowledge is a special case, immune to its own demythologizing. In *The Dolphin*, Lima contests the privileged position of science by not granting it an exalted position among the multitude of discourses given voice in the film—Greek myth, Amazonian myth, cynical realism, surrealism, parody, documentary, and so forth. In so doing, he asserts that the idea that the history of Western science or reason is the history of an exodus from myth, or *Entmythologisierung*, is a myth as well.[5] Thus Lima adds science, and its corollary of technological progress, to the list of myths operative in the Brazilian social imaginary.

The path is a long one that leads to Lima's view that even scientific rationality is simply one shared belief or myth among the many that organize Brazilian culture. The Oedipal leitmotif in the film and its origins in Freud's positivism recall a nineteenth-century Brazilian literature mediated by the positivist discourse of the natural sciences, a propensity exemplified by Euclides da Cunha's *Os Sertões* (1902). Following World War I and the demise of positivism, as González Echevarría explains,[6] the discourse of the natural sciences was replaced in Latin America by the discourse of the social sciences in a search for new beginnings from which to rebuild a fragmented world. This search centered, particularly in the *tristes tropiques* of Amazonia, on myth and language as the bearers of the "authentic" knowledge of the *other*.

This early mediation of the social sciences in Latin American letters incorporated Freudian theory, avant-garde movements of the twenties, and early anthropology and ethnography, as these various discourses converged in the search for national identities and in the attempt to incorporate the rural population with its "popular" or "folk" culture into the modern state. In the case of Brazil, this intersection can be seen in, for example, the Week of Modern Art in São Paulo (1922), Mario de Andrade's *Macunaíma*, and the entire Movimento Antropofágico, of which Raul Bobb (whose *Cobra Norato* deals with the dolphin theme) was a part, and to which the entire Cinema Novo is much indebted.[7] Indeed, the changing treatment of myth and "the people" in the social sciences and in Brazilian literature can be seen in compressed form in the trajectory of Cinema Novo itself from the 1960s to the 1980s—from an initial documentary tendency through a stylistic evolution going from critical realism to the allegorical discourse of tropicalism, including the "cannibalist-tropicalist" phase.[8] All of these genealogical sources are cited and reiterated in *The Dolphin* and so illuminate and authorize Lima's representational choices.

Finally, in line with the Freudian imagery and its evocations discussed so far, from a present-day clinical standpoint, the *boto* tales, and especially the reactions to them on the part of the "subjects," can be described as culture-bound syndromes. This approach treats the belief that one has seen dolphins turn into humans and back again, and that one has had sexual relations with same, as a culture-specific manifestation of a more general

syndrome whose origin is the unconscious.[9] In the psychoanalytic literature, the relativism of the culture-bound approach is not overtly questioned. Simons and Hughes point out that if another culture "were to
develop a cross-cultural scheme for the classification of undesirable =
deviant = 'sick' behavior, it would include Type A behavior as a prime
example."[10] This relativism does not extend, however, to the concept of an
underlying collective unconscious that produces the transcendental phenomenon known as myth. The problem with this type of relativism is that
although it talks about separate mythological systems, it does not consider
which of these systems the theory of cultural relativism or the concepts of
myth and the unconscious belong to. Much as in the Middle Ages when one
could argue about the number of angels that might fit on the head of a pin
but not the existence of angels, today one can argue about the quantity of
meanings that may perhaps fit on the head of a myth, but not myth's existence as a meaning-bearing sign whose origins are in the unconscious.[11]

Once one accepts that myths are culture-bound messages from the
interior, it is but a short slide down a slippery slope to asking what the tales
told at the manifest level reveal about the latent levels of the collective
unconscious of the societies and cultures that produce them.[12] Slater's
definitive study of the dolphin tales, *Dance of the Dolphin,* takes this psychoanthropological approach: "Like a growing number of literary scholars,
anthropologists, and historians," she writes, "I have been especially interested in the larger question of cultural-confrontation and the subversive
possibilities of apparently innocuous symbolic forms; . . . the Dolphin stories provide a privileged understanding of the meanings and mystifications
upon which worlds are built."[13] For Slater, then, these tales reflect neither
"timeless" myths nor something akin to Schelling's self-referential "tauto-
gorical" presences, but rather a sociocultural response to the economic,
social, political, and environmental changes and conflicts taking place in
present-day Amazonia. This approach, following a muted Gramscian
model, suggests the counterhegemonic nature of popular discourse—"cultural-confrontation and the subversive possibilities of apparently innocuous symbolic forms."[14] This approach is distinct from the Frankfurt School
model, which saw the popular sector as basically a passive receiver of cultural messages.

We may contrast Slater's more Gramscian and so Latin American approach with functionalist Eurocentric research of only a decade ago, which insisted on the top-down nature of mythic discourse.[15] On this latter view, myth functions to impose and perpetuate a given set of sociocultural relationships. In other words, myth is the cause and society the effect, while Slater has it the other way round. The psychoanthropological approach, then, aspires to synthesize the symbolist approach of Freudian essentialism with a functionalist approach à la Malinowski.[16]

Though Slater's view in some ways removes myth from the status of archetype—it is no longer both the cause and effect of "patriarchy"—it still trades upon the underlying psychoanalytic postulate that assumes myth to be a transcendental feature of humanity originating in the collective unconscious. This view also assumes that the manifest level or literal folktale is a censored or coded message that needs only to be decoded, by a "qualified" agent, in order to reveal a latent and "deeper" truth, Slater's "privileged understanding." By positing the universal existence of unconscious desires and their symptomatic narrative expression, such as myths, dreams, fantasies, and folktales, this theory tautologically accounts not only for the universal existence of myths, but also for their cause—the unconscious—and their effect, namely to express the content of the collective unconscious. Their various incarnations or contents are explained as the consequence of local contexts, and so we have a tripartite model comprised of the literal tale at the manifest level, and two latent levels, one diachronic at the level of local culture, and one synchronic at the level of a global or universal unconscious. Thus theory (or ideology), which is supposed to explain observed reality, becomes the foundation on which reality is constructed, the preexisting model to which everything must conform. Rather than "dis-covering" an existing object, theory creates it. Slater sees *boto* tales as context-bound responses to change in Amazonia but sees her own reading of them as universal and transcendent.[17]

Following this "folktale as coded message in the present" paradigm, a local reading that necessarily suggests itself is that of the *boto* as gringo or foreigner who wreaks havoc in a traditional way of life through changes imposed by his money and technologically backed "progress." In fact, in *Dance of the Dolphin* Slater devotes an entire chapter to "*The Dolphin as White Man*" in which she develops precisely this conclusion.[18] In the film, just prior to his meeting to tempt Tereza's husband Rufino with the forbidden fruit of the tree of technological knowledge, the multinational *boto* is shown descending from a new high-tech bus, wearing gringo regalia, speaking first English and then Portuguese with a gringo accent, and making his first pause to refresh beneath a Coca-Cola sign (a company ironically listed on the credits as a sponsor, presumably in the name of culture). Lima's representation here indeed coincides with Slater's dolphin-as-white-man equation.

The method used by Lima to portray the *boto* is, however, far from the ethnographic field study method that Slater uses. Indeed, as mentioned above, an important feature of *The Dolphin* is the use of a combination of cinematic techniques—documentary, surrealist, and realist—to relate the events in the motion picture. The *boto*-as-gringo motif is merely one representation among many. For Lima, a reading of the dolphin tales as a reaction to technological progress or technoimperialism is merely one piece of the puzzle. By situating the discourse of technology within a multiplicity of other mythic perspectives and viewing it through the eyes of various subjects, he demonstrates that this reading is simply one more story, one more social construct among many.

Lima's multilayered representational method proceeds, at least in part, from an awareness of the problem of agency, from what Clifford calls the *crise de conscience* in anthropology and ethnography—the revelation of their literary nature,[19] the acknowledgment of the ideological role of the agent or subject of scientific discourse.[20] In Latin America, beginning around 1950, official anthropological stories were undermined by the general movement for liberation in the postcolonial world, especially the Cuban revolution, and the accompanying realization that the official stories tended to be ideologically complicit with First World hegemony in Latin America. Clifford writes, "Henceforth, neither the experience nor the interpretive activity of the scientific researcher can be considered innocent."[21] From this point on, anthropologists themselves become aware of the literary, rhetorical, and ideological nature of their representative practice, and indeed today anthropologists such as Taussig and Geertz, in a self-reflexive metadiscourse, proclaim the literariness of their work.[22] This longing to disavow the authoritative disciplinary voice manifests itself in the multiple discourses represented in *The Dolphin*, indicating Lima's desire to participate in this new self-reflexive metadiscourse.

The move to self-reflexivity is part of a more general critique, beginning with Nietzsche, of the ideological character of modernist representation and its unilinear conception of history, its cult of progress, and so on.[23] Given the putative end of modernity and consequently the foundational crisis mentioned above, how does one legitimize the relation between an object of study and the statements made about that object? Specifically, how does one validate a statement regarding the connection between the dolphin story and other myths, and a corresponding Brazilian sociocultural reality?

As we have seen, Lima's approach is to offer a variety of perspectives on the same events, a cinematic doubling of point of view, of myth, and of the *boto* himself, who appears in a multiplicity of incarnations. In the film, there is a presumably "objective" off-camera narrator who, together with a documentary camera style, gives us one version of the story. This narrator often interviews a group of cynical local fishermen, a kind of Greek chorus, who offer a pragmatic interpretation of events—for example, the *boto* stories are just a cover for otherwise unexplained pregnancies, an excuse for poor fishing catches, a way to dupe gullible believers, and so forth. There are also two dream sequences, which presumably shed light on the inner motivation of the dreamers, Tereza and Corina, and recall the Freudian influence pervading the decoding of myth and folklore. And finally, there is the overall record of events recorded by the camera—the complete film—a succession of events that includes the dreams, the documentary interviews with the chorus, Keystone Cops chase scenes involving the locals and the *boto*, and all the other actions that take place in the film.

The overall picture the film paints, then, is one of multiple perspectives on the "meaning" of the *boto* tales, a kind of historiography of the various approaches to myth, narrative, and film in Brazil. A postmodern reading would have it that this contradictory, even chaotic view makes it difficult to conceive of a *single* correct interpretation. If there is no objective reality lying beneath, or beyond, the images Lima projects, so much the better, for the disorienting effect of a multiplicity of possible readings of the *boto* tales is precisely what provides the emancipatory element in the film. From a postmodern perspective, by showing that the manifest/latent binary is susceptible to infinite regress, and that at each level representation is not value-free but rather the contrary, meaning is liberated from critical authority, be it anthropological, ethnographic, psychoanalytic, or literary.

This implies, however, that the ideal of a common social self-consciousness is unrealizable. In a world of multiple language games there can be only limited, or at least not univocal, understanding of social communication and exchange. Indeed, without a sort of neo-Kantian consensus in matters of signification, a hybrid society cannot find commonly constructed social ground. The solution, the unifying social thread, seems to be, for Lima, the shared foundation of *mythos* or narrative.

If the mythic code or mediation, the citational chain of myth, precedes and conditions the formation of the subject, then myth is indeed a subjectless discourse. If Lima's, and all subject positions, are interpellated through mythic discourse, then *The Dolphin* derives its performative function through the citation of myth, and so in the end Lima is right and we have not so much content as structure, more precisely Oedipus-as-structure. This idealist formulation, however, problematizes the question of social change. Without a subject of discourse, how does an idealist vision explain social change?

Nietzsche writes, referring to the death of the father, "This violence always manifests the need for a belief, for a prop, for a *structure*."[24] But what if the structure were an effect caused by other relationships, rather than that metaphysical prime mover christened by Freud as "the unconscious"?[25] What if the content is destitute of signification? What if the eternal iteration and reiteration of the unconscious is a myth itself, caused by a violence that always needs a belief, a prop, a *structure*?

The question arises, then, whence this violence that needs a belief or structure, that universally creates not the unconscious but narrative props? We can begin to answer by noting that where the psychoanthropological approach insists that the manifest content reveals a latent content to be decoded by "the one who is supposed to know," another perspective might ask what function these tales perform in terms of material system-environment relations. The constant factor in both myth and society, past, present, and future, is the relation between societies and their organic and inorganic environment, their material relations with the real. The violence in this scenario is the violence enacted in establishing and maintaining the system-environment relations between society and nature.

An example of this alternative approach to popular discourse is Roy Rappaport's study of the Tsembaga of New Guinea, a group of Maring speakers.[26] The Maring cosmology revolves around two sets of spirits, the Red Spirits and the Spirits of Rot. These spirits are said to represent dead ancestors, to whom the living owe abiding obligations, principally for aiding the living in time of war. Meeting the symbolic debt to the ancestors requires an ongoing cycle of ritualized warfare and pig sacrifice. The cycle also involves a variety of taboos on certain foods, sexual intercourse, and so on. According to Rappaport, it is owing to the mediation of the cosmological system "that the actual material variables comprising the ecosystem are regulated."[27] The net effect of the six-to-twenty-year cycle of pig production, pig sacrifice, ritual warfare, and return to pig production, with its accompanying taboos, is to provide a sustainable balance between the human population and the carrying capacity of the valley in which the approximately 200 Tsembaga live. Wilden summarizes his analysis of the Tsembaga ritual cycle by observing, "With the exception of natural catastrophes or the coming of the white man, the Maring-Tsembaga system, co-evolved with nature, is quite capable of lasting to the end of time."[28] The Maring cosmology is an inscription or marker that records and, upon being performed, reiterates system-environment relations. The material variables of the ecosystem are regulated inadvertently by following ritual proscriptions. The Tsembaga do the right thing for the wrong reason.

Relatedly, Peggy Reeves Sanday, in *Female Power and Male Dominance,* examines the 186 societies of the standard cross-cultural sample to underscore the fact that the social relations supposedly constructed by myth are instead a product of system-environment relations. "The environmental context of gender symbolism in origin stories is the main focus," she writes. "Origin stories are symbolic manifestations of an outer, inner, or dual orientation to nature."[29] The Oedipal structure, mediated by the Western social imaginary, is only one possible arrangement among many in terms of the relations between narrative, culture, and nature. It is possible that narrative can be seen as a means not only to reveal social relations, but also to offer a form for recording and transmitting through time co-evolved survival procedures regulating material socioenvironmental relations. In the case of Tsembaga society, an efficient ecosystemic structure is passed on from generation to generation through a content that is only indirectly related to the meaning of the content of the Tsembaga myths. In the case of Western society, the code or *gestell* that links reason, theory, narrative, and meaning is perpetuated through time. The performance and the content coincide, and so an endless cycle of mythical return is perpetuated, a perpetual motion machine for attributing the same form to any content, for the endless production of context-free or imaginary meaning.

An Oedipal structure that deals only with social relations posits itself as free of society's environmental context while simultaneously reproducing this imaginary relation of independence. The violence of Tsembaga society needs and gets a belief system, a prop, which though irrational in content serves to carry the coded symbolic information which allows that society to perpetuate system-environment relations. The same may be said of Western societies, with the exception that the belief system is not symbolic of long-term sustainable system-environment relations, but instead a direct reflection—a mirror image or doubling—of agonistic system-environment relations, of an imaginary, specular relationship between society and nature. The Tsembaga achieved a symbiotic relation with their natural environment while the Western *gestell* (code) has produced an agonistic or competitive relation with ours. These differences are reflected in the respective cosmologies and, above all, in the respective social codes or mediations of the two societies, one symbolic and the other imaginary.

We may now ask, then, what does *The Dolphin* do in terms of perpetuating system-environment relations? What structure, or belief system, or prop is transmitted through time in *The Dolphin*? We noted earlier that *The Dolphin* proffers a multiplicity of myths—Greek, Amazonian, scientific—without granting a privileged position to any one account. It does this by offering a number of points of view, again without privileging any of them. Additionally, it rehearses a number of scientific discourses—positivist, anthropological, ethnographic—and cultural discourses—documentary, literary, tropicalist—without appearing to sanction any particular discourse. And finally, it posits a series of antagonists—Oedipal, Dionysiac, *boto*—in such a way as to make these appear both multiple and interchangeable, which indeed they are. In fact, that all these components truly are interchangeable is precisely the mythic and tragic message of *The Dol-*

phin. Both in form and in content, *The Dolphin* iterates the essence of tragedy: it is not the differences but the loss of them that gives rise to violence and chaos in society.

This is the view argued at length by René Girard in *Violence and the Sacred*, and subsequently taken up by a host of other scholars.[30] I emphasize it here to underscore that what *The Dolphin* does is communicate the essence of Western tragedy through time. By positing a crisis of distinctions, Lima reiterates the tragic message, and by positing the *other*, the foreigner, the one who is part insider and part outsider, part human and part beast, as sacrificial victim whose death restores the civic order, he replays the *kathartic* moment in which "mysterious benefits accrue to the community upon death of a human *katharma* or *pharmakos*," since "the purpose of the sacrifice is to restore harmony to the community, to reinforce the social fabric."[31] Finally, what *The Dolphin* does is perpetuate the discourse of tragedy, of the Western *gestell*, in both content and form, a postmodern multiplicity of perspectives that by its very nature reiterates the tragic crisis of distinctions. The postmodern crisis, Lyotard's dissolution of grand narratives or Clifford's *crise de conscience*, is in Girard's terms a sacrificial crisis: the sacrificial crisis can be defined, therefore, as a crisis of distinctions— that is, a crisis affecting the social order. This cultural order is nothing more than a regulated system of distinctions in which the differences among individuals are used to establish their "identity" and their mutual relationships.[32]

In the final analysis, *The Dolphin* posits the unconscious as the prime mover, the ultimate subject that writes the text of society and so constructs sociocultural relations, making the social text an endless chain of citational reiterations. By postulating all knowledge as mythic, and all myth as simultaneously culturally relative at one level and as an essential prime mover at another, Lima remains trapped in the *gestell* of narration as knowledge, the trap of the search for meaning in myth. He remains snared in the view that narration, the expression of the social imaginary, is either the cause or the effect (or both simultaneously) of social relations.

Once myth is accepted as a meaning-bearing sign, and this meaning is decoded and a "truth" revealed, then, given the incompatible variations of myth, it follows that by the principle of noncontradiction not all myths can be true. But this conclusion denies the postulate that all myth bears deeper truths. The obvious solution is to posit a theory of cultural relativism in order to recuperate the notion that all myths are equally true. The problem with this approach is, of course, that any contact with another cultural world undoes the separation that relativism needs. As Lima's film demonstrates, dialogue between different mythic systems must necessarily take place within a common cultural horizon. Furthermore, the effort to relativize—the postmodern move *extraordinaire*—provokes the embodiment of tragedy, a crisis of distinctions. Relativism becomes simultaneously poison and remedy. Lima's solution is, as we have seen, to retreat to a restoration of differences: the *boto* is killed, the *polis* is delivered from the plague that caused the fish to vanish, and the hierarchies return.

An alternate view, such as Rappaport's, would have it that the relations between the human system and the natural environment are the prime movers of social relations, and that myth is an indirect reflection of these relations, a post hoc phenomenon that is merely symbolic of existing system-environment relations. On this view, myth can only be trace and memory, never prime mover, and so can never provide a foundation or authority, or can never be given as full presence—the collective unconscious as beginning and end of myth and, hence, of society. Ultimately, what initially appears to be a postmodern perspective in *The Dolphin*, the multiplicity of differences given voice in the film, becomes the paradigmatic tragic moment as narrative movement converts multiple differences into a crisis of difference insofar as these various differences interact and are put into relation with one another in the course of the film.

The search for meaning in *mythos* or narrative requires a foundation to create and interpret narrative. This foundation, as we have seen, is the agent of representation, be it the individual subject or the collective unconscious, but always an idealist self-generating prime mover. The alternate approach discussed above regards myth and narration as a trace or memory of material ecosystemic relations whose performance perpetuates these co-evolved relations. This view, by looking at what social narrative does, rather than what it says, avoids the metaphysical problems of meaning and agency that prove so inescapable for Lima in *The Dolphin*. This view does not, however, contradict Lima's position that mythic narrative mediates social relations, but instead asserts that myth mediates these relations at one level while at another it is itself mediated by ecosystemic factors. On this view, the way to break the eternal return of mythic iteration and reiteration, an endless chain of different versions—Greek, Brazilian, scientific—of the same story, is to change the material relations between system and environment. The question of social change then moves from the idealist arena of ultimate versus relative meaning to the sociomaterial realm of ecosystemic relations. Finally, I would suggest that it behooves us to make a thoroughgoing analysis of popular discourses to consider not only what these say in sociohistoric terms, but also what they do in ecosystemic terms.

10/ "Useless Spaces" of the Feminine in Popular Culture

Like Water for Chocolate and *The Silent War*

VINCENT SPINA

OTH THE WILDLY POPULAR NOVEL BY THE MEXICAN author Laura Esquivel, *Like Water for Chocolate* (1992), and the almost completely unknown pentology, *The Silent War* (1979–1987) by the Peruvian novelist Manuel Scorza, have at least one thing in common: the figure of woman is central to each text. In the following discussion, I want to study how this figure functions in terms of the idea of culture represented in each work. In neither is culture finally an affair of class or even society; Esquivel's text, which takes place primarily in domestic space, is staged in terms of ceremony and religion, while the site of Scorza's texts, though more varied and far more public, is equally governed by myth and ritual. How does culture participate in this discourse, and how does the figure of woman prove crucial to the process?

Raquel Olea has noted how women have not been part of modernity's social contract, constructed according to the needs of the bourgeoise: "Masculine was, in sum, the space of the power that constructs projects of civilization and society. Feminine, by contrast, was the closed space of the private, of unpaid domestic labor performed without a contract, the space of the reproduction of labor power and of the species."[1] The contrast is by now familiar. Olea goes on to note how, although there were norms and prohibitions proper to each space, it was toward what she terms "the place of useless energies" that maximum social repression was directed, by means of which woman, and through her the family, could be seen as "the basic unit of bourgeois society."[2]

I will suggest that these energies, far from being "useless" in some degraded social sense, are seen by both Esquivel and Scorza as powerfully destructive and creative—prior to "the space of power" that includes bourgeois society and its cultural inscriptions. My reading is at once indebted to and divergent from Huyssen's account in *After the Great Divide* of the historical inscription of mass culture as woman, "in which mass culture appears as monolithic, engulfing, totalitarian," while "modernism appears as progressive, dynamic, and indicative of male superiority in culture."[3] Both *Like Water for Chocolate* and *The Silent War* are in this respect premodern texts, or at least explore respective worlds before the advent of modernity, which is why each can represent woman as a mythic figure of such significance and power for the constitution of culture.

In each novel woman is a shaping force in a narrative from which she has been excluded. Even more crucial, in each novel woman is enshrouded in an idea of mystery that is intimately related to a certain notion of popular culture—notwithstanding that the very fact of such culture is absent in one case except in the form of cookbook recipes, and largely present everywhere in the other case almost exclusively through voices. Huyssen writes that "the claim that the threats (or, for that matter, the benefits) of mass culture are somehow 'feminine' has finally lost its persuasive power."[4] Perhaps so. In the following discussion, I will try to account for the mythic substratum that has made it possible first to imagine culture as "feminine"— whether to celebrate or denigrate it—not only before it was "mass" but before it was culture at all in the modern sense.

A Poetics of the Carving Knife

In his study of Japan, *The Empire of Signs*, Roland Barthes comments on chopsticks, a metonomy for Japanese cuisine considered from the point of view of its preparation and consumption:

> In the gesture of the chopsticks, further softened by their substance—wood or lacquer—there is something maternal, the same precisely measured care taken in moving a child: a force . . . no longer a pulsion; here we have a whole

demeanor with regard to food; this is seen clearly in the cook's long chopsticks, which serve not for eating, but for preparing foodstuff: the instrument never pierces, cuts, or slits, never wounds but only selects, turns, shifts; . . . they never violate the foodstuff: either they gradually unravel it (in the case of vegetables) or else prod it into separate pieces (in the case of fish, eels), thereby rediscovering the natural fissures of the substance.[5]

If we think of Tita, the main character of *Like Water for Chocolate*, and if we consider the detailed descriptions of food preparation in the text, as well as the obvious pleasure and enthusiasm attached to this preparation and the final consumption, the parallels between the novel and Barthes's interpretation of how food is experienced in Japan become apparent.

Yet, as with all human activity, these moments of pleasure in which the food is prepared would not be possible without a prior act of violence that brings the foodstuff—be it animal or vegetable—to the table of the cook. Indeed, the very function of refined preparation may exist not merely to please the palate but to seduce us into forgetting this prior act. Still, though it be effaced, the initial act of violence remains integral to the whole process: the peace of preparation and eating is not possible without that act—they become one act. Thus we are introduced to Mama Elena, Tita's mother and prime antagonist:

> She made her cuts through the rind with such mathematical precision that when she was done, she could pick up the watermelon and give it a single blow against a stone, in a particular spot, and like magic the watermelon rind would open like the petals of a flower, leaving the heart intact on the table. Unquestionably, when it came to dividing, dismantling, dismembering, desolating, detaching, dispossessing, destroying, or dominating, Mama Elena was a pro.[6]

To the extent, then, that the entire food process indicates a phase of preparation—"maternal," according to Barthes—and another phase of destruction, Tita and Mama Elena are not only antagonists but also complementary. They are unified by the whole process, phases of which each represents. Such a unification, of course, is not without precedent. From Celtic Ireland to India, there are goddesses characterized by the union of destruction and creation into a single force.[7] More specifically, a goddess uniting these opposing forces also appears in the Aztec Pantheon: Tlal-teutli, dismembered by Quetzalcoatl and Tezcotlipoca so that parts of her body could be used to create earth and the gods. As compensation, she is thereafter given the human blood she so desired.[8]

To further the identification of these characters within a unified plane of creation and destruction, remember that both Mama Elena and her old-est daughter Rosaura—her spiritual, as well as material, heir—give birth but cannot nurse their children. For Mama Elena, this is true only for Tita, as though upon escaping from her mother's womb on a sea of sorrow born from her own tears, Tita carries away her mother's own power to nurture the life she has created, converting her into the pole of destruction on the plane of their existence as a single force. In contrast, Nacha, the Indian woman who feeds, nurtures, and instructs Tita in the wisdom of food recipes, dies a virgin.

Tita herself, able to produce milk from her breasts for Rosaura's first child and able to feed the second from her kitchen creations, is ironically only capable of a false pregnancy. Thus, contained within the destructive lies an area of fertility, while within the creative pole there can be found a trace of the destructive—barrenness. In this light, the plane takes on the characteristics of the I-Ching symbol: a circle divided between two oppos-ing forces, in each of which lies a portion of the other.

In contrast to this understanding of the relationship between Tita and Mama Elena, critics have tended to view their antagonism as the product of a male-dominated society. Joanne Saltz points out that Mama Elena is an extension of a counterrevolutionary, authoritarian (male) society, and her desire to dominate her daughter stems from the traditions of that society alone.[9] Similarly, Alder Senior Grant sees Tita's death as based on her inability to live without Pedro, demonstrating in this way her "dependencia total del falo" ("total dependency on the phallus").[10]

Of course, both Saltz and Grant acknowledge the novel's attack on male-dominated society, but to reduce the two main characters to mere functions of this society is to lose sight of the important female dynamic revealed by the novel in reference to creation. In this respect, the words of Mama Elena are significant when she boasts to the parish priest that she needs no men on her ranch;[11] it is not merely an offhand remark but a the-sis the novel all but demonstrates, except for the necessity of male sperm.

Nor is the identification of the force of destruction with that of creation lost on Tita. While she tries to kill the quail as gently as possible for the rose petal recipe, Tita realizes that "you cannot be weak when it comes to killing: you have to be strong or it just causes more sorrow."[12]

The space of the struggle between these two characters becomes the kitchen. The immediate cause is Mama Elena's interdiction against Tita's ever marrying Pedro. She decides that he shall marry Rosaura instead, the oldest daughter, and Tita shall remain single so that she can devote her life to the care of her mother, as decreed by tradition. That the kitchen should become the space of their contention comes about quite naturally. First, the death of Tita's father at the time of her birth had forced Mama Elena to take charge of the ranch. Second, Mama Elena must leave Tita to the care of Nacha, the cook, since the shock of her husband's death caused her milk to dry up; this fact establishes Tita's place in the kitchen. Third, Mama Elena establishes her own place there because, by taking over her husband's role, she has become the provider. Finally, Mama Elena's bathhouse, though not in the kitchen itself, is very near to it; in fact, it is in the bathhouse that mother and daughter meet when Tita prepares her mother's bath, then helps her to bathe and dress.

On the one hand, therefore, we have the kitchen fire associated with cooking juxtaposed against the water of the bath. They are opposing elements, yet their metonymic ranges are quite similar. Both are associated with the sources of life and death since they are capable of causing both. Indeed, both are present in the title of the book: the phrase "Like water for chocolate" refers to water being brought repeatedly to the point of boiling so that that chocolate warmed over it in a double boiler will melt and blend smoothly; without the heat of fire, the blending could not take place. And water at the boiling point may either cook or kill. Tita, representing the kitchen fire, thus confronts her mother as the latter rises from her bath. The close association between the two women becomes even more evocative if we remember that the opening of the Tlalteutli myth places the goddess on the primordial waters that covered the earth before time and creation.[13]

It is after the bath scene, when the two women have returned to the kitchen, that they are informed of the death of Rosaura's first child. For the first time, Tita openly defies her mother's dictum not to cry and accuses her of having murdered the baby by sending him and his parents to live away from the ranch. Mama Elena beats Tita, ironically, with a wooden kitchen spoon. Tita suffers an emotional breakdown and is rescued from entering a mental institution by the family doctor, the North American John Brown, who takes her to another kind of kitchen where she regains her taste for life and the will to live.

Brown has converted this other kitchen, located in a secluded part of the household, into a laboratory. It had been built as a retreat for his Kikapoo grandmother. There she cooked and prepared her curative herbs, and there she took refuge from the racist persecution of the rest of the family, which lasted until she cured her father-in-law of a disease that Western medicine had failed to cure. John received his first lessons in medicine there; in fact, he passed most of his childhood in that kitchen, and he has returned there in order to reconcile Western medicine with the Kikapoo wisdom of his grandmother.

In view of John's return to this space and the reason for his return, as well as how he privileges his grandmother's knowledge over that of the West and finally becomes an open follower of his grandmother, it is difficult to understand how Saltz considers his return to the kitchen a "kidnapping" of his grandmother's knowledge.[14] On the contrary, his very being is forged in a space profoundly inscribed within his grandmother's womanness. He grows within this space and becomes a creative personality because of it.

The other principal characters may all be defined in terms of their relation to the same space. Gertrudis, the middle sister, though a revolutionary general in a male army, is always sympathetic toward her sister Tita and, by extension, toward what she represents in terms of the kitchen. Indeed, for Gertrudis the kitchen becomes a space of spiritual renewal (though she herself cannot cook) to which she must return from time to time. She states, "Life would be much nicer if one could carry the smells and tastes of the maternal home wherever one pleased."[15] It is as though the kitchen itself (rather than Mama Elena) becomes the "maternal" space, a dynamic area in which the process of creation and destruction contend with each other, ultimately to complement each other and become a whole. Just so, Gertrudis's life itself resonates with the same contention. In her role as military leader she is a destroyer. Yet her affiliation with the kitchen and with her sister Tita aligns her with the creative aspects of the creation/destruction complex.

Rosaura and Pedro also are defined in terms of their relationship with the kitchen. Rosaura becomes the spiritual heir to Mama Elena, insofar as the latter represents the values of traditional Mexican society. The daughter certainly mirrors her mother's own destructive desire, but she lacks the aggressive power that makes of her mother an active force within the kitchen dynamic. On the contrary, Rosaura eschews the kitchen almost entirely, and in turn the kitchen, in a figurative sense, eschews her: the food it produces for nourishment becomes for Rosaura a slow poison that leads to an ignominious death. Yet, in spite of her association with all that is not life-producing, she is still the physical mother of Esperanza and the grandmother of the narrator of the novel, whose role portends a reconciliation of these opposing forces, a feat accomplished before only by her Great-Aunt Gertrudis.

Pedro, in contrast to the other characters, is the least self-sufficient. In fact, he hardly exists outside the kitchen and apart from what Tita or Mama Elena make of him. What does he do? Does he have an occupation? Esquivel does not even consider these questions. Rather, she brings him to life and to death only in the kitchen and in the presence of either Mama Elena or Tita. Thus, he declares his love for and intention to marry Tita in the kitchen. He is aroused by the sight of her nursing his child in the kitchen. Finally, he dies in that very part of the kitchen complex where the opposing forces of destruction and creation are most concentrated: Mama Elena's bathing room, transformed by Tita into a bedroom for their liaison. And, more ironically, the affair is carried out on Gertrudis's former bed. She is the one character (before Esperanza, and her daughter, the narrator) who most unites the creative and destructive poles of the complex. To increase the irony, Rosaura, from her window, can see the sparks produced in the bedroom when Tita and Pedro make love, but she does nothing about it, believing them to be the ghost of Mama Elena.

Tita's relations with Pedro and John can be comprehended in terms of the power of myth. It is undoubtedly one of the mysteries of the novel why she chooses Pedro instead of John, but this choice does conform to a clear symbolic logic. First of all, it is necessary to discard Saltz's notion that by accepting John Tita would submit herself to male domination—worse still, North American domination.[16] Far from signifying this role, John's central appeal derives from his own formation in a kitchen—his grandmother's—where he has been humanized and sensitized to Tita and her humanity. And here lies the problem. On the level of myth, Tita and Mama Elena exist as contending poles within a space, defined as the kitchen. Mama Elena performs her function by turning outward from this space to what must be brought to the kitchen and destroyed. Tita, on the other hand, turns inward to this space in order to create from what has been destroyed.

As unreconciled types, one cannot perform the function of the other; thus, at the level of myth, Tita cannot turn outward to John and take him as her consort. Pedro, though, on the contrary, has no life outside Tita's space; indeed, he is her creation and, as such, the focus of her love. Out of this love, no life will result; not so much because of some figurative taboo against a figurative incest, but rather because life is the product of an interaction between two distinct beings. Here we have only Tita and her creation, Pedro, who, ultimately, has little existence beyond her, and so must be identified with her. This kind of dilemma is only solved when the dynamic of destruction and creation is incorporated into a single individual such as Gertrudis or Esperanza. These two characters no longer reside as poles within a particular space. Rather, by incorporating the opposing poles within themselves, the space represented by these poles resides within them.

In her essay on this novel, Janice Jaffe is especially interested in how, by dominating their space, women come to dominate their destinies. She compares the preparation of food to creative expression, thus linking Esquivel to Sor Juan Ines de la Cruz, Virginia Woolf, and Helena María Viamontes, for whom cooking and creation become the same process.[17] Salvador Oropesa follows a similar line, noting that, although Esquivel's novel does not deviate from the norms of a male-dominated society that assigns women to the kitchen, it transforms this space by claiming for it a new set of values—those chosen by women themselves.[18]

Furthermore, the level of myth of the novel implies that women can be restored to their original unity, a unity expressed in the Tlalteutli myth. This goddess is certainly a creator, but she is also a destroyer. She is both victim and victimizer. By extension, this kind of restoration demands that all the other dualities be restored to their original wholeness; in the case of Gertrudis, for instance, the novel obviously demands a restoration of the duality between virgin and whore. The novel has no interest in either the traditional Mexican society that Mama Elena represents or the American imperialism that John Brown suggests because its dramatization of life is ultimately prior to the structures of patriarchy or to national dispositions of space. If we ask, nonetheless, how the vision of primoridal unity proposed by *Like Water for Chocolate* can be articulated in political terms, we must turn to *The Silent War*, where the space of woman acquires enough cultural valence to operate in the larger social and cultural realm, even if ultimately remaining marginal—not to say inimical—to it.

The Poetics of the Revolver

Much of the critical reception of *Like Water for Chocolate* can be explicated in terms of Huyssen's historical scheme concerning the divide between modernism and postmodernism:

> The boundaries between high art and mass culture have become increasingly blurred, and we should begin to see that process as one of opportunity rather than lamenting loss of quality and failure of nerve. There are many successful attempts by artists to incorporate mass cultural forms into their work, and certain segments of mass culture have increasingly adopted strategies from on high.[19]

Esquivel, far from being conceded such an "opportunity," has instead been criticized, as Saltz phrases it, "as one example too many of magic realism, 'pop lit' unworthy of serious attention, or a novel of little interest to the male reading public."[20] By contrast, no critic writing about Scorza ever considered his work unworthy. As a sizable list of essays and two dissertations about his work can attest, he has been readily admitted to the company of such important Latin American writers as Julio Cortázar, José Maria Arguedas, Jorge Luis Borges and others.[21] And yet, in spite of the quite different critical treatment accorded to Scorza, in the pentology there is one character, Maca, who can be seen as the embodiment of the principles of the feminine as Huyssen discusses them under the sign of popular culture—principles that make it possible to situate *The Silent War* as offering another version of the female space Esquivel represents in *Like Water for Chocolate*. Of course, the discursive terms are different in each book. In Esquivel, they have to do with innuendo, rumor, and gossip; the larger political world of the revolution is largely effaced. In Scorza, on the other hand, they participate in Indian legend and myth; the larger public world is highlighted.[22]

The five novels chronicle the Indian uprisings that took place during the 1950s and 1960s in the environs of the Cerro de Pasco Mining Corporation in Peru. The violence was a response to intrusions on communal Indian lands by a U.S. company, as well as by local landowners, and each novel ends with a massacre of the Indians. There is a growing awareness among the survivors of their political rights, in conjunction with a gradual progression in the nature of the uprisings, from spontaneous reactions against the encroaching forces to an organized and coordinated movement joining many Indian communities in the Cerro de Pasco region.

The pentology reveals a radicalized form of what the gradual, painful gaining of political consciousness meant for the Peruvian Indian population. The narrative involves a vertiginous display of styles, each one commenting upon, deconstructing, or supporting the others. No sooner is a statement made or a text formed than it is perceived as having become "established" and available for comment—an overheard snatch of dialogue, an anonymous remark made by someone who may have witnessed a particular episode of concern within the general narration, or even a newspaper article. In short, what we have in the pentology is an example of a popular cultural artifact—an "oral text"—made manifest even before it becomes popular and can be placed in an appropriate genre.

We may think here of Mikhail Bakhtin's discussion of novelist discourse, whose goal, he says, is to remain an open-ended document: "The novelist is drawn toward anything that is not yet completed."[23] And yet, it must be conceded, by the act itself of being produced, a certain completion must therefore be realized in any text—some aesthetic notion, or some sort of arbitrary, incipient sequence—at which point other discourses (oral or written) gather about it like the walls around a fortress. The text becomes itself an object to be commented on.

What is interesting in Scorza is how woman appears at precisely this moment of gathering—specifically, the figure of Maca. Her series of appearances and disappearances become, throughout the pentology, a representation of the space in which a peculiar kind of dynamics takes place, before it becomes fully actualized as discourse. Popular discourse, therefore, is disclosed in *The Silent War* as above all a commenting discourse, yet one that paradoxically must exist prior to that which is commented on, locatable as a space for a potential economy of creative or destructive energy.

Consuelo Hernández J. sums up very well why Scorza chose a collage of surfaces to reveal the world of his fiction. By including in his accounts the events that originate in the grand majority, Harnández says, Scorza

> paradójicamente, cuenta "la historia de los anexos y de los márgenes", cerrando así la brecha, el gran abismo que deja la historia oficial, escrita por y para la clase dominante, esa historia que calla los hechos inconfesables para no desprestigiar su "autoridad."

> (paradoxically, relates "the history of the ancillaries and the margins," closing in this way the gap [but will it ever be closed?], the great abyss which is left by official history written by and for the dominant class, the history which silences the unconfessable facts in order that its "authority" not fall into disrepute.)[24]

Maca's history is told not only as abiding in these marginalized texts, but as embodying the narrative of marginalization itself. She first appears in *Garabombo, el Invisible (Garabombo, the Invisible)* where Garabombo has a chance encounter with her, one that has apparently kept him from fulfilling his official duties to his Indian community. In the voice of the narrator we learn that Maca is the illegitimate daughter of Melchior Albornoz, a well-to-do though ne'er-do-well rancher who, because she is only an *hembra* ("female"), was willing to trade her for a dog but could not find the right breed. Albornoz subsequently takes her into his family, but raises her as a boy, almost feral, unaware of the beauty of her blue eyes and dark complexion. One day, while trying to rustle cattle from the Tusi municipality, she is captured and publicly humiliated. At this point, Garabombo encounters her and helps her carry the side of beef the town was forcing her to drag through the streets as punishment.

Humiliated by capture, convinced that the Albornozes family will not take her back, Maca eventually transforms herself into the woman she is, dresses herself in the clothes of an Indian woman—thereby identifying herself with that culture—and disappears within the textual convolutions of the novel. Maca returns in the fourth volume, *Cantar de Agapito Robles (The Song of Agapito Robles)*, but no longer in the voice of the omniscient narrator. Maca's story is now told by Migdonio de la Torre y Corvarrubias del Campo del Moral, whose name is surpassed in extension only by the size of his estates—which in turn are surpassed only by the quantity of young Indian women he has raped. But here, somewhat paradoxically, it is not the voice of a conqueror that speaks, but rather the voice of someone who simply gives testimony. At this point, it is as if he who was the devourer of women has himself been devoured.

Maca becomes the name of what devours him. More significantly, she emerges as the name for the imperative that the five novels represent: a social and political consciousness that will become operative even for those who oppose its benefits for the poor or the subjugated in the country. Maca, as a woman and the product of an illicit, degraded liaison, thus functions in one respect as the metonymic figure for the Indians who, like her, have been raped, persecuted, and denied their place in the paternal home. But she also exists as something else: the origin of a discourse that would articulate its own devaluation and exclusion.

Migdonio pays a kind of impossible tribute to this inexpressible discourse:

> When Maca smiled at me for the first time, she smiled and I swear I then understood what caused, oh fuck, the fall of angels, what would, damn the hour I was born, cause the desperation that now burns me.[25]

It seems clear in this passage that the character not only fears being devoured by what he has devalued, but has also enjoyed it. For her part, Maca herself does not speak. What would it mean if she could? That she could lose her space as representing some primordial unity out of which speech comes, and instead appear inescapably as a form of her own, another style, or—in Bakhtin's novelistic scheme—a merely completed thing? As it is, the peculiar discursive position that Maca occupies here as inspiration to the impossible testimony of another would be lost.

And yet, to the extent that the narrative, through its narrator, seeks to "capture" Maca—that is, name her, and have her yield up her name in her own words—*The Silent War* cannot avoid comprising a "style," either at local points or as a whole. I am thinking here of Jacques Derrida's conception of "style" in the sense of a spur or stylus or stiletto.[26] The stylus marks or names, but also, as expressive of the male principle—in Derrida's case, Nietzsche's—it also mutilates. Thus, for example, in Migdonio's account of Maca's arrest in *Cantar de Agapito Robles,* he adds the following information: upon capture, she was incarcerated and raped; subsequently, she hired the best whores in the region to teach her how to entice and enslave men. Therefore, Migdonio has effectively captured her, named her, and revealed the name to be Eva (Eve), the whore and courtesan.

But Derrida points out that there is more to the question of stylus, or spur. In fact, as her appearances and disappearances in the text of the pentology seem to propose, the desire to capture Maca suggests not only a stylus or a stiletto, but, in addition, a spur in the sense of a rocky trajectory on a shoreline that protects the coast from the onslaught of the waves and ocean. Or, yet again, as a spar from which sails/veils may be hung to conceal something. The stylus that names Maca *whore* is, then, explicable as part of a movement that conceals her behind the veil of the spar. Maca is accorded no power to rename herself, even though she retains the power of naming—the same power that the whole pentology wants to inscribe in terms of the legends, innuendos, myths, which are the very fabric of the story. The result is a pronounced vacancy. Traces of Maca abound, but her space is marked by absence.

Indeed, it seems that for her power she requires this absence as a space to be filled up by a cacophony of male voices that try to invoke her presence. On this basis, at the narrative level, Maca resists capture only to topple the men from their places of power. In the Maca chapters of *Cantar,* she collects an entourage of idiots who roam the streets of the towns she visits. She dresses them in the uniforms of generals and admirals and names them after the official heroes and presidents of the republic. In so doing, she eludes male voices and their attempts to identify her on their terms. Then suddenly Maca disappears, to return one last time in *La tumba del relámpago (Lightning's Grave)*.

In this novel, the pursuit of Maca and the attempts to appropriate her continue more frenetically and more intricately. In the first place, Maca has returned to her family and, once again, has adopted male clothing. Doroteo Silvestre, a cattle merchant and sometime rustler, falls fatally in love with her when he sees her killing a man and then discovers she is a woman. Although before, when she was dressed as a man, no one mistook Maca for a woman (when she dresses as a woman she seduces only men), in this final text, though dressed like a man, enough of her womanly characteristics appear to make Doroteo fall fatally in love with her. On the other hand, a series of women whom she has seduced for her brother Roberto, proceed to find her equally, and fatally, attractive.

In short, Maca has become androgynous. At the same time, as if to enforce her position as the nodal point of popular discourse in the book, we learn from words taken from the Catholic confessional that people have canonized her as a saint. One of the devotees is a prostitute who is herself a former victim of Maca's seductive powers. At one point, Doroteo recounts the following:

> Pero me vio los ojos cegados y su revólver me perdonó. Perdonó mi pecho abierto por la migración de gorriones que, mirándola, se me metían para siempre dentro del corazón.

> (But she saw my blinded eyes and her revolver forgave me; forgave my chest opened by the flocks of sparrows which, upon seeing her, would be finding their way to my heart forever.)[27]

When he asks who the woman was, one of the multitude of anonymous voices in the novel informs him that it was not a woman but a man. He pursues her anyway—to his own death fighting side by side with her. In a parallel chapter, entitled "The Trials *[aflicciones]* of Father Chasán," we hear the voices of a series of prostitutes as they confess to the priest their fatal attraction to Maca/Maco. Thinking that Maca is a man, they have all been seduced into going to bed with her and then tricked into making love to Roberto, her brother, with whom she changes places in the darkened bedrooms.

What are we to make of these developments? Here, once again, I would argue that Maca embodies a mythically situated female space whose undifferentiated energies make possible a rich reversal of roles. There are some young women pursuing a person they believe to be a man in order to appropriate him, as the previous story suggests. But we eventually appear to return to a more normative gender position, since the result is that the women have been in fact possessed by Roberto, even if through the machinations of his sister. Occupying a space where destruction and creation seem to be all of a piece, Maca once again appropriates the discourse of the masculine and then recreates it solely for the sexual benefit of her brother.

In the final volume of the pentology, *La tumba del relámpago*, it is possible to discern a rich intersection with *Like Water for Chocolate*. First, we recall that when Tita and Pedro make love in the bathhouse, Rosaura, Tita's sister and Pedro's wife, sees the sparks that fill the night but thinks that they are Mama Elena's ghost. Later, when Tita and Pedro die in the final fire on the farm after Esperanza's death, Tita is "canonized" through the popular text of her recipe book. Compare, in the episode of Maca's death, the character of Rosaura Canales, an innocent girl "sold" by her parents to Maca, posing as a man. At this time, Maca does not "give" the child to Roberto, but offers her own body to him instead. When she subsequently dies in the fire, she, like Tita, is also canonized—this time, by the voice of the people.

What is the status of these dual canonizations? What do they reveal about the final form of popular discourse that memorializes them? Of course they seem to be religious, and yet if we recall Bakhtin's injunction about the necessary incompletion of the novel as popular discourse, we realize that the novels can be seen as reflections not so much upon their own incompletion as the site upon which this incompletion is founded. *The Silent War* finally confronts the popular discourse that *Like Water for Chocolate* displaces in the form of cookbook recipes, and what we find is that "the people" and woman are reciprocal figures, each struggling to regain control of what they have lost, each continually in danger of being violated and effaced, each subject to the same space, at once degraded and holy.

It is crucial to preserve this space. In making it available to the larger public realm in which it can only be either appropriated or destroyed—at best coded "useless," if we recall Raquel Olea's phrase—*The Silent War* in fact celebrates the space of the female by mystifying it through popular discourse—just as *Like Water for Chocolate* does, only by, in contrast, delaying the appearance of this discourse until the end. As we have seen, the political realm that Esquivel withholds in her narrative, in order to keep the cycle of destruction and creation closed, is the very realm that Scorza repeatedly promotes, in order to open the same cycle. And yet all attempts to identify Maca remain a mystery that popular discourse can only mystify, and, all attempts to implement her power politically come to grief, right to the end, when, after "Saint" Maca in a dream-vision informs the harpist, Lima, that his own Indian community should attack the landowners before the others. Unity among the Indians is broken. The armed forces attack each community individually, and each time the result is the massacre of the Indians.

In the "chapter which needs no name" we at last hear Maca's voice. It is, in effect, not really speech, but a meditation, a conversation she carries out with herself. The reader follows her thoughts:

> Dancing I can calm this anger. If I could, I'd dance until the Last Judgment. To forget what must be forgotten and recall what must be recalled. Have I anything to recall? What do I take with me from this province? From this life? The joy of knowing that I trampled those who trampled others![28]

This is all we know of her directly, in her own voice, grasped among the multiple stylistic inscriptions of five novels. Although in *Like Water for Chocolate* Tita needs Pedro in order to be complete—that is, the novel allows a space to be created in which the image of woman opens herself to some other principle of completion besides herself—*The Silent War* leaves Maca with no man to complete her, except herself. Just so, the novel imagines no voice to complete her except the popular voice of the people.

The pentology is not a love story. It is structured by the need for a politics, rather than a relation between men and women. Nonetheless, through the figure of one woman in particular we can see something of the mythic space underlying both the narrative and the popular imagining of this narrative, whether as a political program, a sexual conflict, or as a religious belief. More crucially, we can see the generative power of this space. Although the discourses of myth and the discourses of popular culture are normally presumed to be opposed, what both *Like Water for Chocolate* and *The Silent War* suggest, albeit in quite different ways, is that popular energies are continually recreated and destroyed through the figure of the mythic woman, under whose auspices we eat and talk, struggle and create, live and die.

11/ Masculinities at the Margins

Representations of the *Malandro* and the *Pachuco*

SIMON WEBB

T HE AIM OF THIS DISCUSSION IS TO EXAMINE THE COMPLEX cultural significations assigned to the popular cultural figures of the *malandro* and the *pachuco*. Associated with popular cultural resistance to dominant culture in Brazil and the United States, respectively, the figures of the *malandro* and the *pachuco* have been mobilized and deployed in the discourses of both hegemonic and subaltern cultures, generating an array of contradictory significations. Their interpretation ranges from vilification as delinquents to celebration as cultural heroes. The meanings of their names have been translated as spiv, wide-boy, rogue, hustler, pimp, black marketeer, gangster, and so forth. The intention here is not to define the essential *malandro* or *pachuco*, but to discuss the ways by which meanings are mapped onto their bodies through the discursive practices of both dominant and subaltern cultures, and how these meanings reflect the interests of hegemonic masculinity and its contestation and negotiation by subaltern cultures. The plural "masculinities" of my title belie an approach to masculinity as a nonessential discursive construction. This approach, suggested by Foucault, denies that gender roles are natural and posits that they are naturalized through the discursive practices of hegemonic groups.

While the *malandro* and the *pachuco* now occupy a mythic space in Afro-Brazilian and Mexican American popular culture, the two figures correspond to subcultural responses within these marginalized ethnic groups to specific historical circumstances. The *malandro* is a figure associated with

Afro-Brazilian culture, specifically with samba music and lyrics, in the period following the abolition of slavery in 1888 to approximately the end of Getúlio Vargas's dictatorship (1930–1945). The *pachuco* figure is associated with the Mexican American population, and in particular with a subcultural response in California of Mexican American youth, known as zoot-suiters, during the U.S. participation in the Second World War (1941–1945).

Both countries witnessed significant structural changes in these periods, Brazil moving from a slave labor to a wage labor economy, and the United States shifting into a war economy involving the entrance of women and members of ethnic minorities into occupations previously regarded as the domain of white males. Both countries experienced a realignment and redefinition of the relationship between dominant and subordinate groups—between classes, races, and genders; and in both cases an attempt was made to repressively incorporate previously marginalized groups into the national work force and the imagined community of the nation.[1]

It is within this context that I will discuss dramatic representations of the *malandro* and the *pachuco*. The nouns *malandragem* and *pachuquismo* indicate that these figures not only symbolized resistance to attempts at incorporation into or interpellation by dominant culture, but also symbolized ways of being that contested those predicated by dominant culture.

Photographs and later representations of *pachucos* and *malandros* indicate that these are ways of being men. There is no attempt to vindicate these masculinities as somehow more liberating or feminist than others. Rather than analyzing or defining traits and characteristics of masculinity, I will emphasize the social processes of engenderment and the contradiction and differences illustrated in resistance to these processes. These differences reflect the view, writes Segal, that "'masculinity' and 'femininity' are constructs specific to historical time and place. They are categories continually being forged, contested, reworked and reaffirmed in social institutions and practices as well as a range of ideologies."[2]

References to Latin American masculinity invariably dismiss it sweepingly as machismo, a term used to homogenize the heterogeneity of Latin American masculinities as one pathological and essential masculinity. Such generalization inhibits a detailed discussion of difference, preventing the decentering of secure and stable hegemonic male identities inherited from idealized traditions.[3]

While some dismiss the *malandro* and *pachuco* subcultures as examples of pathological masculinity or as stylish fads, the complex reactions within the contemporary dominant culture indicate that they were seen as very real threats and were dealt with as such. Segal indicates that conflict between masculinities positing essential identities is inevitable: "The recognition of multiple masculinities cannot simply be reduced to a question of masculine styles. *There is no possible harmony between them.* Inevitably they must confront and attempt to undermine each other. For 'masculinity' . . . gains its symbolic force and familiar status, not from any fixed meanings, but rather from a series of hierarchical relations to what it can subordinate."[4]

As members of ethnic minorities, the *malandro* and the *pachuco* are marginalized by the dominant white culture in both Brazil and the United States. For Homi Bhabha, living on society's margins is an epistemological condition of hybridity, as new identities are constructed to resist and survive marginalization: "The epistemological 'limits' of these ethnocentric ideas are also the *enunciative boundaries* of a range of other dissonant, even dissident histories and voices—women, the colonized, minority groups, the bearers of policed sexualities. It is in this sense that the boundary becomes the place from which something begins its presencing."[5] However, those who are marginalized are also the witnesses and victims of the violence of attempts to impose on them a definition of a homogeneous national culture.

An analysis of the violence inflicted upon the members of these subcultures, then, is important to understanding the history of these figures in relation to the dominant culture. Two dramatic works in which they are central, Luis Valdez's *Zoot Suit* (1978) and Chico Buarque de Hollanda's *Ópera do Malandro* (1978) are examined here. I will attempt to contextualize these representations and the masculinities encoded in them with their authors' concerns at the time of writing. Both were adapted to film (in 1981 and 1986, respectively), and I will use the films for illustration to widen the discussion. First, I will provide some background regarding the appearance of these subcultural manifestations.

The *Pachuco* and the Zoot Suit in the 1940s

Representations of Mexican Americans in white North American culture stretch back before the U.S. invasion and conquest of the northern states of Mexico in the mid-nineteenth century and the treaty of Guadalupe-Hidalgo in 1859. Mexicans had long been seen as a mongrel race in contrast to the Puritan white North American population, not only in skin color but also in moral fiber.[6] After the conquest, the Mexicans living in the southwestern territories became Mexican Americans, inheritors of a Mexican cultural legacy but members (albeit marginal ones) of U.S. society. As such, they were the bearers of the negative image of the colonial discourse that justified the conquest of 1859: as *peons*, bandits, or degenerate Spaniards, they became another ethnic *other* (along with the indigenous people and the black population) against which dominant white North American culture constructed itself as superior. Their image changed little, writes Pettit, "in conquest fiction from the 1850s to the 1940s," and in Hollywood the word *greaser* was used to describe Mexicans until the 1920s.[7]

The political debate of the two decades preceding World War II confirms these images, as illustrated in discussions of Mexican immigration, reflecting the concerns about unemployment resulting from the Wall Street crash of 1929 and the desire of hegemonic culture to privilege its members. A professor of zoology who was asked to describe Mexican immigrants commented: "Without the trace of Caucasian blood . . . [Mexicans are] ignorant, tractable, moderately industrious and content to endure wretched conditions of life which most white laborers would not tolerate. . . . [They are] a menace to public health . . . of low mentality, inherently criminal, and therefore a degenerate race that would afflict American society with an embarrassing race problem."[8] The fact that a zoologist was asked to comment on the Mexican character indicates the view of Mexicans as less than human: the emphasis on inherent criminality, degeneracy, and the race problem marks out the discursive constellation that surfaced in the Sleepy Lagoon trial and riots, discussed below.

Marginalized from mainstream society, Mexican Americans' access to political and economic power was limited, and the small politically organized sector of the Mexican American population expressed assimilationist goals. They had internalized hegemonic cultural values, as "in the 30s there was still a tendency for Mexican Americans to blame themselves and their cultural antecedents for their 'backward condition.'"[9] This tendency was reflected in the Mexican American Movement, founded in 1942, which sought "the involvement of both Mexicans and 'Anglo Americans' . . . [in] combating the 'backward conditions and attitudes' in Mexican communities."[10] In the same year, the zoot-suited Mexican American male, known as the *pachuco*, became a common sight in Los Angeles, attracting considerable media attention. The *pachucos* provoked a negative reaction from those whose outlook were expressed by mainstream Mexican Americans: they saw them as troublemakers sullying the image of the Mexican American and encouraging further discrimination.[11]

The *pachuco* subculture has been explained in many ways. Their clothing and visibility have been seen as a powerful sign of difference: "These youths were not simply grotesque dandies parading the city's secret underworld," Cosgrove observes, "they were the 'stewards of something uncomfortable,' a spectacular reminder that the social order had failed to contain their energy and difference."[12] This explains their rejection by dominant culture and assimilationists alike: their seemingly proud, even arrogant assertion of difference was problematic for a hegemony that did not yet have the terms to define them, and it contradicted the very meaning of assimilation. For Octavio Paz, this resistance to assimilation was the result of the conflict between second-generation immigrants and their parents and the contrasting attitudes of these two generations to dominant culture.[13] Having been exposed to North American social institutions, especially education, and also the realities of institutional racism and limited opportunities in U.S. society, the second-generation immigrants were more aware of the gap between the nation's Constitution and institutional practices.

The Mexican critic Carlos Monsiváis emphasizes the experience of urban modernity in his interpretation of the *pachuco*:

> The *pachuco* emerges as the first important aesthetic product of migration, the bearer of a new and extremist concept of elegance . . . that in the eyes of the Anglos (and the fathers of the *pachucos*) is an outright provocation. The *pachuco*'s audacity in clothing and in gesture permits them to mark out their

new territory with mobile signs, and, like their model, the Harlem dude, challenge discrimination too. *Pachucos* eventually become (not very voluntarily) symbols of cultural resistance, and end up cornered and persecuted in the segregation campaigns that culminate in the Los Angeles Zoot Suit Riots.[14]

Monsiváis's words capture some of the ambiguities and difficulties in discussing the *pachuco*. Wearing the zoot suit symbolized membership in a subculture and a sense of identity for a population rejected by Mexicans as "Americanized" and by Anglos as "Mexican." *Pachuquismo* can be seen in Bhabha's terms as an identity negotiated at the margins of ethnocentric ideas.

However, Monsiváis hints at the danger of labeling the *pachuco* as a symbol of cultural resistance: that is something the *pachuco* reluctantly eventually became. Both Malcolm X and César Chávez, later leaders of the black power movement and the Mexican American farm workers' union, respectively, wore zoot suits and were involved in the 1943 riots. It is likely that participation in the riots led to a heightened awareness of institutional prejudice. However, it is also difficult to measure the extent to which such readings have been imposed upon the subculture in retrospect. Artists like Duke Ellington apparently did associate the zoot suit with resistance to racism. In Los Angeles in 1941 and 1942, before multiracial audiences, Ellington performed a musical extravaganza about zoot-suiting, *Jump for Joy*, which has been seen as important in establishing an antiracist symbolism around wearing the costume. In Tyler's words, "It ridiculed racism and stereotypes. One musical sketch was 'I've got a passport from Georgia and I'm going to the USA.' The message made a clear impact on Mexican and black youth who took up the zoot suit and militant ethic and cultural pride and a rejection of white racism."[15]

There does seem to be a clear link between sporting a suit of a distinctive cut and cultural resistance on the part of its wearer, but again such generalizations must be qualified: wearing the suit signified different things, depending on a host of factors. Gayatri Spivak warns of the dangers of imposing homogeneous readings over subaltern struggles as a move that reflects the discursive practices of dominant cultures always seeking to locate a will and sovereign determining subject in what is "a discontinuous network of strands that may be termed as politics, ideology, economics, history, sexuality and so on."[16] This is especially the case where subcultures and style are involved. Participation in subcultures is not necessarily primarily motivated by politics. It can reflect a range of desires and situations: generational conflict, economic and ethnic marginalization, a desire to mark difference, to belong, to "look good," to be fashionable. Where fashion and style are the visible markers of subcultural membership, market forces, mass production, and advertising also enter the discussion and can "'diffuse' and 'defuse'" the symbolism of styles by taking them out of their cultural context, so that new wearers invest them with different meanings.[17]

The zoot suit, in Cosgrove's words, "is more than an exaggerated costume, more than a sartorial statement, it is the bearer of a complex and contradictory history."[18] (See figure 11.1.) As a result, its origins are widely disputed. It and other subcultural costumes like it have been linked to the gangsters of the U.S. prohibition era, the Brooklyn sharp kid, the Harlem dude, and London's Second World War black marketeers.[19] Clear among this confusion is that the zoot suit is associated with marginal figures and was an international phenomenon before it was associated with the *pachuco*. It was sported by black and white entertainment stars, Duke Ellington, Cab Calloway, Sammy Davis Jr., Danny Kaye, and Frank Sinatra among them, and it was even known as the "*Gone with the Wind* suit" after the clothing worn by Clark Gable in the film.[20] Its fashionability, then, or desirability, is the result of the value invested in it by the culture industry's star system and the sense of transgression derived from its association with a wide variety of marginal, interstitial characters. It is associated with dance hall culture; therefore, as a social hieroglyph a connection exists between the suit, the culture industry, transgression, leisure, and pleasure. The zoot suit is symbolic of the world outside work and the transgression of working life.

The suit itself consists of a long, broad, knee-length square-shouldered coat called "fingertip" because of the long sleeves, baggy pleated trousers ("reet pleats," "drapes"), tightened ("pegged") at the ankle and turned up ("stuffed cuffs"), "pork pie" hats, and a long watch chain to which is attached a key, a watch, or an Italian stiletto pocket knife.

Analysis of the appropriation, redefinition, and relocation of the items that make up the suit by *pachuco* (in California) and the Harlem dude (in New York) should account for how the man's suit was transplanted from the world of work to the world of leisure. The tailored suit is notorious for the social codes surrounding it, being the sartorial symbol par excellence of white-collar work and bourgeois values. These associations are contested and mocked by wearers of the zoot suit, for whom it is a symbol of pleasure and difference. The exaggerated cut of the zoot suit makes it comfortable for dancing and simultaneously makes it a carnivalesque parody of the bourgeois suit's sobriety. Consequently, it has been interpreted as a parody of middle-class life styles and values. Wearing the zoot suit is thus seen by Cosgrove as one of the "everyday rituals . . . [in which] resistance can find natural and unconscious expression. In retrospect, the zoot suit's history can be seen as a point of intersection, between the related potential of ethnicity and politics on the one hand, and the pleasures of identity and difference

Figure 11. Edward James Olmos sports the famous "drape shape" in Luis Valdez's *Zoot Suit* (1981). Copyright © 1998 by Universal City Studios, Inc. Courtesy of Universal Studios Publishing Rights. All rights reserved.

on the other. It is the zoot suit's potential and ethnic associations that make it such a rich reference point for subsequent generations."[21]

Wearing the zoot suit was seen as a provocation by the dominant culture; thus the reaction to it, and its subsequent suturing to the body of the *pachuco*, can best be evaluated in terms of ethnicity and difference. While the zoot suit was widely worn, it seems to have been interpreted as particularly threatening when worn by blacks and Mexican Americans. The United States' involvement in the war meant a large-scale movement by women and members of ethnic groups into industrial labor that was previously the domain of white male workers. This movement gave rise to a moment of historical trauma because it necessitated the realignment of established gender and race relationships. Marcuse describes this type of realignment, which reflected the asymmetrical power relations between dominant and subaltern groups, as a process of repressive desublimation.[22] The process is called desublimation, that is, because heretofore naturalized power relations are made explicit, while it is repressive because hegemonic groups attempt to contain the desires released by this desublimation with minimal loss of power. The release of desire by these processes is not contained without contradiction. Hall writes, "Repressive desublimation is a dangerous, two-sided phenomenon. When the codes of traditional culture are broken, and new social impulses are set free, they are impossible fully to contain."[23] This observation bears a direct correspondence to the zoot suit phenomenon. The movement of Mexican Americans into industry was accompanied by a reinforced emphasis on assimilation by the dominant ideology. The zoot suiter resists such assimilation, sending the message that Mexican Americans are as capable as Anglos, but without being the same. The terms of their response contest dominant racist assumptions and the process of repressive desublimation.

Concurrently, the North American media were projecting an ever more homogeneous national image in an effort to strengthen nationalism and patriotic feeling in order to compensate for the material sacrifices necessitated by war. Thus the social weft of North American society was tugged in opposite directions: as the labor market opened up, cultural nationalism reinforced homogeneity. The strain and anxieties caused by this situation were reflected in the almost hysterical media attacks on the *pachuco*. The zoot suit's visibility made it an easy target for media scapegoating tirades on the enemy within, and wearing it became synonymous with deviancy. In March 1942, Cosgrove reports, "the War Production Board's first rationing act had a direct effect on the manufacture of suits. . . . In an attempt to institute a 26% cut-back in the use of fabrics . . . [which] effectively forbade the manufacture of zoot suits. . . . However, the demand for zoot suits did not decline and a network of bootleg tailors based in Los Angeles and New York continued to manufacture the garments."[24] Thus wearing a zoot suit could be linked by the press to unpatriotic behavior through the association with black marketeering and obvious flouting of rationing.

The association of zoot suits with Mexicans and gangs is also related to crime waves during the war. For the media, the outbreak of crime during wartime was an unacceptable contradiction of the image of a nation united against a common enemy. The Mexican American community was an obvious scapegoat population, given the dominant cultural image of Mexican Americans. During the Sleepy Lagoon murder trial, these discourses were consolidated and firmly stitched onto the body of the *pachuco*. In August 1942 the body of José Díaz was found in Los Angeles. The police charged eighteen members of an L.A. gang in the first mass trial for conspiracy to murder in U.S. history.

The trial, which involved numerous violations of judicial practice, was a blatant example of the collusion between law and hegemonic interests, throwing into relief the discursive practices of hegemony in North American society. Carey McWilliams, a historian sympathetic to the plight of the defendants, states:

> [The trial] took place before a biased and prejudiced judge (found to be so by an appellate court); it was conducted by a prosecutor who pointed to the clothes and the style of the haircut of the defendants as evidence of guilt. . . . For the first weeks of the trial, the defendants were not permitted to get haircuts and packages of clean clothes were intercepted by the jailer on orders of the prosecutor. As a consequence of this prejudicial order, the defendants came trooping into the courtroom every day looking like so many unkempt vagabonds.[25]

The zoot suits were seen as evidence of guilt, and the defendants' clothes and hair were exhibited as unkempt and dirty. Thus their appearance was made "extraordinarily bizarre and marginal," and the very "status conferred by a zoot suit therefore transformed into a liability."[26] The dirtying of the *pachucos* approximated their image to that of Mexican Americans as farm laborers, and away from the threatening symbol of modernity, hybridity, and urban sophistication communicated by the *pachuco*.

The zoot suit riots of 1943 can be interpreted in the same context. The press continued to vilify the *pachuco*. An infamous cartoon serial by Al Capp called "Zoot Suit Yokum" featured a conspiracy by zoot suit manufacturers to take over the country through a national hero dressed in a zoot suit. In the final frames, the hero becomes a villain and public indignation is redirected against "anyone and everything associated with a zoot suit."[27] The cartoon reached an enormous audience, and Mazón believes it was instrumental in the behavior of servicemen toward zoot suiters in June 1943. Al Capp talked openly of his work's scapegoating, commenting on North America's need for "a good-five cent masochist."[28] If "Zoot Suit Yokum" represented that masochist, then so did *pachucos*.

The tendency to associate zoot suiters with the enemies of the American public was repeated throughout the United States. An assimilationist black newspaper in Pittsburgh ran a series of anti–zoot suit cartoons that pictured the black zoot suiter as the enemy.[29] The *Los Angeles Times* "featured a caricature by Paul Ford in which the Japanese premier was portrayed as being a 'sartorial' dresser, favoring above all a zoot suit when riding horseback."[30] May 1943 appears to have been a month of high political tension. The no-strike pledge of the war was broken by coal miners on May 1. Conflicts between civilians and servicemen on the East Coast escalated. Notably, the press failed to report these incidents, which led to seven deaths in a one-month period preceding the riots, and instead concentrated on events featuring zoot suiters in which nobody was killed.

In early June military personnel went into Mexican *barrios* in large groups, stripping zoot suiters and cutting their hair. By the seventh of June, civilians had joined in, and thousands searched for zoot suiters to "de-zoot." Incredibly, despite the number of people involved, the tension of the period, and the sensationalist press reaction, nobody was killed.[31] The zoot suit riots have a symbolic quality about them: the servicemen and civilians physically assaulted the zoot suiters, but their main aim seems to have been to strip them. What appears to have taken place is a symbolic castration:

signs of identity and difference were simply removed. Mauricio Mazón believes that the military personnel merely visited upon the *pachuco* the symbolic castration and initiation suffered on entering the army.[32] While this partially explains the symbolism and ritual behavior of the riots, it fails to account for the different ethnicity of the two groups. Arguably, the zoot suit itself is fetishized, in a recognition and disavowal of difference and society's conflicts; eroticized and vilified in the culture industry and the press, it was the zoot suit that offended, not the marginalized zoot suiter.

Pachucos, then, and the challenge they posed to hegemonic masculinity, were dealt with through coercion and consensus. Continual media attacks labeled them as deviants and criminals, and colonial discourse with its "orientalism" placed the *pachuco* as inferior *other*. Therefore they occupied a cultural space against which wartime hegemonic masculinity defined itself: against artifice and style, plainness and economy; against gang deviancy, group discipline; against leisure, sacrifice; against heterogeneity, homogeneity. The *pachuco* was located as an inferior in a series of binary relations, in a space similar to that occupied by women in the male/female couplet. The *pachuco* is therefore continually subordinated and emasculated in dominant discursive practices; perhaps the aggressive *machismo* associated with *pachucos* could be interpreted as an attempt to resist this institutionalized cultural emasculation.

Blacks, Samba, and *Malandragem* in Brazil

Like *pachuquismo, malandragem* in its historical manifestation in early twentieth-century Brazil can be linked to a historical trauma and processes of repressive desublimation. The abolition of slavery marked a significant stage in the transformation of Brazil from a slave-based society to a state moving toward modern capitalism, a project that Getúlio Vargas attempted to institutionalize and quicken. Freedom after slavery was an ambiguous condition for Brazil's black population. Whereas Brazilians tend to view themselves as free from the racial divisions and institutional segregation of the United States, Brazil inherited a similar residue of colonial discourses. A range of racist ideologies associated with colonial history—from racial and climatic determinism to Social Darwinism and the eugenic discourse that evolved into the conviction among the Brazilian elite that a "whitening" process was the "solution" to Brazil's ethnic diversity—reinforced the opinion that blacks were only good for hard labor. Brazil officially encouraged and subsidized European immigration, giving preference to Europeans in the labor market.

Blacks were therefore marginalized and forced into poorly paid labor. From this situation emerged the myth of the urban black *malandro*, a figure associated with his ability to hustle and live off his wits from illegal or semilegal occupations. *Malandragem* as a way of being incorporates plural and contradictory significations. It can signify anything from utter self-interest and a willingness to exploit all social relationships and values for purely selfish reasons, to a desultory antiessentialism (a refusal to abide by social rules or morality or to fit into models of national identity, scorn for the positivist work ethic), or to subaltern resistance. The refusal to be defined, and instead delight in confounding established codes of behavior, are elevated to a national symbol in Mario de Andrade's *Macunaíma,* in which the protagonist of the same name, a "hero without character" evades simplistic psychological definition and confounds the epistemological assumptions of discourses from exoticism to positivism. His changeability and inconsistency are part of the adaptability that enables him to survive.

Cultural commentators have found many antecedents for the *malandro* figure. Antonio Cândido locates the "first great *malandro* to enter the world of the Brazilian novel" in Leonardo, the son, in *Memórias de um sargento de milícias* (1854–1855).[33] This is a character who illustrates the dialectic of order and disorder in Brazilian society, existing somewhere between them and exposing the relativism of morality and the fallacy of the attempt enshrined in courtly institutions of early nineteenth-century Brazil to impose "order" on Brazilian society. Cândido traces the folkloric origin of Leonardo to a popular hero of Brazilian oral narrative, Pedro Malasartes, whom another Brazilian academic, Roberto DaMatta, recognizes as the *malandro*'s antecedent.[34] Malasartes ruins a landowner to avenge the exploitation of his brother by turning the landowner's very language against him. For example, when asked to clean up a field, he uproots everything, including the valuable crop. By obeying the letter of the law, ruining the landowner in the process, Malasartes exploits the *jouissance* of language and reveals that meaning cannot be fixed, despite the illusion given by the landowner's contractual language, that it can. Malasartes exhibits the discursive slipperiness of the *malandro*, "revealing the relativities and breaches that are always to be found in the power game and in the concrete relationships between the strong and the weak."[35] There are other antecedents to the *malandro*, useful in illuminating aspects of *malandragem*;[36] however, the tendency to universalize deemphasizes the specific historical circumstances and ethnicity of the *malandro* exalted in samba.

Samba, a mixture of African rhythms and Portuguese musical traditions, is an expression of the hybrid culture that stems from the Afro-Brazilian slave experience. Its history is very much contiguous with that of Afro-Brazilians after the abolition of slavery. Its first expression is associated with the *morros* around Rio de Janeiro, where the black population was forced to live after modernization programs demolished Rio's poorer areas. Samba music and lyrics record the experience of the black population in Rio. The *malandro*, "rejecting demeaning manual work and challenging his inferior social position," provided "the greatest source of inspiration" for the *sambista*, and songs featuring the *malandro* predominated during the twenties and thirties.[37] Lisa Jesse describes the role of the mythical *malandro* in Afro-Brazilian culture:

> Although . . . concerned, above all, for his own well being, the *malandro* is . . . opposed to the exploitation of his social class. He challenges any form of manipulation by the state, and thus is worshipped by the rest of the community. He does not want to become a middle class city dweller, preferring instead to indulge in small acts of *malandragem*. . . . The myth of the *malandro* had much more power than the real life spiv, and helped preserve the socio-cultural identity of his community.[38]

The emphasis on the myth in preserving sociocultural identity is an important aspect of the history of the *malandro*: the power of myth helped negotiate the terms of this sociocultural survival by winning and marking cultural space for the community. The frequent mention of the *malandro* in samba lyrics, and the attempts by *sambistas* to portray themselves as *malandros*, resulted in the two terms becoming synonymous.[39] As a result, the performance of the samba was subject to repression by the authorities until 1930.

Samba and *malandragem*, like *pachuquismo* and the zoot suit, were seen

as threatening by dominant institutions as powerful expressions of difference, and perhaps as expressions of a way of being in contrast to and in
competition with dominant masculinity. As with the *pachuco* figure, occasional fights between samba groups stigmatized all *sambistas* and the associated *malandro* with pathological masculinity.

In terms of style, the significations of the *malandro*'s garb bears a striking similarity to those of the zoot suit and are probably influenced by similar precedents. However, Hollywood's influence should not be exaggerated,
as the style is also similar to this description of street performers and sere-
naders from the 1860s to the turn of the century: "Divide-lhe a hirsuta
(cabeleira) como em dois morros . . . o chapéu mal o resguardando do
sereno, caindo-lhe sobre uma das orelhas, e deixando descoberta a outra . .
. traja velho paletó, calças de cor duvidosa, e assenta os pés em vetustas
chinelas de couro" ("His hair is separated into two mounds. . . . His hat
hardly protects him from the drizzle, it falls over one of his ears, leaving the
other uncovered. . . . He wears an old jacket, oddly colored trousers and old
leather slippers").[40] This compares closely to the description in Wilson
Batista's samba "Lenço no pescoço" ("A Scarf Around My Neck," 1933):

> Meu chapéu de lado
> Tamanco arrastando
> Lenço no pescoço
> Navalha no bolso
> Eu passo gingando
> Provoco e desafio
> Eu tenho orgulho
> De ser tão vadio.

> (With my hat askew
> Dragging my clogs
> A scarf around my neck
> A razor in my pocket
> I saunter along
> I provoke and challenge
> I am proud
> To be such a loafer.)

A major difference between the two is the addition of the razor blade. This adds an aggressive touch to the *malandro*'s appearance, emphasized in the verbs *provoke* and *challenge* used in the song. Like the zoot suit, the *malandro* suit became an easy target for police repression. Moreira da Silva's samba, "Olha o Padilha" ("Watch out for Padilha"), tells a story of a *malandro* being stripped of his suit that is remarkably similar to the ritual of the zoot suit riots:

> A calça virou calção
> Na chefatura um barbeiro sorridente
> estava a minha espera
> Ele ordenou raspa o cabelo dessa fera
> Não está direito seu Padilha
> Me deixar com o coco raspado.

> ([My] trousers became shorts.
> In the station a smiling
> barber awaited.
> He ordered my hair to be shaved.
> It's not right Mr Padilha
> To leave me with a bald head.)

Again, the provocation and challenge of the *malandro* made a fetish of his clothing. Unlike the *pachucos*' symbolic challenge to assimilation, samba lyrics indicate that the *malandros* not only resisted attempts at assimilation and were linked to transgression through leisure, but that they challenged the very tenets of positivist capitalism. The positivist work ethic demands the creation of subjects whose characteristics reflect that ethic: loyalty, stability, hard work, self-sacrifice, and dependability. This is anathema to the *malandro*, and many songs reflect an antiwork ethic that subverts the image of the positivist national character institutionalized during the Vargas dictatorship.

The experience of the black population exposed the fallacy of this ethic: for them, work was associated with slavery and the loss, not gain, of freedom and dignity. Work is associated with displeasure, while the *malandro* occupies the world of pleasure: sex, samba, dancing, carnival, gambling,

and drinking are raised to the status of an ethos. Matos sees in this a carnivalized perception of the world that extends beyond the time of carnival
into everyday life. The discourse of samba lyrics and *malandro* clothing, like
the zoot suit, can be seen as homologous, flouting both bourgeois values
and ethics. As with the *pachuco*, such generalizations must be qualified, for
participation in a subculture can reflect multiple and complex motivations.
It is also impossible to be sure how much of the myth reflects values sutured
onto the *malandro* by dominant ideology; like the *pachuco*, the *malandro*
became the measure against which national character was defined during
the Estado Novo.

The ban on samba was lifted under Vargas, as he attempted to enlist the
black population into the social imaginary. Vargas's populist regime (like
Peronism in Argentina) sought to harness the support of the working
classes through processes of repressive desublimation. Workers were organized into trade unions that were coopted and controlled by government
officials. Thus workers' desires were expressed, released, and contained in a
process controlled by the state, which attempted this containment by constructing a new economy of desire in which workers saw their aspirations
reflected in the nation's image: nationalism became the binding force
intended to unite all classes, under the leadership of an all-embracing,
impartial government.

In the attempt to integrate black workers into the national work force,
Vargas made samba and carnival symbols of Brazilian national identity.
The figure of the *malandro* was problematic to Vargas's aims, as *malandragem* resisted the work ethic. Therefore, an attempt was made to write the
malandro and *malandragem* out of samba music. To this end, Jesse writes,
"The Departamento Oficial de Propaganda was established in 1931, which
became . . . the Departamento de Imprensa e Propaganda [DIP] in December 1939. . . . [It] actively encouraged artists and writers to create works
that were national in character by means of subsidies, sponsorships and
prizes."[41] The DIP censored works judged to contradict the regime's ideological parameters, although the success of these policies in expelling
malandragem from samba are widely debated. For Jesse, "The turnaround in
the portrayal of the *malandro* is, without doubt, the clearest example of this
cooption by the state; . . . after 1940 the DIP advised composers to exalt
honest toil in the lyrics and to criticize bohemian lifestyles."[42]

The extent of the changes brought about by censorship was coupled with the effects of music's gradual massification in the nascent culture industry. Record companies recognized in samba a folkloric, picturesque element which they could sell in Brazil and abroad. As a result, the very nature of the composition of samba changed. Early samba was collectively composed, and even after commercialization there was still a tendency to write in partnership with other artists. Collective composition in general conforms neither to bourgeois notions of authorship nor the culture industry's star system and modes of production. The *sambistas* were encouraged to write individual compositions, and the samba's wider diffusion heralded further changes in its production and reception. Jesse reports:

> White, middle class, often well-educated young men such as Noel Rosa and Ari Barroso were attracted to writing and performing samba in particular. . . . These white musicians transformed the samba genre in order to appeal to a more middle-class audience, making its rhythm less syncopated, and its lyrics and melody more sophisticated, and more easily performed by dance hall orchestras. Many black *sambistas* realized that by towing the official line of the Vargas regime, even if only superficially, they could gain access to the new vehicles of the radio and the record industry.[43]

Writing for a more middle-class audience and under the surveillance of censors, the *sambistas* represented the *malandro* and *malandragem* by following two different tendencies. In the first, the *malandro* became conspicuous for his absence, or he became the *malandro regenerado,* a reformed character with a family, house, and job—conforming to the national image, suitably repentant of his pleasure-loving days. This figure, who reflects the exaltation of hard work required by the Department of Propaganda, is typified in the work of white composer Ari Barroso, who became the exportable *sambista* par excellence, working in Hollywood and producing cliché images of a paradisiac Brazil that matched Vargas's national image and the expectations of the "exotic" *other* in Hollywood's culture industry—as in the famous "Aquarela brasileira" ("Watercolor of Brazil," 1939).

The second tendency reflects the practice of *malandragem* itself: in the face of censorship, *malandragem* is reflected in a more ironic and slippery discourse. This works on multiple levels and thus evades censorship while incorporating messages that can be read against the grain to subvert the state ideology of the censors. The white composer Noel Rosa, in Matos's opinion, is one of the more sophisticated composers capable of such ambiguous work. His sambas, which reflect a fascination for the bohemian life style and subjective mobility of the *malandro,* contain a subversive element. His famous "Rapaz folgado" ("Easygoing Guy," 1938) encodes a metatextual call for *sambistas* to reform their external appearance:

> Deixa de arrastrar a seu tamanco
> Pois tamanco nunca foi sandália
> E tira o lenço branco do pescoço
> Compre sapato e gravata
> Jogue fora esta navalha
> Que lhe atrapalha
> Com chapéu de lado deste rata
> Da polícia quero que escapes
> Fazendo samba canção
> Eu já lhe dei papel e lápis
> Arranje um amor e um violão.

> (Stop dragging those clogs
> Clogs were never sandals
> And get that white scarf off your neck
> Buy some shoes and a tie
> Throw that razor away
> It's getting in your way
> With your hat askew I wish
> You'd get out of trouble with the cops
> By writing *samba-canção*
> I've given you a pencil and paper
> Now get yourself a lover and a guitar.)

Advising them to divest themselves of the suit to avoid problems with the police, Rosa indicates that stylistic resistance must be replaced by a more subtle and discursive resistance; he exhorts the *malandro* to use pen and paper and occupy the cultural space opened up through samba to express the ethos of *malandragem*. Appearing to reject *malandragem*, the song passes the censors, but Rosa asks only for superficial reformations of dress, not of ethos, and a change of name from *malandro* and its scape-goated significations to *rapaz folgado*. Rosa was often critical of the vanity of *malandro* style and the *malandro*'s mythification, while being influenced by its ethos. His ironic and playful approach smacks of *malandragem;* the mobility and linguistic dexterity central to *malandro* survival become central to the survival of Rosa's artistic integrity under censorship.

Claudia Matos describes the *malandro* identity in terms matching Bhabha's epistemology of the border: as an interstitial figure and a metaphor and symbol of oppressed fantasy and social conflict, one that contradicts the monologism of the state.[44] However, in her opinion, the *malandro* is a figure who in the end cannot escape the state. *Malandragem*, for her, is effectively repressed, despite the efforts of *sambistas* like Noel Rosa. This interpretation fails to take into account the multiple significa-tions of the symbol, assuming a total victory for hegemony in the battle for signification. This symbolic annihilation is impossible, in my opinion, as the decoding of symbols by those who do not share hegemonic interests or pol-itics deviates from official readings.

Noel Rosa's discourse demonstrates how *malandragem* could adapt and survive repression: the transmutability of the *malandro* is particularly suit-able to such negotiation. Carnival and samba, while coopted, can still be read against the grain as subversive, and the *malandro* can still be mobilized and deployed in the discourse of popular resistance, even as hegemony also mobilizes and exploits the same popular cultural practices and symbols for its own discursive purposes. The antiessentialism in *malandragem* evades hegemonic attempts to simply dismiss it as delinquency. Both Matos and Jesse, concentrating on recorded samba, fail to mention how live perfor-mances of samba could also mock and flout censorship and maintain the subversive content of its expression: a type of samba known as *samba de breque* incorporates a break in the song that allows performers to improvise and provide ironic commentary on the lyrics themselves and on contempo-rary events.

The change in content of the samba under censorship had a direct bearing on the codification of masculinity in its lyrical discourse. While the antiessentialism, subjective mobility, and linguistic dexterity of the *malan-*

dro are often discussed and celebrated, little mention is made of the fact that *malandragem* rarely, if ever, involved a deconstruction of monolithic and phallocentric representations of women. As the *malandro* represented an *other* against which hegemonic masculinity constructed itself, and the worker the *other* against which the *malandro* constructed his masculinity, in the end both relied upon the subjection of woman both as a passive and as an inferior *other* against which to anchor their vying subjectivities. Jesse writes:

> Samba lyrics reflect and perpetuate the prevalent sexist attitudes of the time they were written. The countless sambas which deal with . . . domestic violence provide a clear illustration of this; . . . the tone of such songs is very light hearted, trivializing the issue; . . . the flirtatious antics or infidelities of women were seen as a just cause of this violence or else women were portrayed as masochists who provoke it.[45]

Jesse discusses the stock stereotypes of women in samba that reflect its male-centered discourse: they are the drudge and the *malandra*, corresponding to the couplet Madonna/whore in patriarchal culture. Characteristics of *malandragem* in women seem to be unacceptable for *sambistas:*

> The *malandra* unlike her male counterpart, is not praised for her free wheeling, hedonistic existence, but is condemned, instead, for her heartless treatment of her lovers. She behaves unacceptably when she pursues an identical lifestyle to that which is perfectly respectable and even expected of her male opposite number. Her activities, it is always implied, pose a threat to the fabric of society as a whole. In flouting patriarchal control, such women become dangerous to society. The *malandro*, in contrast, provides an alternative lifestyle that helps to offer a solution to the pressures to accept poorly paid, demeaning, manual labor. Furthermore, the *malandro* stud is revered for his sexual prowess and control over women.[46]

The *malandro*'s combination of patriarchal and antiestablishment values puts him in a complex position sexually. The *malandra* is desired for her unconventional sexuality, while her presence as desiring subject is unacceptable to the masculine code of sexual prowess and control over women.

The drudge, on the other hand, confirms (through submissive contrast to) his masculinity but is unacceptable for the very same reasons, being symbolic of marriage, responsibility, the home, work, and the absence of pleasure so reviled by *malandragem*. Marriage and romantic love are often associated with the loss of participation in samba itself: "O casamento e a esposa são criticados porque roubam o homem à fruição [do] próprio samba. E samba quer dizer não somente fruição, mas contato com a 'turma'; integração no grupo, no ser coletivo" ("Marriage and wives are criticized because they rob men of enjoying . . . samba itself. Samba not only means enjoyment, but contact with the gang, integration in the group, in the collective being").[47] Marriage robs the *malandro* of samba, participation in which is a marker of identity: thus marriage is seen as a form of symbolic castration.

The link between the drudge, romantic love, and the establishment indicates that the negative portrayal of women in samba may be linked to censorship. It is possible that failure in love could be a veiled reference to the failure of state ideology to overcome conflict through love of the nation. Forbidden to talk explicitly of poverty and problems contradicting the national image, the failure of relationships and the unceasing vilification of women in the form of the drudge may represent deflected resistance to the state. If this were so, it seems to have been more unconscious than otherwise, as often no differentiation is made between the drudge as symbol of the establishment and the drudge as woman; therefore, the trope in samba is woman = establishment. Sambas do not split the signifier *woman* and the signified *establishment*. This a blind spot in an ethos that thrives on destabilizing essentialism and exploiting the split between signifier and signified, revealing a masculinity similar to hegemonic masculinity in its naturalization of female subjugation.

Valdez, the *Pachuco*, and *Zoot Suit*

Mauricio Mazón described the zoot suit riots as a process of "symbolic annihilation." This mirrors the conclusions made by Matos on the disappearance of the *malandro*: it indicates the total victory of hegemony in the battle for signification. Yet the power of attraction exerted by these figures still revolves around their subversive potential, indicating that the dominant culture was unable to assign a definitive and fixed meaning to them. Both figures have been repeatedly discussed by cultural commentators since their appearance. Octavio Paz's essay on *pachucos*, in which he blames them for their persecution because they are incapable of assimilation, illustrates an internalized "orientalism" similar to that of the Mexican American Movement. He sweepingly rejects any racist implications to their repression, stating, "Y no se crea que los rasgos físicos son tan determinantes como vulgarmente se piensa" ("And don't believe that the physical characteristics are as determining as most people think").[48] Paz writes that wearing the zoot suit signifies a desire for victimization: as victim the *pachuco* is finally recognized by the society that ignores him. This interpretation is uncomfortably close to Al Capp's "five-cent masochist." It justifies repression and eliminates the need for serious discussion of racial issues by using a pseudo-psychological approach that places the *pachuco* in the position of disobedient child.

Luis Valdez gives a radically different interpretation of the *pachuco* in *Zoot Suit*. He reverses the negative hegemonic representation and posits the *pachuco* as a positive figure resisting domination. Valdez's work and his construction of male subjectivity must be examined, taking into account his commitment to the Chicano movement. This movement was the first large-scale, radical, organized expression of Mexican American interests. Emphasizing a history of racial subordination, the Chicano movement sought to make the mechanisms of this subordination explicit, to contest them, and to positively realign the Mexican American subject position within North American society. This involved the construction of a Chicano identity in which Mexican Americans could recognize themselves and in whose name they could be mobilized to renegotiate their relationship with the dominant culture. In Muñoz's words, "The search for identity and the dilemmas that it posed are the keys to understanding the Chicano student movement of the 1960's. To a large degree, the movement was a quest for identity, an effort to recapture what had been lost through the socialization process and imposed by U.S. schools, churches, and other institutions."[49] It was to this project that Valdez was committed, co-writing a nationalist manifesto, *El Plan Espiritual de Aztlán*, which greatly influenced the identity politics of the movement. (See figure 11.2.)

Zoot Suit attempts to relocate an essential Mexican American identity lost through socialization in North America. The drama centers on the Sleepy Lagoon trial, and its protagonist, Henry Reyna, is based on the leaders of the gang charged for murder. It thus rewrites those events, focusing on Henry and his community's experience of the case. Henry's experience is mediated through his relationship with the character El Pachuco, Valdez's theatrical embodiment of the *pachuco* myth itself. He is invisible to the other characters, appearing only to Henry (and the audience) throughout the drama, advising, criticizing, and arguing with him at crucial moments. Reversing the tendency to portray the *pachuco* as a powerless victim, Valdez's character narrates parts of the play, has the control of a director, is omniscient and authoritative, and constructs his own history of events. He can freeze the action by flicking his fingers, which he does at times, to discuss things with Henry or to address the audience.

To some extent the *pachuco* is presented as the object of desire of Chicano identity.[50] In his opening soliloquy to the audience, El Pachuco postures as such:

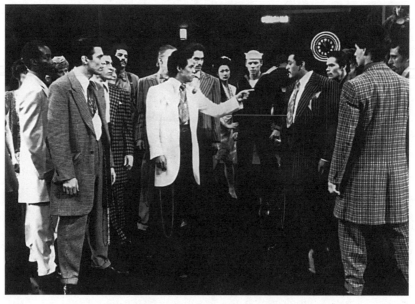

Figure 11.2 Uniform cut, variable style: the zoot suit as worn by *pachuco* gangs. Copyright © 1998 by Universal City Studios, Inc. Courtesy of Universal Studios Publishing Rights. All rights reserved.

PACHUCO: It was the secret fantasy of every *bato* [dude]
In and out of the *chicanada* [Chicano community]
To put on a zoot suit and play the myth
más chucote que la chingada
[more *pachuco* than any son-of-a-bitch].[51]

Thus the desire to be a zoot suiter is that of every *bato* (dude), not just of a small minority, and the myth is given a mystic quality or "coolness": "more *pachuco* than any son-of-a-bitch." This final line is spat out with extraordinary aggression by Edward James Olmos in the film, and reflects the patriarchal values deeply embedded in the term *la chingada,* as the violated woman discussed by Octavio Paz in *El laberinto de la soledad.*[52] This opening statement, Fregoso writes, is indicative of Valdez's construction of male subjectivity: "*Zoot Suit* foregrounds the male subject by essentializing male desire as the *pachuco.* As the film unfolds we discover the ways in which the *pachuco* 'plays out' a male centered fantasy about the *pachuco* reality."[53] The opening scenes of the film version corroborate this reading. El Pachuco's role as director points to an element of metatheatricality that is perhaps reminiscent of Brechtian distancing techniques, as the audience is made aware that they are watching a representation of reality. This distancing is used at times to encourage a deconstructive approach from the audience, especially in the absurd trial scene when the *pachuco* actually calls for an action replay of a comment made by the judge.

At other times, however, the audience is encouraged to identify with the *pachuco,* and a more humanistic, didactic approach is taken. For Fregoso, the model for audience identification is set in the opening scenes of the film, as a father/son pair are shown entering the theater and taking their seats: the camera flicks back to them periodically throughout the film, a technique that not only accentuates the film's theatricality, but also posits a masculine identification between audience and film: "The self-reflectivity of the film, as expressed by the *pachuco,* . . . also signals the extent to which a masculine context governs the production of identity; . . . this film is about men: the *pachuco* personifies the 'myth' of Chicano manliness."[54]

This identification ignores *pachuca* experience. As a result, the portrayal of women is consistent with the centrality of males (discussed above in the context of *malandragem*) and the traditional position of women in

Mexican society. Henry's mother, girlfriend, and ex-girlfriend roughly correspond to the mythical female Mexican trinity of long-suffering mother, virgin, and whore *(la chingada)*. Women are appendages to male characters, as the trio of adoring female singers who accompany the *pachuco* character illustrate in Valdez's film (see figure 11.3).

Della, the virginal girlfriend whom Hank has asked to marry him, is contrasted to Bertha, his ex-girlfriend, whose aggressive sexuality and tough *pachuca* attitude are negatively portrayed, much as the *malandra* is depicted. When Della complains that Henry treats her like a "square" and attempts to initiate sexual activity, Henry reacts to her threat of becoming

Figure 11.3 The *pachuco* as object of desire. Copyright © 1998 by Universal City Studios, Inc. Courtesy of Universal Studios Publishing Rights. All rights reserved.

a desiring subject by dragging her to the car and telling her to get in the back seat, shouting, "Is that what you want, to be like Bertha?" Female desire is limited to passive adoration of Henry and El Pachuco. Fregoso reads this as subsuming female desire to the universal male identity posited in El Pachuco as part of Chicano cultural nationalism, collapsing multiple Chicano identities into a single historical subject.[55]

These interpretations again emphasize that any essentialist portrayal of masculinity must construct itself against a subjugated *other*, upon which the values excluded from that masculine codification are projected. But this says little about the conflicts involved in constructing such an identity. Valdez exhibits a masculinity that both protects and imprisons its subjects, as illustrated in the relationship between Henry and El Pachuco. There is both resistance and complicity in Henry's attitude. When El Pachuco offers Henry advice and encourages him to take up an aggressive stance, it is often to help him defend himself from possible white attacks.

In this instance, what is often dismissed as pathological *machismo* can be seen as a form of resistance. El *pachuco* mocks Henry's decision to join the navy, asking him why he should fight for a society that does not recognize him. He is aggressively cynical toward Henry's dealings with Anglos, reasoning that if hopes are not raised, neither are they dashed and trauma can thus be avoided. He encourages Henry's aggression toward George, the peoples' lawyer, when George evades Henry's questioning:

EL PACHUCO: He didn't answer your question, *ese* [this guy].
HENRY: You still didn't answer my question, mister. Who's paying you? And how much? (41)

This aggression is a strategy to avoid being trapped by evasion; it clarifies relationships. Henry is suspicious of trickery in George, a lawyer and symbol of white male hegemony: his aggression and defiance are defenses against possible institutional racism. This aggression is linked to Chicano brotherhood, as witnessed in gang bonding throughout the play, again in the face of external threats, and can be associated with the defense of the Mexican American community, not just with excessive aggression and pathological masculinity.

Henry reacts fiercely to any contradiction of his image as an active, independent agent. When Alice tells Henry he was imprisoned because the press are sensationalizing the *pachucos* to sell newspapers, the following exchange takes place:

> ALICE: Somebody is using you as a patsy.
> HENRY: Who are you calling a patsy? (49)

Henry sees his masculinity threatened by this comment, and El *pachuco*'s immediate reaction is to encourage him to aggressively reassert this masculinity:

> EL PACHUCO: *Puro pedo*. She's just a dumb broad only good for you know what.
> HENRY: Look, Miss Bloomfield, just leave me alone, all right? (49)

This aggressive refusal to be seen as a victim provides protection from intrusion by white institutions, but it also imprisons Henry in an ossified code of behavior that does not change with the contingencies of the moment and which freezes *others*, notably women, into stereotypical subject positions. Henry seems at times aware of the crippling effect of such ossification in personal relationships, and he clashes with El Pachuco. Whereas El Pachuco advises him to reject help from George and Alice, Henry accepts it. El Pachuco's reaction is to insult Henry's virility:

> EL PACHUCO: Hang tough. *(Grabs his scrotum.)* Stop goin soft.
> HENRY: Who's goin soft? . . .
> EL PACHUCO: . . . the classic social victim, eh?
> HENRY: *(Furious but keeping his cool.)* Mira, ese. Hank Reyna's no loser. I'm coming out of this on top. *Me entiendes*, Mendez?
> EL PACHUCO: *(Forcefully.)* Don't try to out-*pachuco* ME, *ese*. (51)

Thus resistance is involved in Henry's negotiation of the myth of the *pachuco*'s identity and his reality: a critical dialogue of sorts is maintained that prevents Henry from moving along a self-destructive path by always adhering to El Pachuco's masculine code of conduct. There is, then, conflict between the two. This conflict climaxes when Henry is in solitary confinement and seems to lose his sense of self. It is a moment when his identity slips perilously close to revealing that, cut off from society, there is no self on which to rely. Losing his composure and cool, violating the strict economy of gesture and emotion embodied in El Pachuco, Henry sobs to himself, "I'm Henry Reyna, I'm Henry Reyna." El Pachuco's reply is enigmatic and does not tally with the essentialism of Valdez's work: "A dream, *carnal* [buddy], a dream." The fictive nature of identity is emphasized, and Hank's reaction is to reject El Pachuco: "*Sabes que, ese,* I got you all figured out. I know who you are, *carnal.* You're the one that got me here. And you know what: you're me, my worst enemy and my best friend, myself. So get lost. Get lost."

The conflict is not resolved: the moment is diffused by El Pachuco clicking his fingers and reminding Henry he's in a play: "*Orale, pues* [Hey, listen], don't take the *pinche* [mere] play so seriously, Jesus." He then brings about a scene in which the L.A. zoot suit riots are represented. This moment is crucial in the construction of a Chicano national identity and is intended to provide a symbolic answer to Henry's identity crisis. El Pachuco is pictured in conflict with sailors, who insult him and then "de-zoot" him. In this moment of symbolic castration, El Pachuco rises to reveal his "true" identity: as Aztec music plays, he stands up wearing an Aztec loincloth. Valdez places El Pachuco as the inheritor of the Aztec history of resistance to conquest by the Spaniards. Fregoso describes this action as an archaeological project, a search for origins, reflecting a humanistic view of the essential self to be uncovered when the effects of socialization are stripped away.[56] This fixed point of origin predates colonization and subjugation: the Aztec world. It is an approach that does not see identity as constructed, but ironically this scene appears at a moment in the play when the fiction of identity has just been revealed.

Straining to construct an essential Chicano cultural identity, Valdez's play reveals the very mechanism of that construction. In the end, however, Henry and El Pachuco are reconciled after Henry leaves jail. The didactic message is that the gangs have found their identities in jail: ironically, they have "learned a lesson" even though they are not guilty. Henry has vicariously found his "true" identity, and the others have become more class- and race-conscious, rejecting *pachuco* individualism in favor of a commitment to fight for the Chicano community:

JOEY: We've learned our lesson . . . well, anyway, I've learned my lesson. No
more *pachuquismo* for me. Too many people depending on us to help out. The
raza here in Los. The whole Southwest, Mexico, South America! . . . If you get
us out of here, I figure the only thing I could do is become a union organizer.
(74)

Thus, the *pachuco* is appropriated as a figure of resistance into the Chicano movement, but *pachuquismo*'s individualism and aggressiveness is not
deemed conducive to Chicano unity. While the form of *Zoot Suit* points to
the hybridity and richness of Mexican American culture, the content is limited by essentialist nationalism. Valdez's reversal of the negative portrayal
of the *pachuco* is a necessary historical revision to counter negative stereotypes in North American culture. But this gesture falls short of its subversive intentions because it shares the same epistemology of identity as the
dominant culture. As revisionist history, *Zoot Suit* realigns the position of
the Chicano subject in North American history and society, but it leaves the
structure of that history intact.

Valdez's project is politically strategic: it is an attempt to improve the
power balance in favor of the Chicano community. But it does not "undermine the law of symbolic language,"[57] and therefore the phallocentric values of dominant discourse permeate the construction of gender in *Zoot
Suit*. The *pachuquismo* of *Zoot Suit* challenges the authority of hegemonic
masculinity but does not subvert it.

Chico Buarque, the *Malandro*, and *Ópera do malandro*

Chico Buarque de Hollanda's play, *Ópera do Malandro*, was written in
very different circumstances from those that produced Valdez's *Zoot Suit*.
Based loosely on Brecht's *Threepenny Opera*, Buarque's material reflects his
strong political commitment, but, unlike Valdez, he is not limited by cultural nationalism to present a model of identity. This is partly due to the fact
that *Ópera* was written in 1978 during the period in modern Brazilian history known as the *abertura*, a transition stage to democracy after fourteen
years of military dictatorship. While Valdez played an active part in Chicano organization, the Brazilian dictatorship prohibited and repressed
political activities among the population. Therefore there were no visible

counterhegemonic groups for Buarque to be committed to, as resistance went underground—both literally, in the organization of guerrilla groups, and linguistically, as artistic language had to utilize again the language of *malandragem* called for in Noel Rosa's "Rapaz folgado" to outwit the censors, with whom Buarque clashed continually.

Buarque's approach to *malandragem* is reminiscent of Rosa's. While celebrating the language and discursive slipperiness of the *malandro*, he is critical of the myth, and his portrayal of Max the *malandro* in *Ópera* is not particularly sympathetic. However, he uses the space occupied and passed through by the *malandro*, that of society's margins, to instigate a *malandro*-like attack on establishment values and morality.

Buarque uses a white actor, Edson Celulari, to play Max in the film, which, along with the emphasis on Max's black marketeering exploits, marks his criticism of *malandragem*'s exploitation when its ethos is displaced from the community and conditions from which it sprang.[58] Max's characterization emphasizes the self-serving and social climbing nature of *malandragem;* he defends nobody but himself and uses everybody in the process. His black marketeering involves importing North American consumer goods. The play is set during the time of Vargas's Estado Novo, and the references to Vargas's dictatorship provide allegorical criticism of later dictatorships in Brazil.

Thus the play can be seen as working on different levels. Max as the black marketeer in typical *malandro* style exploits the gap between supply and demand caused by Vargas's emphasis on national production. At the same time, Max is shown to be pretentious, as his spattering of English words is mocked by his gang, and Buarque thus mocks the snob value of Max's black market consumer goods and criticizes the pro–North American policy of the Médici dictatorship. Rather than opposing capital and the establishment, as the popular *malandro* often does, Max acts as the penetrating vanguard of capitalism, importing products on the black market that he later imports legally when his band of smugglers becomes an import-export company. Thus, Max's antiestablishment attitude is merely exploiting the limits placed on capital and the free market by the state. His role is transgressive only in the sense of what Marshall Berman describes as "the paradoxically 'unprincipled' principle of free trade,"[59] acting as a dynamic agent that eventually creates a channel for bringing the products of consumer capitalism into Brazil. His *malandragem*, then, corresponds to an ethos of unprincipled entrepreneurialism. Buarque shows that the difference between him and his "legal" counterpart, the brothel keeper Duran, is only minimal; and it is easily reversed when Max is at last accepted as a successful businessman.

Max's characterization is reminiscent of Cândido's dialectic of *malandragem* between order and disorder. Buarque's work continually blurs these boundaries. Max, Duran, and Chaves, the police inspector, operate in similar ways: both Max and Duran pay bribes to Chaves to overlook their illegal activities. Chaves and Max are shown to be childhood friends, and the film skillfully emphasizes the similarities and bond between the two. In the scene in which both use a public convenience, as one looks into a mirror, the other looks back. As they urinate, their gestures are exactly the same. Again they represent two sides of the same coin; they even share sexual partners. The scene is also a hilarious pun on their similar relationship to phallic power.

The difference between Max and Duran is that the latter is an institutionalized pimp running a massive prostitution network, whereas Max is involved in small-time street pimping. While the prostitutes adore Max and hate Duran and Chaves, the parallels among the three are made explicit by Fichinha and Geni:

> FICHINHA: Olha, o Max pode até ser bom de cama. Mas, no fundo no fundo, patrão, feitor, e domador de circo é tudo a mesma coisa.
> GENI: Tudo a mesma coisa. Duran, Max e o escambau, no fim, eles, acabam de se entendendo. E nós, ó!

> (FICHINHA: Look, Max may well be good in bed. But, deep down, master, boss, and circus tamer are all one and the same.
> GENI: All one and the same. Duran, Max, and that swindler, in the end they're the ones who understand each other. And us—oh, well!)[60]

Buarque, then, is highly critical of Max's style of *malandragem*. All three figures live off and exploit women; all three share a masculinity constructed on and subsisting from women's subordination.

It is through the voices and experiences of the prostitutes and other marginal characters in the play that Buarque gives voice to his criticism of that masculinity and the society that constructs and supports it. The portrayal of Duran as an institutionalized pimp can be simultaneously read as a criticism of the morality of the bourgeoisie, the Estado Novo, and Brazil's later dictatorship. Duran can be seen as an allegory of a populist leader. He sees himself as working in the interests of his prostitutes, providing them with contracts, benefits, and social documentation, and therefore contributing to Brazil's economic growth. His first words reflect this: "É isso mesmo, tem que dar um basta nessa malandragem. No dia em que todo brasileiro trabalhar o que eu trabalho, acaba a miséria" ("This ought to bring an end to *malandragem*. The day when every Brazilian works like me, the suffering will end").[61] Like Vargas, he attempts to organize the workers to serve his own ends. In the play he wants them to march on Workers' Day to publicly denounce Chaves's corruption; privately, it is a bid to blackmail the police inspector into killing Max for marrying his (Duran's) daughter. His behavior constantly swings from benevolence to authoritarianism. The analogies with populist leaders are more obvious in the film and closely associated with fascism: Duran's character is Otto Strüdel, a German immigrant usually framed sitting under a portrait of Hitler.

Duran/Strüdel's financial well-being is based on prostitution. His source of income undermines his wife Vitoria's constant bourgeois moralizing about maintaining a decent household and being an honest Christian. Furthermore, the prostitutes provide what Duran sees as a release valve for workers tired of humdrum jobs and boring domestic lives. He thus implicitly admits that both jobs and wives do not provide plenitude and satisfaction, while simultaneously expressing his support for an ideology that claims they do.

There is a complex constellation of significations surrounding the portrayal of the prostitutes. Judging from their experience, relationships between men and women are described purely in terms of power and violence, as in the song "Se eu fosse o teu patrão" ("If I Were Your Boss"), where a master/slave relationship explicitly based on violence develops into a description of an equally violent, if more perfidious, male/female relationship in which beneath an appearance of happiness lies treachery and hate.

Buarque's portrayal of Duran's organized prostitution also alludes to the pervasive nature of dictatorships, illustrating how censorship and repression are linked not only to political activity, but also to sexuality and to sexual practices. Duran's control of the world of prostitution, which undermines the repressive morality of the dictatorship by its very existence, belies the manner in which ideology can permeate the most intimate private experience. Sex is very much regarded as a worker's sacrifice in the song "Viver do amor" ("To Live to/for Love"). Sung by the prostitutes to Fichinha as she joins their number, it equates sex to the work of civil servants, to the sweat and blood of hard labor, and to holy sacrifice. Thus the rhetoric of politics is inscribed in the most intimate of acts. The organization of prostitutes and these lyrics are evidence of the attempt to contain desire and excess within controllable parameters, a process comparable to repressive desublimation. Politics and sexuality become linked, as sex and desire are de-eroticized and associated with work, sacrifice, and slavery. Thus, on the one hand Buarque shows sexuality undermining bourgeois morality, and on the other hand he shows how the discursive practices of that morality seek to undermine the subversiveness of sexuality.

Just as institutionalized boundaries between order and disorder, morality and immorality are questioned and blurred, so they are between the sexes. The song discussed above ("Se eu fosse o teu patrão") serves to destroy notions of male and female roles as natural and complementary, instead focusing on the violence that binds the male/female binary. The presence of Geni, a transvestite character, further blurs these divisions. Geni's role is central to the dénouement of the plot as (s)he finally betrays Max. In the process, (s)he taunts Chaves, who cannot understand Geni's sexuality within his own conventional understanding of gender roles. Geni appears to provoke aggression in Chaves simply by being there, provoking him at one point to shout, "Sai da minha frente, vai, cai fora!" ("Get out of my face, go on, get out!").[62] The strength of this reaction indicates the anxiety triggered in Chaves by Geni's difference. In a hilarious scene, Geni extorts money for information regarding Max's whereabouts and then proceeds to extort more from Chaves for his insults:

> GENI: Olha, era só dois contos. Mas agora que o inspetor me chamou de veado puto eu vou ter que exigir uma indenizaçao. Fica tudo por quatro contos e eu me dou por satisfeita.

CHAVES: Se não é veado, o que é que é? É machão?
GENI: Nem veado nem machão. Eu sou plurissexual.

(GENI: Look, it was only two *contos*. But now the inspector called me an old fag-got I'll have to demand compensation. Let's call it four and be done with it.
CHAVES: If you're not a faggot, what are you? A man?
GENI: Neither faggot nor man. I'm plurisexual.[63]

Geni then goes on to demand apologies for the insults, making a complete fool of Chaves and his division of sexuality into heterosexual/homosexual categories.

In the film, Geni is shot by Chaves in the same scene in which Max is exiled to Argentina: the two acts are powerfully symbolic of the violence enacted to enforce homogeneity on a national community. The image of the *malandro*'s rotting body in the song "O *malandro* no. 2" ("The *Malandro* No. 2") that ends the opera is a symbol of this violence:

> O *malandro*
> Tá na greta
> Na sarjeta
> Do país
> E quem passa
> Acha graça
> Na desgraça
> Do infeliz. . . .
> O coitado
> Foi encontrado
> Mais furado
> Que Jesus
> E do estranho
> Abdômen
> Desse homem
> Jorra pus.)
>
> (The *malandro*
> Is in the hole

In the gutter
Of the country
And whoever passes
Finds amusement
In the disgrace
Of this miserable one. . . .
The poor thing
He was found
More sliced up
Than Jesus
And what's strange is
The abdomen
Of this man
gushes pus.)

The vocabulary of decay and disease encodes Buarque's view of Max's rotten *malandragem,* and also the violence done to the body of the *malandro* by the Estado Novo. Buarque uses the religious imagery of Christ's sacrifice to hint that Brazilian national identity was founded on the figurative death of the *malandro.* This rotten image counters the *happy ending* when Max and Teresinha literally sing the praises of consumer capitalism and boast of their newfound wealth.

Unlike Valdez, then, Buarque deconstructs notions of essentialist identity, applying this deconstruction to gender as well as national identity and not splitting the two. His use of Brechtian distancing techniques is coupled with a call to political activity, but not through identification with a male hero. The opening scenes of the play are metatheatrical, as João Alegre, the "producer," addresses the audience and formally thanks a high-society lady (the actress who plays Vitoria) for sponsoring the play. Later, after Duran has organized the workers and then cannot prevent them from marching, Vitoria again steps into this metatheatrical role and demands that the play be stopped, as it is getting out of hand (that is, not reflecting a bourgeois aesthetic). João Alegre refuses to stop the play and is asked to resign.

The process of repressive desublimation is seen to fail, but this time it is the split between art and life, another boundary constructed by the bourgeoisie, that is transgressed: Buarque indicates that the desires released in this work must go beyond it as art and influence the world outside the theater. This is particularly important, given the split between left-wing hegemony and mass political movements in the 1964–1968 period brought about by the dictatorship, and also in the fragile climate of the *abertura*, where tentative moves were made to set up collective political groups and rebuild what was destroyed under the more repressive regime of the dictatorship after 1969.[64]

Buarque's work seems itself to be a product of the epistemological conditions of the border or marginality, challenging hegemonic masculinity and the assumptions of dominant ideology from their "enunciative boundaries."

Conclusion

As marginal figures, the *malandro* and the *pachuco* resonate with a sense of uncontained energy and difference; in Bhabha's words, they are "in excess of the sum of their parts." They encode identities that are signs of new, hybrid cultural formations. As such, their bodies bear the history of a battle for signification: they are the space in which a number of different discourses meet, clash, fragment, and mix. Both were subcultural manifestations of identity that came into being as a reaction to processes of repressive desublimation in Brazil and the United States. Their differences to hegemonic masculinity both indicate the existence of a plurality of masculinities and decenter notions of masculine essence that underlie the epistemology of hegemonic identity politics. The threat they posed to hegemonic masculinities and therefore to dominant culture resulted in a very similar process of repression in both countries. They were situated either in a similar place to women in the male/female binary and culturally emasculated, or conversely, dismissed as evidence of pathological masculinity and equated with machismo, a term that conflates all Latino masculinities into one pathological code of conduct, thereby dismissing them and their differences.

The repeated representation and re-representation of these figures by writers such as Chico Buarque and Luis Valdez point to the subversive potential still carried by these myths. The differences in representation between the *Ópera do Malandro* and *Zoot Suit* illustrate that their subversive quality depends on the purposes of the representation, and again this negates the fiction of essentialism in identity. Valdez's representation of Chicano cultural nationalism sutures the spectator into a masculine identification with El *pachuco*. Buarque is far more critical of the *malandro* but uses the associated marginal world to interrogate the unquestioned assumptions of gender identity typified in *Zoot Suit*.

Finally, the zoot suit and *malandro* outfit is associated with resistance to repression that goes beyond the United States and Brazil. Octavio Paz remarks of his astonishment in 1945 on finding French youth wearing the zoot suit. His assumption that they were merely aping North American fashion was rebuffed: "Casi todas [personas] me dijeron que esa moda era exclusivamente francesa y que había sido creado al fin de la ocupación. Algunas llegaban hasta a considerarla como una de las formas de la "Resistencia"; y su fantasía y barroquismo una respuesta al orden de los alemanes" ("Nearly everyone told me this was an exclusively French fashion, and was created around the end of the occupation. Some went as far as to consider it one of the forms of "Resistance"; and its fantasy and baroque nature a response to the order of the Germans").[65] Thus the French zoot suit has its own history of resistance. There are similarities with many other popular cultural figures of the time—the Jamaican rudie, the Cuban *curro*, and others. There is also a striking similarity between the history of the samba and the tango in Argentina. The parameters of the comparison undertaken here could, then, be much wider and illustrate many more examples of difference in masculinities, nation, and popular culture.

Notes

Introduction

Unless otherwise indicated, translations are by the authors.

1. Martins, "For a Popular Revolutionary Art," quoted in Johnson and Stam, *Brazilian Cinema*, 60. Compare Armand Mattelart, introduction to *Communication and Class Struggle*, ed. Mattelart and Siegelaub. See also Franco, "What's in a Name?"

2. Sarlo, *Escenas de la vida posmoderna*, 18.

3. Ibid., 20.

4. Ibid., 22.

5. Denning, "The End of Mass Culture," 258. Of course, there is no end of debate in Anglo-American cultural studies circles about this claim, much less what follows from it. See Nelson and Grossberg, *Marxism and the Interpretation of Culture*, and a summary statement of postmodern logic in Jameson, *Postmodernism*. See also Beverley, "The Politics of Latin American Postmodernism," in *Against Literature*.

6. Bennett, "The Politics of 'the Popular,'" 18.

7. Ibid. Sarlo puts the same point more expansively: "Popular culture does not have a past paradigm to which it can refer: it is impossible to restore an authenticity which would only produce manifestations of a folkloric kitsch which would not interest even its protagonists. The same way the high culture (written culture) does not go back through its classics except through processes of transformation, deformation, and irony, the popular cultures cannot think about their origin except through the present" (*Escenas de la vida posmoderna*, 129).

8. Ibid., 87.

9. Ibid., 113.

10. Cited in Bary, "Forum," 270. Beverley makes the same point for a specifically Latin American context: "There is the related danger that—as in the case of Baudrillard's books on the United States—the production of a postmodernism 'sublime' in relation to Latin America may involve the aesthetic fetishization of its social, cultural, and economic status quo (as abject, chaotic, heterogeneous, carnivalesque, etc.), thereby attenuating the urgency for radical social change and displacing it into cultural dilettantism and quietism" (*Against Literature*, 106–07).

11. Rowe and Schelling, *Memory and Modernity*, 97–98. Rowe and Schelling make the following distinction: "However, *Studies in Latin American Popular Culture*, the only

academic journal dedicated to popular culture in Latin America, defines the popular as solely pertaining to urban mass culture and the culture industry. This is in line with the longer-established *Journal of Popular Culture*, which deals predominantly with the culture of the United States and Canada." The significance of this distinction has a long history in cultural studies. See, for example, Brantlinger, *Crusoe's Footprints*. On the distinction among the terms *folk art*, *popular art*, and *mass art*, see the introduction to Naremore and Brantlinger, *Modernity and Mass Culture*.

12. Beverley, Oviedo, and Aronna, introduction to *The Postmodern Debate in Latin America*, 4.

13. Martín-Barbero, *De los medios a las mediaciones*, 27.

14. Rowe and Schelling, *Memory and Modernity*, 97.

15. Yúdice, "Postmodernity and Transnational Capitalism," 23.

16. Rowe and Schelling, *Memory and Modernity*, 4.

17. Yúdice, "Postmodernity and Transnational Capitalism," 20. Compare Emily Hicks: "Latin American culture in particular is essentially heterogeneous, a culture that articulates borders between widely disparate traditions. The contemporary culture of Mexico, for example, emerges from what can be considered a multilayered semiotic matrix: the Mixteco Indians, Spain, the Lacandonian Indians, McDonald's, *ballet folklórico*, and punk rock. The heterogeneous cultures of Latin America exist in the spaces that emerge between a desire for memories of pre-Columbian cultures, a respect for the continuing traditions of indigenous cultures, and a problematic relationship with Spanish and other European cultures and the New World culture of the United States" (*Border Writing*, xxiv).

18. Rowe and Schelling, *Memory and Modernity*, 2. See Jameson's inaugural essay, "Reification and Utopia" as well as his *Postmodernism*. Compare Neil Larsen's comment in his foreword to Hicks, *Border Writing:* "This is a utopian project, in the best and worst senses of the word. It reproduces the classical ideological pattern of severing the transformation of consciousness from the constraints imposed by the transformations of social being" (xviii). It is precisely this "severance" that we are emphasizing here.

19. McCabe, *High Theory/Low Culture*, 4.

20. Compare McCabe, discussing the difference Gramsci's well-known conceptions of the national-popular and the hegemonic make to earlier forms of social analysis: "The differentiation of cultural artefacts becomes a simple gauging of their political effects. The Gramscian argument describes a cultural terrain in which the dominated's resistance of the dominant is always in terms of meanings already politically defined" (ibid., 5–6). The essays in this volume further confirm the enormous utility of the idea of hegemony at the present moment in cultural studies, at the expense of what McCabe characterizes as either the Hegelian notion that culture is available as a knowable totality or the Marxian position that the study of culture must proceed as a class analysis.

21. Sarlo, *Escenas de la vida posmoderna*, 129.

22. Franco, *The Modern Culture of Latin America*, 282.

23. Albo, "Our Identity Starting from Pluralism in the Base," 28.

24. Dorfman and Mattelart, *Para leer al Pato Donald.*

25. In a classic article, Arjun Appadurai puts the same case more grandly: "The crucial point, however, is that the United States is no longer the puppeteer of a world system of images, but is only one node of a complex transnational construction of imaginary landscapes. The world we live in today is characterized by a new role for the imagination in social life. To grasp this new role, we need to bring together: the old idea of images, especially mechanically produced images (in the Frankfurt School sense); the idea of the imagined community (in Anderson's sense); and the French idea of the imaginary (imaginaire), as a constructed landscape of collective representations, which is no more and no less real than the collective representations of Émile Durkheim, now mediated through the complex prism of modern media" ("Disjuncture and Difference in the Global Cultural Economy," 4–5). See also Albo, *Modernity at Large,* based on this essay.

26. Anibal Quijano, "Latin American Identity," in *The Postmodern Debate in Latin America,* ed. Beverley, Oviedo, Aronna, 216.

27. Beverley, *Against Literature,* 111.

28. Just as significant is the case of Brazil, the other United States–sized Latin American nation. For example, see *The Brazilian Puzzle,* ed. Hess and Da Matta. In Hess's afterword, he solves the "puzzle" by "seeing Brazil not in evolutionary terms as a developing counterpart of the developed West, but instead as a different mix of general characteristics shared by each country in different ways and to different degrees" (297). In cruder words: culturally, Brazil is simply part of the United States, provided that (as Hess goes on to say) the United States is part of Brazil, or "becoming Brazilianized," in terms of its poverty, crime, and national debt.

29. On Carnival, see Da Matta, *Carnivals, Rogues, and Heroes;* see also Guillermoprieto, *Samba;* and Caesar, "Bringing it All Down." The *testimonio* is discussed in two essays in Beverley, *Against Literature.*

30. A model of such work might be Slater, *Stories on a String;* one might also consult Beverley and Zimmerman, *Literature and Politics in the Central American Revolutions;* Foster's work on Argentina; to Simpson, *Xuxa: The Megamarketing of Gender, Race, and Modernity,* each of which varies widely in terms of political nuance and theoretical orientation; Slater could, for example, be classified as doing a rather specific practice of folklore, while Simpson a broad form of cultural studies.

31. McCabe, *High Theory/Low Culture,* 9.

32. Schwarz, "Brazilian Culture: Nationalism by Elimination," in *Misplaced Ideas,* ed. Gledson, 16.

33. Sarlo, *Escenas de la vida posmoderna,* 109.

Chapter 1. The Case of the *China Poblana*

1. Andrade, "Se levantará un monumento," in Carrasco Puente, *Bibliografía de Catarina de San Juan y de la China poblana,* 4.

2. Ibid.

3. Maza, *Catarina de San Juan*, 12.

4. Ibid.

5. León, "Catarina de San Juan," in Carrasco Puente, *Bibliografía de Catarina de San Juan y de la China poblana*, 60–61.

6. Castillo Graxeda, *Compendio de la vida . . . [de] Catarina de San Juan*, 34–35.

7. León, "Catarina de San Juan," in Carrasco Puente, *Bibliografía de Catarina de San Juan y de la China poblana*, 40.

8. Carrasco Puente, *Bibliografía de Catarina de San Juan y de la China poblana*, 64–65.

9. Alarcón, "Chicana's Feminist Literature," 182.

10. Cypess, *La Malinche in Mexican Literature*, 12–13.

11. Carrasco Puente, *Bibliografía de Catarina de San Juan y de la China poblana*, 40.

12. Castillo Graxeda, *Compendio de la vida . . . [de] Catarina de San Juan*, 60.

13. Arenal and Schlau, *Untold Sisters*, 339.

14. A. Ramos, *Primera, Segunda y Tercera partes de los Prodigios de la Omnipotencia y milagros de . . . Catharina de San Juan.*

15. Carrasco Puente, *Bibliografía de Catarina de San Juan y de la China poblana*, 34–35.

16. Castillo Graxeda, *Compendio de la vida . . . [de] Catarina de San Juan.*

17. León, "Catarina de San Juan y la china poblana," in Carrasco Puente, *Bibliografía de Catarina de San Juan y de la China poblana*, 41.

18. Castillo Graxeda, *Compendio de la vida . . . [de] Catarina de San Juan*, 44.

19. Ibid.

20. Allen, "Feminist Criticism and Postmodernism," 280.

21. Keen, *La imagen azteca*, 196–99.

22. Maza, *Catarina de San Juan*, 132.

23. Ibid., 134–35.

24. Carrasco Puente, *Bibliografía de Catarina de San Juan y de la China poblana*, 39.

25. Castillo Graxeda, *Compendio de la vida . . . [de] Catarina de San Juan*, 41.

26. Carrasco Puente, *Bibliografía de Catarina de San Juan y de la China poblana*, 51.

27. José Puigarri, *Monografía histórica e iconográfica del traje*, in Carrasco Puente, *Bibliografía de Catarina de San Juan y de la China poblana*, 62.

28. García Icazbalceta, *Vocabulario de mexicanismos*, in Carrasco Puente, *Bibliografía de Catarina de San Juan y de la China poblana*, 60–61.

29. Fanny Calderón de la Barca, *Life in Mexico*, in ibid., 72.

30. Ibid., 76–77.

31. Nervo, "Guadalupe (la chinaca)," in Carracso Puente, *Bibliografía de Catarina de San Juan y de la China poblana*, 84–85.

32. Ibid.

33. Ibid.

34. Ibid.

35. Sommer, *Foundational Fictions*, 7.

36. Carrasco Puente, *Bibliografía de Catarina de San Juan y de la China poblana*, 4–8.

37. Alarcón, "Chicana's Feminist Literature," 189.

Chapter 2. *Caipira* Culture

The author wants to thank Beatriz Cordeiro, of Curitiba, for her help in locating and obtaining material about Mazzaropi in Brazil, and Fantasy Video, of Maringa, for their generosity in making their Mazzaropi collection available, at no cost, for a long time. *Obrigada.*

1. Catani, "A aventura industrial e o cinema paulista," 290.

2. Stam, *Tropical Multiculturalism*, does not even mention Mazzaropi and his work.

3. *El Justicero* (1967), directed by Nelson Pereira dos Santos, and *Todas as mulheres do mundo (All Women of the World*, 1967), directed by Domingos de Oliveira, and *Macunaíma* (1969), directed by Joaquim Pedro de Andrade, and *Azyllo muito louco (Crazy Nuthouse,* 1970)—directed by Nelson Pereira dos Santos, are a few examples of Cinema Novo films that use humor.

4. Leone, "Caliças no País das Maravilhas," 66, emphasis added.

5. *Folha de São Paulo,* June 14, 1981.

6. *Orfeu da Conceição (Black Orpheus),* which won the Grand Prize at the Cannes Film Festival in 1959, is an interesting case of a "Brazilian" film that appeals mainly to foreigners. It is almost totally unknown in Brazil. The story, an interpretation of the myth of Orpheus and Eurydice as it happens during a carnival in Rio de Janeiro, was originally a musical play written by Brazilian poet Marcus Vinícius de Moraes and published in 1956 under the title *Orfeu da Conceição.* The film *Orfeu negro* has a hauntingly evocative music score by Antonio Carlos Jobin and Luís Bonfá. The dialogue and the acting, however, are stilted and wooden to any native Portuguese speaker. Neither the producer, Sacha Grodine, nor the director, Marcel Camus, is Brazilian, so one could argue that the most famous Brazilian movie is, in crucial aspects, not Brazilian at all, even though made in Brazil, in Portuguese, with Brazilian actors and Brazilian music, after an original Brazilian play.

7. See Johnson, *The Film Industry in Brazil,* 168, table 22, which shows that foreign films attracted at least twice as many spectators as the Brazilian films during this period. Table 25 shows that in 1980 Brazilian films captured only 30.8 percent of the market.

8. On Cinema Novo, see ibid.

9. Qtd. in Festa, "Brazilian Cinema Loses Its Way," 6, emphasis added.

10. Ibid.

11. Bernadet, *Brasil em Tempo de Cinema,* 38; Martins, "Artigo sobre Aristocratas," 158.

12. Vieira and Stam define *chanchada* as "a derogatory epithet created by hostile mainstream critics." The genre, intimately linked to the world of carnival, refers "to a

body of films (made between the early 30s and continuing in modified form up to the present) featuring predominantly comic plots interspersed with musical numbers" (Vieira and Stam, *Brazilian Cinema,* 25).

13. Compare the example of Mexico, where North American film was also appropriated for specific Mexican needs. Just as in this period Brazilian films featured the *chanchada* and melodrama (and Argentinian films developed the tango melodrama genre in the 1930's), the Mexican films of the period between 1930 and 1950 also relied heavily on melodrama. Ana López writes, "This was the first indigenous cinema to dent the Hollywood industry's pervasive presence in Latin America; the first consistently to circulate Latin American images, voices, songs, and history; the first to capture and sustain the interest of multi-national audiences throughout the continent for several decades" ("Celluloid Tears," 29–30). The exportation of cinema and film technology has been, since its inception, appropriated as a means of disciplining—or coercing—the budding third world movie industry. López points out that whereas the Office of the Coordinator of Inter-American Affairs (a branch of the State Department) encouraged the development of Mexican cinema, with loans and unlimited access to raw film stock, it mounted a campaign against Argentina. Interestingly, since Brazil posed no special threat or interest to the United States during the Second World War, neither restrictive nor protective measures were taken in relation to the Brazilian cinema.

14. The limitation of quotas of raw film stock was used during World War II to punish Argentina's "subborn neutrality," writes López. At the same time, the Mexican movie industry was encouraged with "loans, equipment, and an unlimited supply of raw film stock." These restrictions "effectively curtailed Argentina's productive capacity: by the end of the war, Mexican films had practically replaced the once popular Argentine features in the Latin American market" (ibid., 48).

15. Another example is the "Cinema Marginal," which occurred in Brazil between 1969 and 1973. See F. Ramos, *Cinema Marginal.*

16. Lambert, *Latin America,* 85; Burns, *A History of Brazil,* 467.

17. F. Ramos, "Os novos rumos do cinema brasileiro," 351.

18. The translation of the name of Graciliano Ramos's novel, *Vidas Secas,* as *Barren Lives* suggests that the lives portrayed are not ever going to bear fruit. However, the adjective *secas* (dry) does not necessarily mean barren. Indeed, the end of the novel makes it clear that the lives of the characters will continue and perhaps even prosper somewhere else beyond the dry, drought-ridden farm where they spend the action of the story.

19. See Rocha, *Revolução do cinema novo (Revolution of Cinema Novo).*

20. Schroeder de Oliveira, *Mazzaropi, A saudade de um povo,* 95.

21. "Ação popular tenta preservar acervo artístico," *Jornal do Comércio,* Sept. 1, 1984.

22. This is typical of a developing cinema. As López reminds us, the mother is also an obsessive presence in Mexican cinema, and she represents various identity anxieties peculiar to the Mexican history as a country founded on the rape of the mother (López,

"Celluloid Tears," 32–34). See also Jean Franco, *The Modern Culture of Latin America*.

23. Being a "Turk" is a joke in itself. In provincial Brazil, anybody who speaks with a different accent and is not either German (any blue-eyed person) or Japanese, is called a "Turk"; Arabs, Jews, or any foreigner with dark hair and/or deals in commerce are lumped under this term. When *Candinho* was made—if not today—for Brazilians outside the major urban centers, the concept of "foreign" was as sketchy as the the concept of the totality of Brazilians. On *caipiras'* views of foreigners, see Cândido, *Os parceiros do Rio Bonito*, esp. 84–87.

24. Querino Neto, "Mazzaropi," 56. Querino Neto argues that Mazzaropi bought the right to use this character from the Medicamentos Fontoura company, for which Monteiro Lobato had developed his Jeca Tatuzinho in 1919. The credits for *Jeca Tatu* mention that the the film is based on Monteiro Lobato's story, but nothing is said about purchasing the rights to use it.

25. The word *caipira* sounds like the Tupi word *caipora*, from which it most likely derives. Caipora, or Curupira, is the name of a devil/trickster whose feet are turned toward the back of his body. In the mythology, the *caipora* tricks his victims into believing that he is going when he is coming, and thus he can catch them by surprise and defeat them. *Caipira* has become the favorite epithet applied to those people who are shy, live in the interior of the country, and are not accustomed to the social ways of the city. Another word used interchangeably with *caipira* is *jacu*, also of Tupi origin (Cunha, *Dicionário Etimológico Nova Fronteira da Língua Portuguesa*). In the language of Brazil, *jacu* is also the name of a very shy bird, common in most forests.

26. See Cândido, *Os parceiros do Rio Bonito*, 57–66. Although Cândido does not mention Mazzaropi, when he was doing his research and collecting data for his book (1947–1954), the artist was presenting *caipira* culture and its problems on the screen, especially through Jeca Tatu. See also Cornélio Pires, *Conversas ao Pé do Fogo (Conversations by the Fire)*, from which Cândido quotes profusely in *Os parceiros do Rio Bonito*.

27. "Gente," *Fatos e Fotos*, December 25, 1978.

28. *Cangaceiro* is name given to bandits from the Northeast of Brazil. Their most famous leader was Virgulino Lampião, whose gang terrorized the backlands of the Northeast—*o sertão*—for years during the 1930s. *Cangaceiros* wore distinctive leather outfits and acquired a reputation for defending social justice, since they purported to rob the rich and distribute the loot among the poor.

29. These three films recall the scene in *Candinho*, when he is made to confront other "Brazilians" who can barely speak Portuguese but who are given more privileges because they seem to enjoy a higher social position. Of course, the texts might be seen as suggesting that there is no problem with accepting persons not born in Brazil into full citizenship, as long as the local *caipira* does not become a foreigner in his own land.

30. Williams, *Marxism and Literature*, 114.

31. Querino Neto, "Mazzaropi," 56.

32. Mazzaropi, quoted in ibid., 58.

33. "O cinema nacional perde seu Jeca," *Folha de São Paulo*, June 14, 1981.

34. Fiske, *Reading the Popular,* 135.

35. Mulvey, "Melodrama In and Out of the Home," 93.

36. "Cannibalism," or "Antropofágia," is the name of a literary movement that had its origin in São Paulo in the 1920s. The members of the group heading the movement were mostly part of the "coffee aristocracy" (*aristocracia do café,* the landed elite who owned enormous coffee-producing farms). The movement called for recognition of the cannibalization of the foreign in Brazilian culture. See Martins, *The Modernist Idea;* Jackson, "Three Glad Races."

37. M. de Andrade, *Macunaíma,* 127. This novel, published by a Brazilian modernist in 1928, was made into film by Joaquim Pedro de Andrade in 1969, winning critical acclaim (receiving the best actor and best screenplay awards from the INC—National Cinema Institute—for that year) and enormous box office success.

38. I obtained this data in informal research done in 1993–1994 in several video stores in Maringá and Londrina, state of Paraná; Campinas, state of São Paulo; Recife, state of Pernambuco; Natal, state of Rio Grande do Norte; and Fortaleza, state of Ceará.

Chapter 3. The Case of Venezuelan *Telenovelas*

Unless otherwise noted, translations in this chapter are by Eva Bueno.

1. López, *La radio,* 256.

2. Martín-Barbero, *De los medios a las mediaciones,* 84.

3. Capriles, "La (Tele)Novela por entregas," III:4.

4. Garmendia, "La telenovela en Venezuela."

5. Beltrán Carías, "José Antonio Guevara," B-27.

6. Modleski, *Loving with a Vengeance,* 33.

7. Héctor Abad Faciolince, "La telenovela," 63.

8. Pasquali, *El orden reina,* 289.

9. Colomina, "Prójimos exquisitos vx. telenovelas," 40.

10. Martín-Barbero, *De los medios a las mediaciones,* 20.

11. Adler, *Understanding Television,* 83.

12. Martín-Barbero, *De los medios a las mediaciones,* 28; this means that in Latin America the hour of the *telenovela* becomes also an aesthetic phenomenon, which magnifies daily life through mediation. "What television produces does not answer solely to demands made by the industrial system or by commercial stratagems, but to exigencies which come from the cultural needs and ways of seeing" (ibid., 20); furthermore, television itself "does not work unless it assumes—and by assuming legitimates—requests from the receiving groups; however, on the other hand, it cannot legitimate these requests without resignifying them in terms of the hegemonic social discourse" (ibid., 20).

13. Martín-Barbero, *De los medios a las mediaciones,* 14.

14. Colomina, "Telenovelas," 4.

15. Ibid., 6; compare Adler's statement that the rules and conventions of melo-

drama must be seen as "the enabling conditions for an encounter with forbidden or deeply disturbing materials: not an escape into blindness and easy reassurance, but an instrument for seeing" (*Understanding Television,* 76). In sum, the melodrama becomes "a peculiarly significant public forum, complicated and immensely enriched because its discourse is aesthetic and broadly popular: a forum or arena in which traditional ways of feeling and thinking are brought into continuous, strained relation with powerful institutions of change and contingency" (ibid.).

16. Rowe and Schelling, *Memory and Modernity,* 232.

17. See also Barros-Lémez, *Vidas da papel.*

18. Allen, *Speaking of Soap Operas,* 9.

19. González, *Llorar es un placer,* 37.

20. López, *La radio,* 236.

21. Another antecedent of the radionovela was the *radioteatro.* It was composed of "dramas and comedies written for the theater, with the necessary cuts made for the radio time, and with slight modifications in the dialogue, made on the printed book which the artists used" (López, *La radio,* 101). Common formulas include the "drama of recognition" (of the son by the father, or of the mother by the son); melodramatic themes of love and of the universal archetypes of man and woman. Radionovelas were peopled by persecuted and innocent heroines, good and virtuous heroes, and the violent and revengeful villains. Furthermore, they replaced the idyllic past where the nobles, the prince and the great lady with the space of the home; it substituted the foreign city, the club life, the high society for a whole set of social relations meant to help people elevate themselves to better social positions.

22. Quiroz, "La telenovela peruana," 118.

23. Klagsbrunn, "The Brazilian Telenovela," 17.

24. Mazziotti, *El espectáculo de la pasión,* 13.

25. Martín-Barbero, *De los medios a las mediaciones,* 40.

26. Mazziotti, *El espetáculo de la pasión,* 16.

27. The success of this *telenovela* does not rest solely in the opportunistic use of current subjects nor in the symbiosis between actor and stereotype; rather, it can be argued that its success rests in the very well planned and executed commercial campaign which presented its characters. Each ad "was a micro-program full of humor and malice. It was a space disposed to stir controversy and a brilliant way to convert the audience into accomplices of the *telenovela*" ("Contra la pared," 88). During its first six months, the *telenovela* maintained an average of 60 percent of the audience, and it made no less than ten million bolívares every day in the twenty minutes of commercials (ibid., 111).

28. Hellinger, *Venezuela: Tarnished Democracy,* 194.

29. Ibid., 189–97.

30. See Lovera De-Sola, *El oficio,* 61–82.

31. *Por estas calles* developed characters that did not fit the usual patterns: Mauro Sarría Vélez, a drug dealer who falls in love with the protagonist of the story; Natalio Vega, a commissioner who imposed his private justice, and, finally, for the first time ever

in Venezuelan *telenovela*, a protagonist couple composed of nonwhites, Eloína Rangel and Eudomar Padilla.

32. Giarroco, "La Telenovela," n.p.

33. Cárdenas, "Por estas calles," 12.

34. Prieto, "Vuelve la telenovela cultural," 50.

35. Liscano, "Otra vez," 7.

36. Prieto, "Vuelve la telenovela cultural," 51.

37. García Mackle, "Por estas calles," 5.

38. Levy, "Denuncia y romance en *Por estas calles*." B-21.

39. Prieto, "Vuelve la telenovela cultural," 51.

40. Montañes, "El fenómeno de *Por estas calles,* 32.

41. "Contra la pared," *Producto,* 82.

42. The Venezuelan *telenovela*, until 1977, was in the hands of a series of Cuban and Argentine writers to whom what mattered was not the reality of the country, but the possibility of telling a love story full of obstacles. *Por estas calles* evidently changed both the focus and the techniques of the *telenovela*.

43. Giarroco, "La Telenovela," n.p.

44. Colomina, "Telenovelas," 23.

45. The Mexican *telenovela, Nothing Personal* (1996), "is the most popular night time *telenovela* produced by TV Azteca, a new network born three years ago . . . [the *telenovela*] broke with the formula that Mexican serial melodramas have used for decades: grownup fairy tales in which true loves are united in the end and poor girls marry rich men. Instead, *Nothing Personal* is immersed in the raw politics and violence of modern Mexico. . . . .The producers wove a plot laced with references to current political scandals. . . . The *telenovela* winds on through a maze of corrupt police and international drug traffickers all too familiar to Mexicans from their everyday lives" (Preston, "Soap Heroine Spurns Script, and Plot Thickens," A-4).

46. Anonymous letter, *El Heraldo,* 4.

47. García Márquez, "Hay que hacer culebrones, pero de buena calidad," B-24.

48. Martínez, "Ultimo capítulo," B-18.

49. Martínez, "Ibsen privadito," 11.

50. Ibid.

51. Cabrujas, qtd. in Hippolyte, "José Ignacio Cabrujas," 260.

52. Rowe and Schelling, *Memory and Modernity,* 109.

53. Giarroco, "La telenovela."

Chapter 4. From *Mafalda* to *Boogie*

1. In 1993, Ricardo Piglia published *La Argentina en pedazos,* a selection of the most celebrated Argentinian cartoonists, which includes his own collaborations with the graphic humor magazine, *Fierro,* a leading publication in the field.

2. Joaquín Salvador Lavado, or Quino, was born in Mendoza Province. Discovering a fondness of graphic humor at the age of three, he studied at the School of Fine Arts in Mendoza, then tried his luck in Buenos Aires. Unable to get work as an artisan, he joined the army, then landed a job in the capital as a graphic humorist. In 1962, *Mafalda*, his most well-known creation, was born. Although the immensely popular comic strip was translated into several languages and even made into a film, Quino decided to end it in 1973 because he felt it was becoming redundant and he had ceased to enjoy its creation. He left Argentina, sojourned in Italy, and is now a Spanish citizen.

3. From a younger generation than Quino, Roberto Fontanarrosa continues the wave of authors—including Quino, as well as Caloi, Viuti, Crist, and others—who combine wit, sarcasm, and humor not only to safeguard the Southern Hemisphere's tradition of graphic humor, but also to elevate the comic strip to the level of the weekly literary reviews. In addition to Boogie, Fontanarrosa has created other popular characters, such as the gaucho Inodoro Pereyra, especially favored in Argentina. In addition, he has written several novels, has published nine volumes of Inodoro Pereyra, five of Boogie, a text on the eternal Argentine passion of soccer, a mock treatise on classics, and a manual for long-lasting relationships.

4. Martín-Barbero, *De los medios a las mediaciones*.

5. The numbering follows Quino's system of identification for *Mafalda* episodes.

6. Resnick and Speck, "Quino after Mafalda."

7. De Certeau, *The Practice of Everyday Life*.

8. Dorfman and Mattelart, *Para leer al Pato Donald (How to Read Donald Duck)*.

9. Hernández, *Para leer a Mafalda*, 13.

10. Dorfman and Mattelart, *Para leer al Pato Donald*, 77.

11. Steimberg, *Leyendo historietas*.

12. See where, for example, thanks to her innate competence as a *flaneuse*, Mafalda seems to deduce that the country marches backward (462), or, elsewhere, that there is the possibility of truths unknown to the masses (1030).

13. Saldías, *Páginas literarias*, 63.

14. López Peña, *Teoría del argentino*, 29.

15. It is only thanks to *Boogie's* success that Fontanarrosa has achieved wide recognition. "Inodoro Pereyra," his other character—vastly more popular in Argentina—reproduces a hypernationalistic context, making its assimilation in neighboring countries more difficult.

16. There are no page numbers for *Boogie* cartoons, so strips are identified by title, followed by the number of the volume in which they appeared. See Fontanarrosa, *Boogie el aceitoso*, vols. 1–2, 5.

17. "Una vieja película" was published in a Mexican weekly, *Proceso* 869 (June 28, 1998): 66.

18. See Martín-Barbero, *De los medios a los mediaciones*, 233, for a definition.

Chapter 5. Framing the Peruvian *Cholo*

1. One such on-line source, Ceramica Chulucanas, http://www.ascinsa.com/chulucanas, advertises the ceramic art from the Chulucanas region. Davies and Fini, *Arts and Crafts of South America*, identify thirty-nine locations in thirteen countries where such art is for sale.

2. David Rockefeller, qtd. in Appiah, *In My Father's House*, 138.

3. Jauss, "History of Art and Pragmatic History," 418.

4. The term *cholo* carries other meanings outside Peru; among Mexicans and Mexican Americans, the term refers to derelicts or gang members, while in Colombia, one group of indigenous people is called the Cholo Indians.

5. Mörner, *The Andean Past*, 63.

6. Handelman, *Struggles in the Andes*, 278.

7. Bunster and Chaney, *Sellers and Servants*, ix.

8. Vargas Llosa, *El Pez en el Agua*, 11; translated by Helen Lane as *A Fish in the Water: A Memoir*, 5.

9. Appiah, *In My Father's House*, 38.

10. Ibid., 44.

11. Mörner, *The Andean Past*, 63, emphasis added.

12. Orlove ("Putting Race in Its Place") uses the term in exploring the history of Peruvian geography as it relates to ordering impulses, including the "hegemonic impulse" that organizes the terrain with regard to social prerogatives, particularly racism.

13. Handelman, *Struggles in the Andes*, 278.

14. We rely on Heidegger ("The Origin of the Work of Art") who argues that artist, art, and the works themselves create each other. Thus, as we put forth each of these separately, we attempt to understand their interdependence.

15. Remember Frantz Fanon's notion that the artist who takes on his people as subject "cannot go forward resolutely unless he first realizes the extent of his own estrangement from them" (qtd. in Appiah, *In My Father's House*, 61).

16. Among this group of artists are Arcadio Boyer, Jorge Vega Iman, Segundo Cambo Celi, Segundo Gallardo Gallo, Abel Sanchez, Kayo Olaya, Nacho Olaya, and Mauricio. Boyer, for example, has gained international fame with exhibitions throughout South America, Europe, and the United States. Consult the Galería de Arte in Lima: galeria@ascinsa.com.pe.

17. Davies and Fini, *Arts and Crafts of South America*.

18. Among those artists are Santodio Paz and Max Inga.

19. Davies and Fini, *Arts and Crafts of South America*, 124–25.

20. Brochure from "El Artesano" gallery, Lima.

21. Davies and Fini, *Arts and Crafts of South America*, 125.

22. "El Mar y las Escenas en la Pintura Regional," vi.

23. See Alloula, *The Colonial Harem*, for a discussion of how visual arts can be used

to send a message back to the colonizer—specifically, how the colonizer's gaze can be revealed in the gaze of the colonized.

24. Heidegger, "The Origin of the Work of Art," 34.

25. Jameson, *Postmodernism*, 7.

26. Appiah, *In My Father's House*, 142.

27. Donum Fine Arts and Crafts catalogue: www.gift-shop.com/donum/pottery.

28. The phrase is also used to describe and criticize an abusive relationship occurring in the mestizo or white community.

29. Berger, *Ways of Seeing*, 60–61.

30. Vargas Llosa, "Questions of Conquest," 52.

31. Donum Fine Arts and Crafts catalogue.

32. Appiah, *In My Father's House*, 143.

33. Ibid.

34. Duthurburu, *El Mestizaje en El Peru*, 82.

35. Jameson, *Postmodernism*, 48.

Chapter 6. You're All Guilty

1. See the *Miami Herald* and *El Nuevo Herald* for the week of July 12, 1996.

2. *Miami Herald*, July 12, 1996.

3. Ibid., July 14, 1996.

4. González Echevarría, "Autobiography and Representation," 569.

5. González Echevarría, *Alejo Carpentier: The Pilgrim at Home*, 280.

6. I use the term *postrevolutionary* to refer to all culture affected by the revolutionary process since 1959.

7. Guevara, *Obra revolucionaria*, 636.

8. Leante, "Confesión en clave de morse."

9. In "Beyond the Rupture," Los Angeles Torres refers to the double notion of betrayal that Cuban American border crossers face in communities in South Florida and Cuba: "There is little room for negotiations between power structures in the exile community and those in Havana. One does not let you go back because the act of returning is treason; the other doesn't let you return because the act of leaving is treason" (434).

10. De Man, *Allegories of Reading*, 279.

11. Manzor-Coats discounts the theory that Cuban culture is "drastically split into two: the one produced 'there,' in the island, and the one produced 'here' in the U.S. Cuban colony." Such a theory is anachronistic and fails to recognize that much of Cuban culture has been produced outside the island ("Performative Identites: Scenes Between Two Cubas," 748).

12. Jorge Mañach writes, "Since its operation consists of reducing the importance of things, in other words, in stopping these things from affecting us too much, *choteo* arises in all situations where the Cuban spirit is affected by an . . . inflexible authority" (cited in ibid., 85).

13. Acosta, "Cine: Titón y la obsesión de hacer 'otro cine' en Cuba."

14. Wockner, "Cuban Drags Let Their Hair Down." According to the Associated Press, the international success of the film has been followed by "drag shows" both in underground and above-ground cabarets. Even the "traditionally conservative unions, strongly tied to the (Communist) party, are hiring transvestites to entertain their members." In addition, a drag queen named Margot became one of the main characters on Cuba's most popular TV program, "El Sabadazo" (ibid.).

15. West, "Strawberry and Chocolate," 16.

16. Ibid.

17. Other Cuban films like *Death of a Bureaucrat* (1966) and *Se permuta* (1984) do not subvert Cuba's political myths, but rather ridicule those who are unwilling or unable to live according to revolutionary ideals.

18. *Strawberry and Chocolate* can be compared to Néstor Almendros's film, *Improper Conduct* (1984), which documents the infamous UMAP work camps (Unidades Militares de Ayuda de Producción), thereby registering both the repression and the personal tragedy of thousands of Cuban homosexuals and transvestites.

19. Smith, "The Language of Strawberry," 31.

20. Wockner, "Cuban Gays Are Out and Precocious."

21. Perugorría, according to Paul Julian Smith, has been "at pains to point out in interviews that he is not himself gay" (qtd. in ibid., 31).

22. Could the directors' choice of actors reflect the concern that a homosexual actor could not look gay enough for a straight audience? Directors have, after all, presented Al Jolson in blackface and Orson Welles playing Othello. *Strawberry and Chocolate*'s ending is particularly revealing in this respect when Diego and David sit down at the Copellia, playfully inverting the roles, as if being gay was equivalent to acting effeminate and speaking with a lisp.

23. Jimper, "Rotten Strawberries and Bitter Chocolate."

24. E. González, "Framing Carpentier," 427.

25. Ibid., 424; González Echevarría, *The Pilgrim at Home*, 286–87.

26. *El arpa y la sombra (The Harp and the Shadow)*, 299.

27. Bakhtin, *Art and Answerability*, 146. Although there are some differences, Bakhtin would call this character a *pretender*, a term he uses to describe the condition of falsity of self. This is the case of the subject who confuses (or openly chooses) the social self in exchange for the inner self. The pretender also rejects responsibility for his or her condition; he or she is answerable neither to the self nor to the other. The pretender finds an alibi for existence, trying to live in no definite space (Morson and Emerson, *Mikhail Bakhtin*, 180–81). Bakhtin's analysis of the pretender examines the socially alienated figures of Dostoevsky's *Notes from the Underground, Poor Folk* (*Problems of Dostoevsky's Poetics*, 181–269), and in *The Idiot* (*Art and Answerability*, 146).

28. Bakhtin, *Art and Answerability*, 146.

29. Carpentier, *El arpa y la sombra*, 283.

30. Without specifically discussing the confession in *El arpa y la sombra*, Julie Jones also observes the juxtaposition of styles in this novel ("Carpentier's *El arpa y la sombra*," 92).

31. Carpentier, *El arpa y la sombra*, 291.

32. Ibid., 325.

33. For similar characterizations in Carpentier's work, see the chapter on the narrator in *Los pasos perdidos* in Pérez-Firmat, *The Cuban Condition*.

34. Carpentier, *El arpa y la sombra*, 335.

35. Cabrera Infante, *Mea Cuba*, 18.

36. Ibid., 19.

37. Ibid., 480.

38. Ibid., 437.

39. De Man, *Allegories of Reading*, 75–76.

40. Cabrera Infante, *Mea Cuba*, 77.

41. Ibid., 78.

42. Ibid.

43. Ibid., 332–33.

44. Two AM radio stations in Miami, WQBA-AM (La Cubanísima) and Radio Mambí (WAQI-AM), played a strong role in opposing Rosita Fornés's visit to Miami. Both consider themselves hard-liners, adamantly opposing dialogue and the United States' establishing diplomatic relations with Castro's Cuba. However, the *Miami Herald* states that this extreme position is not nearly as strong as it once was. The primary audience for Radio Mambí, the highest-rated AM station, are persons sixty-five and older.

45. Zéndegui, *Todos somos culpables (We're All Guilty)*, 151.

46. Behar, "Queer Times in Cuba," 856.

47. De Man, *Allegories of Reading*, 280.

Chapter 7. The *Cueca* of the Last Judgment

The author thanks the University of Toledo Research, Awards, and Fellowships Programs (URAFP), the Biblioteca Nacional de Santiago de Chile, and the Biblioteca de Teatro de la Universidad Católica de Chile for their support. All translations in this chapter, unless otherwise noted, are by Eva Bueno.

1. See Constable and Valenzuela, *Chile Under Pinochet*. The Comisión de Verdad y Reconciliación (Commission of Truth and Reconciliation), created soon after democracy was restablished in Chile, collected proof that 1,068 people were killed and 957 "disappeared," "victims of the agents of the State or of people working for the State" (Informe Rettig, *Informe de la Comisión Nacional de Verdad y Reconciliación*, 883).

2. See De la Luz Hurtado and Ochsenius, *T.I.T. Taller de Investigación Teatral* for a list of plays written and staged in the period.

3. The theatrical objective of TIT was to develop a theater with national and popu-

lar themes based on actual life. At the time, the theater was going through a deep crisis and trying to find solutions for the crisis (ibid.).

4. Agosín, "Agujas que hablan," 527.

5. Ibid. See also Agosín, "El bordado de la resistencia" and "Narraciones en Tapiz."

6. Agosín, "Agujas que hablan," 525.

7. Benavente and T.I.T., *Tres Marías y una Rosa*, 206. Further references to the play will be given in the text. Members of the Taller de Investigación Teatral were Soledad Alonso, Luz Jiménez, Myriam Palacios, Loreto Valenzuela, and Raúl Osorio.

8. Rojo had poses the idea that the art of *arpillería* displayed in the play is also "a theatrical poetics. . . . This is an *arpilleras' art* which contains in its midst a theatrical art." This of course suggests that the "history of the Taller de Arpilleras—Arpilleras Workshop—is not essentially different from the history of the Taller de Investigación Teatral—The Workshop for Theatre Research" (*Muerte y resurrección*, 101).

9. Cirlot, *Diccionario de símbolos*, 310.

10. Bakhtin, *Problems*, 104.

11. Ibid.

12. See *Ercilla*, February 9, 1977, 14.

13. Lafourcade, "¿Por qué atacan a Florcita Motuda?"

14. *Tres Marías y una Rosa*, 245. *Fondas* are rustic wooden structures covered with leaves built in parks or private yards especially for the commemoration of the Chilean independence day on September 18–19. Traditional foods and drinks are sold in *fondas*, which also serve as spaces where people gather to dance the *cueca*.

15. Brecht, *Escritos sobre teatro*, 190. Elsewhere Brecht compares the spectator of the dramatic theater with that of the epic theater, who responds as follows: "I should never have thought so.—That is not the way to do it. —This is most surprising, hardly credible.—This will have to stop.—This human being's suffering moves me, because there would have been a way out for him.—This is great art: nothing here seems inevitable.—I am laughing about those who weep on the stage, weeping about those who laugh" (qtd. in Esslin, *Brecht*, 136).

16. Brecht, *Escritos sobre teatro*, 153.

17. Ibid., 91.

18. Iser, *The Act of Reading*, 169, 170.

19. Gadamer, *Warheit und Methode*, 251.

20. The writer and journalist Patricia Verdugo suffered one of the most dramatic and well-known cases: the cadaver of her father, a Socialist Christian union leader, appeared floating in the Mapocho. This gave her the strength to write a series of books in which she investigated and denounced the attacks on human rights committed by the military dictatorship. See her testimony in Narváez, *La invención de la memoria*, 105.

21. Goldmann, "La sociología y la literatura," 12.

22. Ibid., 14.

23. Benavente, "'Ave Felix,'" 313–18.

24. This note, entitled "Política," appeared in the section "Top Secret," *La Segunda,* July 31, 1979.

Chapter 8. Tango, Buenos Aires, Borges
References to tangos will first give the name of the lyricist, then the composer.

1. For example, the *Insight City Guide* for Buenos Aires includes an essay by Judith Evans.

2. On the recurring themes of the tango, see Corbatta, "El tango: letras y visión del mundo"; Sábato, *Tango, disusion y clave.*

3. See Matamoro, *La ciudad del tango,* on the relationship between the tango and Buenos Aires; Lara and Roncetti de Panti, *El tema del tango en la literatura argentina,* provides the best overview of the tango from a literary point of view.

4. Alfredo Le Pera and Carlos Gardel, "Volvió una noche," in Albuquerque, *Antología de tangos,* 248–49.

5. Foster, "Narrative Rights."

6. Under the broad aegis of masculinism, the will to sexual allegiance is always more of an imperative for men than it is for women, as men are more called upon to prove their masculinity than women their femininity. This does not mean to imply that a woman's femininity is never called into question in societies such as those associated with the tango; it only means that the tango never makes any issue of femininity, much less the question of a woman's sexual worth in terms of the ability to bear children. Virtuous mothers are fairly common in the tango— Alfredo Le Pera and Carlos Gardel, "Silencio en la noche" ("Silence in the Night"), for example—and bad women who run out on husband, home, and children may be mentioned, but there is little interest in decrying barren women.

7. This "voyeurism," in turn, underscores both the relationship between private and public, as well as how public domains exercise the right to contemplate the private, even if only through how real lives are modeled on the fictional characters of cultural texts. Nevertheless, we must distinguish between the public enactment of cultural products and the features of public life–private life made public that they model.

8. Homero Manzi and Aníbal Troilo, "Barrio de tango," in Albuquerque, *Antología de tangos,* 99.

9. Cf. Mafud, *Sociología del tango*; Castro, *The Argentine Tango*; Vila, "Tango to Folk"; Collier, "The Popular Roots of the Argentine Tango."

10. "Cafetín de Buenos Aires" ("Café of Buenos Aires") by Enrique Santos Discépolo and Mariano Mores, in Albuquerque, *Antología de tangos,* 8.

11. See López Badano, *Violencia de género en los medios de comunicación social argentinos,* on masculine violence in the tango.

12. See Katz, *The Invention of Heterosexuality.*

13. The tango has noticeably little to say about gays, except for vague references to

men who are feminized not by virtue of their sexual preference, but by belonging to higher classes—that is, the sleek and fancy dudes who steal women away from their neighborhood lovers, only to abandon them for fresher meat after dishonoring them, often leaving them pregnant, with little choice but to become prostitutes.

14. See Bossio, *Los cafés de Buenos Aires.*

15. Cf. Charly García's magnificently outrageous rock version of the Argentine national anthem, one of the primary icons of the armed forces; see Fernández Bitar, *Historia del rock en Argentina*; Marzullo and Muñoz, *El rock en la Argentina.*

16. Paoletti, "Borges y la ciudad del tango," 98.

17. Goloboff, "La ciudad de Borges"; Salas, "Buenos Aires, mito y obsesión"; Albert Robatto, *Borges, Buenos Aires y el tiempo*, 61–110.

18. Of greater interest for a purely formal analysis would be how Borges metonymizes Buenos Aires: how he selects specifically salient features and then undertakes to conjugate those features with sets of associations. In this way, Borges confirms his belief that texts evoke other texts, beginning with how lexemes evoke other lexemes (or, on an even more fundamental level, how sememes—basic units of meaning that underlie lexemes—evoke other sememes) as well as how the human comprehension of experiential reality takes place along a sliding scale of signifiers.

19. Dorfman, "Borges y la violencia humana."

20. Altamiranda, "Jorge Luis Borges"; Brant, "The Mark of the Phallus."

21. Therefore, there is little room for Borges in books on Buenos Aires where literary compositions accompany photographs or other representations of the city, such as *Buenos Aires, mi ciudad* (Universidad de Buenos Aires, 1963) and Miguel Rep, *Y Rep hizo los barrios* (published in 1993 by the oppositional daily *Páginas/12*). In the former, where nostalgic black-and-white photographs evoke the cityscape of the 1950s and 1960s (the end of seigneurial Buenos Aires, brought about by the emergence of the popular classes under Peronism), Borges appears four times. In the latter volume, where the photographs evoke the neoliberal transformations imposed by the military dictatorships and vigorously continued by current administrations, Borges is not represented once among forty-eight texts.

22. Cf. Savigliano, *Tango and the Political Economy of Passion*, 31, on Borges and the *compadrito.*

23. Borges, "El hombre de la esquina rosada," in *Historia universal de la infamia, Obras Completas*, vol. 3.

24. Borges, "Fundación mítica de Buenos Aires," in *Obras Completas*, 3:81.

25. Ibid.

26. "'El tango," from *El otro, el mismo* (1964) in *Obras Completas*, 3:888.

27. Ibid.

28. Ibid., 3:889.

29. Once more, we understand that violence in the tango is always about the affairs of men—and not just in the end, but from beginning to end, which is why a tango about

women's lives in any feminist sense of the phrase would be inconceivable. Even a tango like "Malena," for example, concerns Malena as a participant in the male-dominated world of the tango: "Malena baila el tango"—"Malena dances the tango."

30. Originally, *milongas* were the parties in which tango was danced. The word has a connotation of bajo fondo—lascivious dancing and dangerous women (prostitutes). These same women who danced in these dance halls for a fee, were metonimically called "milongas." Thus the tango "Milonguita"—and many others that speak about the life experience of these young women from the suburbs who, starting in the first decades of the twentieth century, came to the modern center of the city of Buenos Aires to dance in high class nighclubs—cabarets.

31. "El tango," from *El otro, el mismo* (1964), in *Obras Completas*, 3:889.

Chapter 9. Myth, Modernity, and Postmodern Tragedy in *The Dolphin*

1. Dolphin do drive fish from an area, rounding them up with scout dolphins who chase them from the shallows near the beach to the waiting pack members (Ellis, *Dolphins and Porpoises*, 8–9; Bel'Kovich, "Herd Structure, Hunting, and Play," 42–43).

2. Segal, "Sex Roles and Reversals in Euripides' *Bacchae*," 190.

3. Girard, *Violence and the Sacred*, 10–12. In "La Pharmacie de Platon," Derrida shows how philosophy, from Plato to Nietzsche (who took a contrary stand), has attempted to establish an absolute difference between the two meanings of *pharmakon*— "poison" and "remedy"—when in fact both meanings designate the scapegoat, and so difference is ultimately undermined by symmetry.

4. I refer to the myth of Iphigenia and not specifically to Euripides' posthumously produced play *Iphigenia in Aulis*, though the parallels are striking.

5. Vattimo, *The Transparent Society*, 28–44, and *passim*, develops this view in great detail. Here I follow his meditations.

6. González Echevarría, *Myth and Archive*, 150.

7. Cinema Novo (New Cinema) refers to the films made by young Brazilian cineastes such as Carlos Diegues, Joaquim Pedro de Andrade, and Walter Lima Jr. from the early 1960s to approximately 1972. In general terms, Cinema Novo was a movement against commercial or Hollywood films and the values they represented. It specifically addressed many of the social and artistic issues assiduously avoided by mainstream film.

8. Johnson and Stam, *Brazilian Cinema*, 32–50. King explains, "Cannibalism refers back to the Modernist movement of the 1920s culture when . . . Oswald de Andrade posed the provocative 'Tupy or not Tupy, that is the question' as part of his anthropophagous manifesto. Cannibalism is a form of wilful cultural nationalism, suggesting that the products of the first world can be digested and recycled by the colonized, as a way of countering economic, social, and cultural imperialism" (*Magical Reels*, 113). Products of the First World presumably include their myths.

9. Simons and Hughes, *The Culture-Bound Syndromes*, 10–15.

10. Ibid., 11.

11. The notion of myth as language reaches its apogee in Lévi-Strauss, *Anthropologie Structurale,* which contains his study of Oedipus. See also Vernant, *Myth and Society in Ancient Greece* 203–60.

12. If the Freudian approach proclaims myths to be the symptomatic expression of "lower" unconscious desires, an alternative position, as with Eliade and Jung, would have it that myth is the expression of something "higher" beyond human understanding: the absolute, totality, the sacred.

13. Slater, *Dance of the Dolphin,* 9, 6.

14. Ibid., 9.

15. Examples are Zeitlin, "The Dynamics of Misogyny: Myth and Mythmaking in the *Oresteia*"; Lerner, *The Creation of Patriarchy;* and Case, "Classic Drag."

16. Malinowski, *Argonauts of the Western Pacific,* points out the gap between interpretations of a symbolist kind and the role myths actually play in societies in which they have stayed alive. Malinowski argues the role myth plays in a living society is very much different from that of bearer of eternal metaphysical truth assigned it in the symbolist interpretive field.

17. Slater may well object that my reading is hardly deprivileged.

18. Souza, *A resistível ascenção do Boto Tucuxi,* portrays the *boto* as another type of outsider, this time from the capital. Souza satirizes the power-hungry politician Gilberto Mestrinho who, in real life, in 1990 recaptured the governorship of Amazonas by taking the dolphin as his trademark.

19. Clifford, *The Predicament of Culture,* 22.

20. As Clifford describes it: "In the 1920s, the new field worker–theorist brought to completion a new powerful scientific and literary genre, the ethnography, a synthetic cultural description based on participant observation [which] may be briefly summarized as follows: . . . First, the persona of the field worker was validated, both publicly and professionally. In the popular domain, visible figures like Malinowsky, Mead, and Griaule communicated a vision of ethnography as both scientifically demanding and heroic, . . . the field worker was to live in the native village, use the vernacular, stay a sufficient (but seldom specified) length of time . . . the new ethnographer tended to focus thematically on particular institutions. . . . In the primarily synechdochic rhetorical stance of the new ethnography, parts were assumed to be microcosms or analogies of wholes" (ibid., 29–31).

21. Ibid., 41.

22. In Latin American literature, examples of this metadiscourse include works such as *Yo el supremo* and *Rayuela.*

23. Specifically, this was Nietzsche's position after *The Birth of Tragedy,* beginning with *Human All Too Human.*

24. Nietzsche, quoted in Deleuze and Guattari, *Anti-Oedipus,* 107.

25. Aristotle argued that since thought is both the subject and object of its opera-

tions, it iterates itself and so becomes the "prime mover." The psychoanthropological approach to the dolphin tales maintains Aristotle's equation with one slight permutation: "thought" becomes unconscious thought.

26. Rappaport, *Pigs for the Ancestors.*

27. Ibid., 254.

28. Wilden, *Man and Woman,* 103.

29. Sanday, *Female Power and Male Dominance,* 56, 67.

30. See C. Segal, "The Menace of Dionysus"; Bushnell, *Prophesying Tragedy.*

31. Girard, *Violence and the Sacred,* 287, 8.

32. Ibid., 49.

Chapter 10. *Like Water for Chocolate* and *The Silent War*
Translations from *The Silent War* are by Vincent Spina.

1. Olea, "Feminism: Modern or Postmodern?" 194.

2. Ibid.

3. Huyssen, *After the Great Divide,* 58.

4. Ibid., 62.

5. Barthes, *Empire of Signs,* 17–18.

6. Esquivel, *Like Water for Chocolate,* 93.

7. See Walker, *The Women's Encyclopedia.*

8. Joseph Campbell, *Primitive Mythology,* 224–25. Walker *(The Women's Encyclopedia)* also cites Campbell in her entry on Tlalteutli, and both agree on her importance in the mythology.

9. Saltz, "Laura Esquivel's *Como agua para chocolate,*" 32–33.

10. Grant, "La mujer-texto en *Como agua para chocolate,*" 51.

11. Esquivel, *Like Water for Chocolate,* 79.

12. Ibid., 45.

13. Campbell, *Primitive Mythology,* 224.

14. Saltz, "Laura Esquivel's *Como agua para chocolate,*" 38.

15. Esquivel, *Like Water for Chocolate,* 175.

16. Saltz, "Laura Esquivel's *Como agua para chocolate,*" 38.

17. Jaffee, "Hispanic American Women Writers' Novel Recipes," 228.

18. Oropesa, "*Como agua para chocolate* de Laura Esquivel," 259.

19. Huyssen, *After the Great Divide,* ix.

20. Saltz, "Laura Esquivel's *Como agua para chocolate,*" 30.

21. For discussions of Scorza in relation to other Latin American writers, see Schwartz, "Writing Paris into Contemporary Latin American Narrative"; Rojas-Trempe, "La alteridad indígena y mágica"; Campra, "América Latina: La identidad y la máscara"; and Fox-Lockert, "Vision del paisaje andino peruano en José María Arguedas y Manuel Scorza."

22. *The Silent War* is comprised of the following: (1) *Redoble por Rancas (The Uprising*

in Rancas [1983], 3rd ed. [Barcelona: Plaza y Janes Editora, 1987]); (2) *Garabombo, el Invisible* (*Garabombo, the Invisible* [Barcelona: Plaza y Janes Editora, 1984]); (3) *El Jinete Insomne* (*The Sleepless Horseman*, [Barcelona: Plaza y Janes Editora, 1984]); (4) *Cantar e Agapito Robles* (*The Song of Agapito Robles* [Barcelona: Plaza y Janes Editora, 1984]); (5) *La tumba del relámpago* (*Lightning's Grave* [1979], 4th ed. Bogotá: Sigo Veintiuno Editores, 1985).

   23. Bakhtin, *The Dialogic Imagination*, 27.

   24. Hernández J., "Crónica, historiografía e imaginación en las novelas de Scorza," 151, my translation.

   25. *Garabombo, el Invisible*, 14.

   26. Derrida, *Spurs: Nietzsche's Styles*, 36–40.

   27. *La tumba del relámpago*, 52.

   28. Ibid., 223.

Chapter 11. Masculinities at the Margins

   1. The concept of the nation as imagined community is borrowed from Anderson, *Imagined Communities*.

   2. L. Segal, "Changing Men," 635.

   3. L. Segal, *Slow Motion*, x.

   4. L. Segal, "Changing Men," 635.

   5. Bhabha, *Location of Culture*, 1.

   6. Pettit, *Images of the Mexican American*, 12.

   7. Ibid., 113.

   8. Muñoz, *Youth, Identity, Power*, 22–23.

   9. Ibid., 33.

   10. Ibid., 37.

   11. Ibid.

   12. Cosgrove, "The Zoot Suit and Style Warfare," 79.

   13. Paz, *El Laberinto de la Soledad*, 14. Given the history of California, "second-generation immigrants" is an ambiguous term, as many Mexican American communities are older than the Guadalupe-Hidalgo treaty. However, because of continued and large-scale immigration, there was a large population of second-generation immigrants in the early twentieth century, and they were important in the Mexican American culture of the thirties and forties.

   14. Monsiváis, "Tin Tan: Pachuco," 185.

   15. Tyler, "Zoot Suit Culture and the Black Press," 26.

   16. Spivak, *In Other Worlds*, 204.

   17. Clarke, "Style," 185.

   18. Cosgrove, "The Zoot Suit and Style Warfare," 77.

   19. See Hall, *Resistance Through Rituals*; Tyler, "Zoot Suit Culture and the Black

Press"; and Mazón, *The Zoot Suit Riots*.

20. Tyler, "Zoot Suit Culture and the Black Press," 27.

21. Cosgrove, "The Zoot Suit and Style Warfare," 77.

22. Herbert Marcuse, qtd. in Hall, *Resistance Through Rituals* 65.

23. Hall, *Resistance Through Rituals*, 65.

24. Cosgrove, "The Zoot Suit and Style Warfare," 80.

25. Carey McWilliams, qtd. in Mazón, *The Zoot Suit Riots*, 21.

26. Mazón, *The Zoot Suit Riots*, 28.

27. Ibid., 36.

28. Al Capp, qtd. in ibid., 34.

29. See Tyler, "Zoot Suit Culture and the Black Press."

30. Mazón, *The Zoot Suit Riots*, 52.

31. Ibid., 78.

32. Ibid.

33. Cândido, *Os parceiros do Rio Bonito.* 53.

34. DaMatta, *Carnivals, Rogues and Heroes* chap. 5.

35. Ibid., 233.

36. See Vasconcellos, "A malandragem e a formação da música popular brasileira," 518, on the *malandro's* antecedents.

37. Jesse, "The Discourse of Carioca Samba in the Vargas Era," 27.

38. Ibid., 29.

39. Ibid.

40. Tinhorão, *Música Popular,* 24–25.

41. Jesse, "The Discourse of Carioca Samba in the Vargas Era," 53–55.

42. Ibid., 59.

43. Ibid.

44. Matos, *Acertei no milhar,* 178.

45. Jesse, "The Discourse of Carioca Samba in the Vargas Era," 43.

46. Ibid., 42.

47. Matos, *Acertei no milhar,* 178.

48. Paz, *El Laberinto de la Soledad,* 14.

49. Muñoz, *Youth, Identity, Power,* 61.

50. Fregoso, "*Zoot Suit*—The 'Return to the Beginning,'" 270–72.

51. Valdez, *Zoot Suit,* in *Zoot Suit and Other Plays,* 25. Further references to the play will be given in the text.

52. *Zoot Suit* (Universal Pictures, 1981), written and directed by Luis Valdez, starring Edward James Olmos.

53. Fregoso, "The Representation of Cultural Identity in *Zoot Suit*," 666.

54. Fregoso, "*Zoot Suit*—The 'Return to the Beginning,'" 271).

55. Ibid., 274.

56. Ibid., 271.

57. Moi, "A New Type of Intellectual," 292.

58. The film, *Ópera do malandro,* of MK2 Productions and TF1 Films Productions, was released in 1986. The screenplay was written by Chico Buarque, Ruy Guerra, and Orlando Senna, and was directed by Ruy Guerra.

59. Berman, *All That Is Solid Melts into Air,* 112.

60. *Ópera do malandro,* 128.

61. Ibid., 27.

62. Ibid., 153.

63. Ibid., 356.

64. Schwartz, "Writing Paris into Contemporary Latin American Narrative," chap. 10.

65. Paz, *El Laberinto de la Soledad,* 19–20.

Bibliography

"Ação popular tenta preservar acervo artístico." *Jornal do Comércio*, 9.1.84.

Acosta, Dalia. "Cine: Titón y la obsesión de hacer 'otro cine' en Cuba." Online. Available: http://worldnews.net/wnews/rrlist/interpress/ipwire/miscelaneas/Cine:%20Titon 20y%20la%20obsesion%20de%20hacer%20'otro%20cine'%20en%20%20Cuba %20%20%20-%2019-04-96%20 15:03.

Adler, Richard P., ed. *Understanding Television. Essays on Television as a Social and Cultural Force*. New York: Prager, 1981.

Agosín, Marjorie. "Agujas que hablan: Las arpilleristas chilenas." *Revista Iberoamericana* 51 (1985): 523–29.

———. "El bordado de la resistencia: mujer, tapiz y escritura." *Plural* 233 (1991): 39–46.

———. "Narraciones en un tapiz: *Tres Marías y una Rosa*." *Alba de América. Revista Literaria* 7 (1989): 151–57.

———. *Tapestries of Hope, Threads of Love: The Arpillera Movement in Chile, 1974–1994*. Albuquerque: University of New Mexico Press, 1996.

Aguilera, Francisco de, S.J. *Sermón en que se da noticia de la vida admirable, virtudes heróicas y preciosa muerte de la venerable señora Catharina de San Juan, que falleció en perfección de vida y murió con aclamación de santidad en la ciudad de Puebla de los Angeles a cinco de enero de este año de 1688*. Mexico City: Impresa Nueva de Diego Fernández de León, 1688.

Alarcón, Norma. "Chicana's Feminist Literature: A Re-Vision Through Malintzin/ or Malintzin: Putting the Flesh Back on the Object." In *This Bridge Called My Back: Writings by Radical Women of Color*, ed. Cherríe Moraga and Gloria Anzaldúa, 182–190. New York: Kitchen Table Women of Color Press, 1983.

Albert Robatto, Matilde. *Borges, Buenos Aires y el tiempo*. Río Piedras, P.R.: Editorial Edil, 1972.

Albo, Xavier. "Our Identity Starting from Pluralism in the Base." In *The Postmodern Debate in Latin America*, ed. Beverley, Oviedo, and Aronna, 18–33.

Albuquerque, M. A. *Antología de tangos*. 8th ed. Mexico City: Medina, 1970.

Allen, Carolyn J. "Feminist Criticism and Postmodernism." In *Tracing Literary Theory*, ed. Joseph Natoli, 278–305. Urbana: University of Illinois Press, 1987.

Allen, Robert C. *Speaking of Soap Operas.* Chapel Hill: University of North Carolina Press, 1950.

Alloula, Mark. *The Colonial Harem.* Trans. Myrna Godzich and Wlad Godzich. Minneapolis: University of Minnesota Press, 1986.

Altamiranda, Daniel. "Jorge Luis Borges." In *Latin American Writers on Gay and Lesbian Themes: A Bio-Critical Sourcebook,* ed. David William Foster, 72–83. Westport, Conn.: Greenwood Press, 1994.

Almeida, M. A. de. *Memórias de um sargento de milícias.* São Paulo: Editora Moderna, 1987.

Anderson, Benedict. *Imagined Communities: Reflections on the Origin and Spread of Nationalism.* Rev. ed. London: Verso, 1991.

Andrade, Mário de. *Macunaíma.* Trans. E. A. Goodland. New York: Random House, 1984.

Andrade, Luis G. "Se levantará un monumento a la china poblana." In Carrasco Puente, *Bibliografía de Catarina de San Juan y de la China poblana,* 3–9.

Appiah, Kwame Anthony. *In My Father's House: Africa in the Philosophy of Culture.* New York: Oxford University Press, 1992.

Appadurai, Arjun. "Disjuncture and Difference in the Global Cultural Economy." *Public Culture* 2 (spring 1990): 1–23.

———. *Modernity at Large. Cultural Dimensions of Globalization.* Minneapolis: University of Minnesota Press, 1996.

Arenal, Electra, and Stacey Schlau. *Untold Sisters: Hispanic Nuns in Their Own Works.* Albuquerque: University of New Mexico Press, 1989.

"Art and Technology of the Chulucanas Pottery." Galería El Artesano, Lima, Peru, 1988.

Bakhtin, Mikhail. "Author and Hero in Aesthetic Activity." In *Art and Answerability,* trans. Liapunov; ed. Michael Holquist and Vadim Liapunov. Austin: University of Texas, 1990.

———. *The Dialogic Imagination.* Austin: University of Texas Press, 1981.

———. *Problems of Dostoevsky's Poetics.* Trans. R. W. Rotsel. Ann Arbor: Ardis Publishers, 1973.

Barros-Lémez, Alvaro. *Vidas de papel. El folletín del siglo XIX en América Latina.* Montevideo: Monte Sexto, 1992.

Barthes, Roland. *Empire of Signs.* New York: Hill and Wang, 1982.

Bary, Leslie. "Forum." *PMLA* 112 (March 1997): 269–70.

Behar, Ruth. "Queer Times in Cuba." *Michigan Quarterly Review* 33, no. 4 (1994): 837–58.

Bel'Kovich, V. M. "Herd Structure, Hunting, and Play: Bottlenose Dolphins in the Black Sea." In *Dolphin Societies: Discoveries and Puzzles,* ed. Karen Pryor and Kenneth S. Norris, 17–78. Berkeley and Los Angeles: University of California Press, 1991.

Beltrán Carías, Graciela. "José Antonio Guevara: Es una historia de filiaciones." *El nacional* (Caracas), September 7, 1986.

Benavente, David. "'Ave Félix' (Teatro Chileno post-golpe)." *Pedro, Juan y Diego, Tres*

Marías y Una Rosa, 277–323. Santiago: Ediciones ChileAmérica CESOC, 1989.

Benavente, David, and T.I.T. *Tres Marías y una Rosa*. In *Teatro chileno de la crisis institucional 1973–1980 (Antología crítica)*, 196–248. Minnesota/Santiago: University of Minnesota/Ceneca, 1982.

Bennett, Tony. "The Politics of 'the Popular' and Popular Culture." In *Popular Culture and Social Relations*, ed. Colin Mercer and Janet Woollacott, 6–21. Milton Keynes: Open University Press.

Berger, John. *Ways of Seeing*. New York: Penguin, 1972.

Berman, Marshall. *All That Is Solid Melts into Air*. [1982]. London: Verso, 1985.

Bernardet, Jean-Claude. *Brasil em Tempo de Cinema*. Rio de Janeiro: Civilização Brasileira, 1966.

Beverley, John. *Against Literature*. Minneapolis: University of Minnesota Press, 1993.

Beverley, John, José Oviedo, and Michael Aronna, eds. *The Postmodern Debate in Latin America*. Durham: Duke University Press, 1995.

Beverley, John, and Marc Zimmerman. *Literature and Politics in the Central American Revolutions*. Austin: University of Texas Press, 1990.

Bhabha, Homi K. *Location of Culture*. London: Routledge, 1994.

Bopp, Raul. *Cobra Norato. Nheengatu da margem esquerda do Amazonas*. São Paulo: Irmãos Ferraz, 1931.

Borges, Jorge Luis. *Historia universal de la infamia*. In *Obra completa*, vol. 3.

———. *Obra completa*. Buenos Aires: Emecé Editores, 1974.

Borges, Jorge Luis, and Silvina Bullrich. *El compadrito: su destino, sus barrios, su música*. [1945] Buenos Aires: Compañía General Fabril Editora, 1963.

Bossio, Jorge Alberto. *Los cafés de Buenos Aires*. Buenos Aires: Editorial Schapire, 1968.

Brant, Herbert J. "The Mark of the Phallus: Homoerotic Desire in Borges' `La forma de la espada.'" *Chasqui* 25 (1996): 25–38.

Brantlinger, Patrick. *Crusoe's Footprints: Cultural Studies in Britain and America*. New York: Routledge, 1990.

Braceli, Rodolfo. *Fontanarrosa, entrégate (Y vos también, Boogie. Y usted también, Inodoro)*. Buenos Aires: Ediciones de la Flor, 1992.

Brecht, Bertold. *Escritos sobre teatro*. Ed. Jorge Hacker. Buenos Aires: Nueva Visión, 1970.

Brufman, Gustavo y Mariana Hernández. "Roberto Fontanarrosa: el oficio de hacer reír." *Chasqui* 44 (1993): 70–75.

Buarque, Chico. *Ópera do malandro*. São Paulo: Círculo do livro, 1978.

Buenos Aires, mi ciudad. With photographs by Sameer Makarius. Buenos Aires: Editorial Universitaria de Buenos Aires, 1963.

Bunster, Ximena, and Elsa M. Chaney. *Sellers and Servants: Working Women in Lima, Peru*. New York: Praeger, 1985.

Burns, E. Bradford. *A History of Brazil*. 2nd ed. New York: Columbia University Press, 1980.

Bushnell, Rebecca. *Prophesying Tragedy: Sign and Voice in Sophocles' Theban Plays*. Cornell: Cornell University Press, 1988.

Cabrera Infante, Guillermo. *Mea Cuba*. Barcelona: Plaza y Janes, 1993.

Cabrujas, José Ignacio. "La telenovela en Venezuela." Interview with Nelson Hippolyte Ortega, Caracas, July 22, 1993.

Caesar, Terry. "Bringing It All Down: The 1986 World Cup in Brazil." *Massachusetts Review,* summer 1998, 277–86.

Calderón de la Barca, Fanny. *Life in Mexico during a Residence of Two Years in That Country.* [1843]. Boston and London: Dent, 1970.

Campbell, Joseph. *Oriental Mythology.* New York: Penguin Books, 1982.

———. *Primitive Mythology.* New York: Penguin Books, 1985.

Campra, Rosalba. "América Latina: La identidad y la máscara: Con entrevistas a Borges, Bosch, Carpentier, Cortazar, Galeano, Sábato, Scorza, Vina y Walsh Coyoacan." *Siglo Veintiuno,* 1987.

Cândido, Antonio. *Os parceiros do Rio Bonito.* Rio de Janeiro: José Olympio Editora, 1964.

———. *On Literature and Society.* Trans. and ed. Howard S. Becker. Princeton: Princeton University Press, 1995.

"Capítulo Final." *Por estas calles.* Dramatic Production by Radio Caracas Televisión.

Capriles, Oswaldo. "La (Tele)Novela por entregas." Parts I, II, III. *Papel Literario, El Nacional* (Caracas), May 2, June 14, June 28, 1987.

Cárdenas, José Rodolfo. "Por estas calles." *El Mundo* (Caracas) October 1, 1992.

Carpentier, Alejo. *El arpa y la sombra (The Harp and the Shadow).* Vol. 4 of *Obras completas de Alejo Carpentier.* Mexico City: Siglo XXI, 1983.

Carrasco Puente, Rafael. *Bibliografía de Catarina de San Juan y de la China poblana.* Mexico City: Secretaria de Relaciones Exteriores, 1950.

Case, Sue-Ellen. "Classic Drag: The Greek Creation of Female Parts." *Theater Journal* 37 (1985): 317–27.

Castillo de Graxeda, José del. *Compendio de la vida y virtudes de la venerable Catarina de San Juan.* Puebla: Gobierno del Estado de Puebla, 1987.

———. *La verdadera historia de la China poblana.* Mexico City: Centro Mexicano de Estudios Culturales, 1989.

Castro, Fidel. Speech at the University of Havana. Castro Speech Database (Austin: University of Texas). Online. Available: gopher: //lanic.utexas.edu:70/0R0-16434-/la/Cuba/Castro /1963/19630313.

———. Interview. "Part 6 of Interview." By Tomás Borge. Castro Speech Database (Austin: University of Texas). Online. Available: gopher://lanic.utexas.edu:70/0R0-16434-/la/ Cuba/Castro/1992/19920607.

Castro, Donald S. *The Argentine Tango as Social History, 1880–1955: The Soul of the People.* Lewiston, Maine: E. Mellen Press, 1991.

Castro Morales, Efraín. "Introducción." In *Compendio de la vida y virtudes de la venerable Catarina de San Juan,* ed. José Castillo de Graxeda. Puebla: Gobierno del Estado de Puebla, 1987.

Catani, Afrânio Mendes. "A aventura industrial e o cinema paulista (1930–1955).

'Anexo II—Amácio Mazzaropi: 30 anos de presença no cinema brasileiro.'" In *História do Cinema Brasileiro*, ed. Fernão Ramos. São Paulo: Art Editora, 1987.

Cirlot, Juan Eduardo. *Diccionario de símbolos*. Barcelona: Labor, 1988.

Clarke, John. "Style." In *Resistance Through Rituals: Youth Subcultures in Post-war Britain*, ed. Stuart Hall et al. [1975]. London: Routledge, 1993.

Clifford, James. *The Predicament of Culture: Twentieth-Century Ethnography, Literature, and Art*. Cambridge: Harvard University Press, 1988.

Collier, Simon. "The Popular Roots of the Argentine Tango." *History Workshop; A Journal of Socialist History* 34 (fall 1992): 92–100.

Colomina, Marta. "Prójimos exquisitos vx. telenovelas." *El Diario de Caracas*. June 16, 1993.

———. "Telenovelas: Imagen de Venezuela en el mundo." Unpublished essay. Caracas, 1994.

Constable, Pamela, and Arturo Valenzuela. *Chile Under Pinochet. A Nation of Enemies*. New York: Norton, 1991.

Corbatta, Jorgelina. "El tango: letras y visión del mundo." *Hispanic Journal* 15 (1994): 63–72.

Connell, R. W. "The Big Picture: Masculinities in Recent World History." *Theory and Society* 22 (1993): 597–623.

"Contra la pared." *Producto* 111 (December 1992).

Cosgrove, Stuart. "The Zoot Suit and Style Warfare." *History Workshop: A Journal of Socialist and Feminist Historians* 18 (1984): 77–91.

Cunha, Antônio Geraldo da. *Dicionário Etimológico Nova Fronteira da Língua Portuguesa*. Rio de Janeiro: Nova Fronteira, 1982.

Cunha, Euclides da. *Os sertões*. São Paulo: Editora Brasiliense, 1985.

Cypess, Sandra Messinger. *La Malinche in Mexican Literature: From History to Myth*. Austin: University of Texas Press, 1991.

Dahl, Gustavo. "Cinema Novo e Estruturas Econômicas Tradicionais." *Revista Civilização Brazileira* 5 (1966): 76–84.

DaMatta, Roberto. *Carnivals, Rogues and Heroes: An Interpretation of the Brazilian Dilemma*. Trans. John Drury. South Bend: Notre Dame University Press, 1991.

Davies, Lucy, and Mo Fini. *Arts and Crafts of South America*. San Francisco: Chronicle Books, 1995.

De Certeau, Michel. *The Practice of Everyday Life*. Berkeley: University of California Press, 1984.

Deleuze, Gilles, and Félix Guattari. *Anti-Oedipus: Capitalism and Schizophrenia*. Trans. Robert Hurly, Mark Seem, and Helen R. Lane. Minneapolis: University of Minnesota Press, 1983.

De Man, Paul. *Allegories of Reading. Figural Language in Rousseau, Nietzsche, Rilke, and Proust*. New Haven: Yale University Press, 1979.

———. "Excuses (Confessions)." In *Allegories of Reading*, 278–301.

———. *The Rhetoric of Romanticism*. New York: Columbia University Press, 1984.

Denning, Michael. "The End of Mass Culture." In *Modernity and Mass Culture*, ed. Naremore and Brantlinger, 253–68.

Derrida, Jacques. "La Phamarcie de Platon." *La Dissémination*, 71–179. Paris: Seuil, 1968.

———. *Spurs: Nietzsche's Styles*. Chicago: University of Chicago Press, 1979.

Donaldson, Mike. "What Is Hegemonic Masculinity?" *Theory and Society* 22 (1993): 643–57.

Dorfman, Ariel. "Borges y la violencia humana." *Imaginación y violencia en América*, 38–64. Santiago de Chile: Editorial Universitaria, 1970

Dorfman, Ariel, and Armand Mattelart. *Para leer al Pato Donald*. Buenos Aires: Siglo Veintiuno Argentina, 1972.

———. *How to Read Donald Duck. Imperialist Ideology in the Disney Comic*. New York: International General, 1991.

Duthurburu, José Antonio del Busto, *El Mestizaje en El Peru*. Piura: Universidad de Piura, 1993.

Echevarría, Roberto González. "Autobiography and Representation in *La Habana para un Infante difunto*." *World Literature Today* 61 (1978): 569.

Eco, Umberto. *Apocalypse Postponed*. Bloomington: Indiana University Press, 1994.

Ellis, Richard. *Dolphins and Porpoises*. New York: Knopf, 1982.

"El Mar y las Esenas en la Pintura Regional." *El Tiempo* (Lima), Sept. 5, 1993.

Esquivel, Laura. *Like Water for Chocolate*. New York: Anchor Books, 1992.

Esslin, Martin. *Brecht: The Man and His Work*. New York: Anchor Books, 1971.

Evans, Judith. "Tango." *Buenos Aires*. Singapore: APA Publication /Insight Cityguides, 1988, 147–51.

Faciolince, Héctor Abad. "La telenovela. El bienestar en la incultura." *Número* (Bogotá) 9 (May 1996).

Fernández Bitar, Marcelo. *Historia del rock en Argentina: una investigación cronológica*. Buenos Aires: Ediciones El Juglar, 1987.

Festa, Regina. "Brazilian Cinema Loses Its Way." *Media Development* 40 (1993): 5–8.

Fiske, John. *Reading the Popular*. Boston: Unwin Hyman, 1989.

Flieger, Jerry Aline. "The Purloined Punchline: Joke as Textual Paradigm." *MLN* 98 (1983): 941–67.

Fontanarrosa, Roberto. *Boogie el aceitoso*. Vols. 1–2 [1974]. 3rd ed. Buenos Aires: Ediciones de la Flor S.R.L., 1982.

———. *Boogie el aceitoso*. Vol. 5. Buenos Aires: Ediciones de la Flor S.R.L., 1982.

Foster, David William. *From Mafalda to Los Supermachos. Latin American Graphic Humor as Popular Culture*. Boulder: Lynne Rienner, 1989.

———. "*Mafalda*: An Argentine Comic Strip." *Journal of Popular Culture* 14 (1980): 497–507.

———. "'Narrative Rights' in the Argentine Tango." *Symposium* 37 (1983–84): 261–71.

Foucault, Michel. *The History of Sexuality*, Vol. 1: *An Introduction*. Trans. Robert Hurley. London: Penguin, 1981.

———. *Language, Counter-Memory, Practice.* Trans. Donald F. Bouckard and Sherry Simon. New York: Cornell University Press, 1977.

Fox-Lockert, Lucía. "Vision del paisaje andino peruano en José María Arguedas y Manuel Scorza." *Cuadernos de Aldeeu* 2–3 (May–Oct. 1983): 337–45.

Franco, Jean. "The Incorporation of Women: A Comparison of North American and Mexican Popular Narrative." In *Studies in Entertainment: Critical Approaches to Mass Culture,* ed. Tania Modleski. Bloomington: Indiana University Press, 1986.

———. *The Modern Culture of Latin America: Society and the Artist.* New York: Frederick Praeger, 1967.

———. "What's in a Name? Popular Culture Theories and Their Limitations." *Studies in Latin American Popular Culture* 1 (1982): 5–14.

Fregoso, Linda. "The Representation of Cultural Identity in *Zoot Suit.*" *Theory and Society* 22 (1993): 659–74.

———. "*Zoot Suit*—The 'Return to the Beginning.'" In *Mediating Two Worlds,* ed. John King and Ana Lopez. London: BFI Publishing, 1993.

Gadamer, Hans-Georg. *Warheit und Methode. Grunzüge einer philosophischen Hermeneutik.* Tübingen: Mohr, 1972.

García Icazbalceta, Joaquin. *Vocabulario de mexicanismos comparado con los otros paises hispano americanos.* Mexico City: N.p., 1905.

Galvão, Maria Rita, and Jean-Claude Bernardet, eds. *O Nacional e o Popular na Cultura Brasileira.* São Paulo: Brasiliense, 1983.

García Mackle, Miguel. "Por estas calles." *El Nacional* (Caracas), January 27, 1993.

García Márquez, Gabriel. "Hay que hacer culebrones, pero de buena calidad." *El Nacional* (Caracas), September 15, 1977.

Garmendia, Salvador. "La telenovela en Venezuela." Interview with Nelson Hippolyte Ortega. Caracas, July 22, 1993.

Geertz, Clifford. *Works and Lives: The Anthropologist as Author.* Stanford: Stanford University Press, 1988.

Giarroco, Alberto. "La telenovela en Venezuela." Interview with Nelson Hippolyte Ortega. Caracas, July 10, 1993.

Girard, René. *Violence and the Sacred.* Trans. Patrick Gregory. Baltimore: Johns Hopkins University Press, 1977.

Goldmann, Lucien. "La sociología y la literatura: situación actual y problemas de método." In *Sociología de la creación literaria.* ed. Lucien Goldmann et al., 11–21. Buenos Aires, Nueva Visión, 1971.

Goloboff, Gerardo Mario. "La ciudad de Borges." In *La selva en el damero: espacio literario y espacio urbano de América Latina,* ed. Rosalba Campra, 215–23. Pisa: Giardini, 1989.

González, Eduardo. "Framing Carpentier." *Modern Language Notes* 101 (1986): 424–29.

González, Reynaldo. *Llorar es un placer.* Habana: Letras Cubanas, 1988.

González Echevarría, Roberto. *Alejo Carpentier: The Pilgrim at Home.* Austin: University of Texas Press, 1990.

———. "Autobiography and Representation."

———. *Myth and Archive: A Theory of Latin American Literature.* New York: Cambridge University Press, 1990.

———. "Ultimos viajes del peregrino" *Revista Iberoamericana* 57 (1991): 119–34.

Guevara, Ernesto. *Obra revolucionaria.* Ed. Roberto Fernández Retamar. Mexico City: Ediciones Era, 1979.

Guillermoprieto, Alma. *Samba.* New York: Vintage Books, 1990.

Gutiérrez Alea, Tomás, and Juan Carlos Tabío, dirs. *Fresa y chocolate.* With Jorge Perugorría, Vladimir Cruz, Mirta Ibarra. ICAIC, 1993.

Hall, Stuart, et al., eds. *Resistance Through Rituals: Youth Subcultures in Post-war Britain.* 1975. London: Routledge, 1993.

Handelman, Howard. *Struggles in the Andes: Peasant Political Mobilization in Peru.* Austin: University of Texas Press, 1975.

Heidegger, Martin. "The Origin of the Work of Art." In *Poetry, Language, Thought.* Trans. Alfred Hofstadter. New York: Harper Colophon, 1975.

Hellinger, Daniel C. *Venezuela: Tarnished Democracy.* Boulder, Colo.: Westview Press, 1991.

Henríquez, Camilo. "El teatro en Chile." *La Aurora de Chile,* September 10, 1812.

Hess, David, and Roberto Da Matta, eds. *The Brazilian Puzzle. Culture on the Borderlands of the Western World.* New York: Columbia University Press, 1995.

Hernández, Pablo José. *Para leer a Mafalda.* Buenos Aires: Ediciones Meridiano, 1975.

Hernández J., Consuelo. "Crónica, historiografía e imaginación en las novelas de Scorza." *Cuadernos hispanoamericanos* 453 (Sept. 1995): 149–58.

Hicks, D. Emily. *Border Writing. The Multidimensional Text.* Minneapolis: University of Minnesota Press, 1991.

Hippolyte, Nelson O. "José Ignacio Cabrujas: la muerte de la telenovela." *Revista Iberoamericana* 174: 258–63.

Hurtado, María de la Luz, et al., eds. *Teatro Chileno de la crisis institucional 1973–1980 (Antología Crítica).* Minnesota/ Santiago: University of Minnesota/ Ceneca, 1982.

Hurtado, María de la Luz, and Carlos Ochsenius. *T.I.T. Taller de Investigación Teatral.* Santiago: Ceneca, 1980.

Hurtado, María de la Luz, and Carlos Ochsenius. *Nómina de obras teatrales montadas entre 1968 y 1980 por compañías profesionares y aficionadas en salas comerciales.* Santiago: Ceneca, 1980.

Huyssen, Andreas. *After the Great Divide.* Bloomington: Indiana University Press, 1986.

"Ibsen privadito." *Portada* 8 (Caracas), March 30, 1993.

Informe Rettig. *Informe de la Comisión Nacional de Verdad y Reconciliación.* Santiago: La Nación/ Ediciones del Ornitorrinco, 1991.

Inge, M. Thomas. *Comics as Culture.* Jackson: University Press of Mississippi, 1990.

Iser, Wolfgang. *The Act of Reading. A Theory of Aesthetic Response.* Baltimore: Johns Hopkins University Press, 1978.

Jackson, K. David. "Three Glad Races: Primitivism and Ethnicity in Brazilian Modernist Literature." *Modernism/modernity* 1 (1994): 89–112.

Jaffee, Janice. "Hispanic American Women Writers' Novel Recipes and Laura Esquivel's *Como Agua para Chocolate.*" *Women's Studies, an Interdisciplinary Journal* 22 (1993): 221–34.

Jameson, Fredric. *Postmodernism, or The Cultural Logic of Late Capitalism.* Durham, N.C.: Duke University Press, 1991.

———. "Reification and Utopia in Mass Culture." *Social Text* 1 (1979): 128–42.

Jauss, Hans Robert. "History of Art and Pragmatic History." *Contemporary Critical Theory.* Trans. David Henry Wilson. Ed. Dan Latimer. New York: Harcourt Brace, 1989.

Jesse, Lisa. "The Discourse of Carioca Samba in the Vargas Era (1930–1945): The Works of Ataúlfo Alves, Noel Rosa and Ari Barroso." Ph.D. diss., Liverpool University, 1995.

Jimper, Albert. "Rotten Strawberries and Bitter Chocolate." Online. Available: http://www.qrd.org/qrd/world/wockner/quote.unquote/029-02.22.95.

John Puccini, Darío. "Manuel Scorza, el cronista de la epopeya india." *Revista de crítica literaria latinoamericana* 21–22 (1985): 63–71.

Jones, Julie. "Carpentier's *El arpa y la sombra*: Variation on a Theme." *Perspectives on Contemporary Literature* 12 (1986): 87–93.

Johnson, Randal. *Cinema Novo X 5; Masters of Contemporary Brazilian Film.* Austin: University of Texas Press, 1984.

———. *The Film Industry in Brazil; Culture and the State.* Pittsburgh, Pa.: University of Pittsburgh Press, 1987.

Johnson, Randal, and Robert Stam. *Brazilian Cinema.* Rutherford, N.J.: Farleigh Dickinson University Press, 1982.

Katz, Jonathan Ned. *The Invention of Heterosexuality.* New York: Penguin, 1995.

Keen, Benjamin. *La imagen azteca.* Mexico City: Fondo de Cultura Económica, 1984.

King, John. *Magical Reels: A History of Cinema in Latin America.* London: Verso, 1990.

Klagsbrunn, Marta. "The Brazilian Telenovela: A Genre in Development." In *Serial Fiction in TV. The Latin American Telenovelas,* ed Anamaria Fadul, 12–32. São Paulo: School of Communication and Arts of the University of São Paulo, 1993.

Lacan, Jacques. "The Function of Language in Psychoanalysis." In *The Language of the Self,* ed. A. Wilden. Baltimore: Johns Hopkins University Press, 1968.

Lafourcade, Enrique. "¿Por qué atacan a Florcita Motuda?" *Qué pasa,* February 17, 1977, 34–35.

Lambert, Jacques. *Latin America: Social Structures & Political Institutions.* 4th ed. Trans. Helen Katel. Berkeley: University of California Press, 1974.

Lara, Tomás, and Inés Leonilda Roncetti de Panti. *El tema del tango en la literatura argentina.* 2nd ed. Buenos Aires: Secretaría de Cultura, Secretaría de Estado de Cultura y Educación, 1970.

Larsen, Neil. "Foreword." In *Border Writing. The Multidimensional Text*, ed. D. Emily Hicks, xi–xxi. Minneapolis: University of Minnesota Press, 1991.

Lavado, Joaquín Salvador. *Mafalda*. Buenos Aires: Ediciones de la Flor, 1967–1974.

———. *10 años con Mafalda*. Barcelona: Editorial Lumen, 1973.

Leante, César. "Confesión en clave de morse." *El País* (Madrid), January 6, 1997.

León, Nicolas. "Catarina de San Juan y la china poblana: Estudio etnográfico crítico." *Cosmo* 7:41–43 (1921–22): 81–85, 211–20, 324–28.

———. "Catarina de San Juan y la china poblana: Estudio etnográfico crítico." In Carrasco Puente, *Bibliografía de Catarina de San Juan y de la China poblana*.

Leone, Eduardo. "Caliças no País das Maravilhas." *Revista USP* 1 (Sept.–Nov. 1993): 62–69.

Lerner, Gerda. *The Creation of Patriarchy*. New York: Oxford University Press, 1986.

Lévi-Strauss, Claude. *Structural Anthropology*. Trans. C. Jacobson and B. G. Schoepf. Garden City, N.Y.: Anchor, 1963.

Levy, Tal. "Denuncia y romance en *Por estas calles*." *El Nacional* (Caracas), June 3, 1992.

———. "Otra vez: Por estas calles." *Papel Literario de El Nacional* (Caracas), January 17, 1993.

Lindstrom, Naomi. "Social Commentary in Argentine Cartooning: From Description to Questioning." *Journal of Popular Culture* 14 (1980): 509–23.

Lockwood, Lee. *Castro's Cuba, Cuba's Fidel*. New York: Vintage, 1969.

López, Ana M. "Celluloid Tears: Melodrama in the 'Old' Mexican Cinema." *Iris: A Journal of Theory on Image and Sound* 13 (summer 1991): 29–51.

———. "Our Welcomed Guests. Telenovelas in Latin America." In *To Be Continued. . . Soap Operas Around the World*, ed. Robert C. Allen, 256–75. London: Routledge, 1995.

López, Oscar Luis. *La radio en Cuba*. Havana: Letras Cubanas, 1981.

López Badano, Cecilia. *Violencia de género en los medios de comunicación social argentinos. Apuntes sobre la historia de un imaginatio popular discriminatorio*. Buenos Aires, forthcoming.

López Peña, Arturo. *Teoría del argentino*. Buenos Aires: Editorial Abies, 1958.

Los Angeles Torres, María de. "Beyond the Rupture: Reconciling with Our Enemies, Reconciling with Ourselves." *Michigan Quarterly Review* 33 (1994): 419–36.

Lovera De-Sola, R. J. *El oficio de ser venezolano*. Caracas: Ediciones Librería Destino, 1994.

McCabe, Colin, ed. *High Theory/ Low Culture: Analysing Popular Television and Film*. Manchester: Manchester University Press, 1986.

McCloud, Scott. *Understanding Comics*. New York: Harper Perennial, 1993.

Madrid, Lelia. "'Fundación mítica de Buenos Aires' o la utopía de la historia." *Bulletin of Hispanic Studies* 69 (1992): 347–56.

Mafud, Julio. *Sociología del tango*. Buenos Aires: Editorial Américalee, 1966.

Major Dundee. [Film.] Dir. Sam Peckinpah. USA: Jerry Bressler Productions, 1964.

Malinowski, Bronislaw. *Argonauts of the Western Pacific*. New York: Dutton, 1922.

Mañach, Jorge. *La crisis en la alta cultura cubana e Indagación del choteo*. Miami: Ediciones

Universal, 1991.

Manzor-Coats, Lillian. "Performative Identites: Scenes Between Two Cubas." *Michigan Quarterly Review* 33 (1994): 748–61.

Martín-Barbero, Jesús. *De los medios a las mediaciones: comunicación, cultura y hegemonía.* Mexico City: Ediciones G. Gili, [1987] 1991.

Martínez, Ibsen. "Ultimo capítulo de *Por estas calles.*" *El Nacional* (Caracas), March 9, 1993.

Martins, Carlos Estevam. "Artigo sobre Aristocratas." *O Nacional e o Popular na Cultura Brasileira,* ed. Galvão and Bernardet, 152–67. São Paulo, Brasiliense, 1983.

———. "For a Popular Revolutionary Art." In *Brazilian Cinema,* ed. Johnson and Stam, 59–61. Rutherford, N.J.: Farleigh Dickinson University Press, 1982.

Martins, Wilson. *The Modernist Idea.* Trans. Jack E. Tomlins. New York: New York University Press, 1970.

Marzullo, Osvaldo, and Pancho Muñoz. *El rock en la Argentina: la historia y sus protagonistas.* Buenos Aires: Editorial Galerna, 1986.

Masotta, Oscar. *La historieta en el mundo moderno.* Buenos Aires: Editorial Paidós, 1970.

Matamoro, Blas. *La ciudad del tango; tango histórico y sociedad.* Buenos Aires: Editorial Galerna, 1982.

Matos, Claudia. *Acertei no milhar: malandragem e samba no tempo de Getúlio.* Rio de Janeiro: Paz e Terra, 1982.

Mattelart, Armand. "Introduction: For a Class and Group Analysis of Popular Communication Practices." In *Communication and Class Struggle,* ed. Armand Mattelart and Seth Siegelaub, 2:17–67. New York: International General, 1983.

Maza, Francisco de la. *Catarina de San Juan: Princesa de La India y Visionaria de Puebla.* Mexico City: Editorial Libros de Mexico, 1971.

Mazón, Mauricio. *The Zoot Suit Riots: A Psychology of Symbolic Annihilation.* Austin: Austin University Press, 1986.

Mazziotti, Nora, ed. *El espectáculo de la pasión. Las telenovelas latinoamericanas.* Buenos Aires: Colihue, 1993.

Mercatante, Anthony S. *Good and Evil.* New York: Barnes and Noble, 1996.

Modleski, Tania. *Loving With a Vengeance. Mass Produced Fantasies for Women.* Hamden: Archon Books, 1982.

Moi, Toril. "A New Type of Intellectual: The Dissident." Foreword to *The Kristeva Reader.* Oxford: Blackwell, 1993.

Monsiváis, Carlos. "Tin Tan: Pachuco." *Travesía* 3 (1994): 178–98.

Montañes, Mónica. "El fenómeno de *Por estas calles.* A las nueve de la noche todos se miran en el espejo." *El Diario de Caracas,* February 9, 1993.

Mörner, Magnus. *The Andean Past: Land, Society, and Conflicts.* New York: Columbia University Press, 1985.

Morson, Gary Saul, and Caryl Emerson. *Mikhail Bakhtin: Creation of a Prosaics.* Stanford: Stanford University Press, 1990.

Mulvey, Laura. "Melodrama In and Out of the Home." In *High Theory/Low Culture;*

Analysing Popular Television and Film, ed. Colin McCabe. Manchester: Manchester University Press, 1986.

Muñoz, Carlos, Jr. *Youth, Identity, Power: The Chicano Movement.* London: Verso, 1989.

Murasaki (Shikibu). *The Tale of Gengi.* New York: Knopf, 1981.

Naremore, James, and Patrick Brantlinger, eds. *Modernity and Mass Culture.* Bloomington: Indiana University Press, 1991.

Narváez, Jorge, ed. *La invención de la memoria.* Santiago: Pehuén, 1988.

Nelson, Cary, and Lawrence Grossberg, eds. *Marxism and the Interpretation of Culture.* Urbana: University of Illinois Press, 1988.

Nervo, Amado. "Guadalupe (la chinaca)." *El Mundo.* 5.2.3 16 July 1899: 40. In Carrasco Puente, *Bibliografía de Catarina de San Juan y de la China poblana.*

Nietzsche, Friedrich. *The Birth of Tragedy and the Case of Wagner.* Trans. Walter Kaufmann. New York: Vintage, 1967.

———. *Human All Too Human: A Book For Free Spirits.* Trans. R. D. Hollingdale. Cambridge: Cambridge University Press, 1986.

"O cinema nacional perde seu Jeca." *Folha de São Paulo,* June 14, 1981.

O'Flaherty, Wendy Doniger. *Women, Androgynes and Other Mythical Beasts.* Chicago, The University of Chicago Press, 1980.

Olea, Raquel. "Feminism: Modern or Postmodern?" In John Puccini, Darío. "Manuel Scorza, el cronista de la epopeya india." *Revista de crítica literaria latinomaricana* 21–22 (1985): 63–71.

Ópera do malandro [film]. Dir. Ruy Guerra. Brazil/France: MK2 Productions, 1986.

Orlove, Benjamin S. "Putting Race in Its Place: Order in Colonial and Postcolonial Peruvian Geography." *Social Research* 60 (1993): 301–36.

Oropesa, Salvador. "*Como agua para chocolate* de Laura Esquivel como lectura." *Chasqui* 24 (October 1995): 23–35.

Paoletti, Mario. "Borges y la ciudad del tango." *Revista de Occidente* 69 (1987): 87–100.

Pasquali, Antonio. *El orden reina. Escritos sobre comunicaciones.* Caracas: Monte Avila, 1991.

Paz, Octavio. *El Laberinto de la Soledad.* Mexico City: Fondo de Cultura Económica, [1950] 1993.

Pérez-Firmat, Gustavo. *The Cuban Condition: Translation and Identity in Modern Cuban Literature.* Cambridge: Cambridge University Press, 1989.

Pettit, Arthur G. *Images of the Mexican American in Fiction and Film.* Austin: Texas University Press, 1980.

Pires, Cornélio. *Conversas ao Pé de Fogo. Estudinhos, Costumes, anedotas, Cenas de Escravidão.* São Paulo: N.p. 1981.

Preston, Julia. "Soap Heroine Spurns Script, and Plot Thickens." *New York Times,* December 2, 1996.

Prieto, Hugo. "Vuelve la telenovela cultural. Todo un remake." *Domingo Hoy* (Caracas), May 31, 1992.

"Publicaciones." *Amigos,* April 1994, 82–83.

Puigarri, José. *Monografía histórica e iconográfica del traje*. In Carrasco Puente, *Bibliografía de Catarina de San Juan y de la China poblana*.

Querino Neto, Antonio. "Mazzaropi." *Revista Set Cinema e Vídeo* 5 (1983): 56.

Quijano, Anibal. "Modernity, Identity, and Utopia in Latin America." In *The Postmodern Debate in Latin America*, ed. Beverley, Oviedo, and Aronna, 201–16.

Quiroz, María Teresa. "La telenovela peruana: antecedentes y situación actual." In *El espetáculo de la pasión*, ed. Nora Mazziotti. Buenos Aires: Colihue, 1993.

Ramos, Alonso. *Primera y Segunda Parte de los Prodigios de la Omnipotencia y milagros de la Gracia en la Vida de la V. Sierva de Dios Catharina de San Juan, natural del Gran Mogor difunta en la Imperial Ciudad de los Angeles de la Nueva España*. Mexico City: Impresa Nueva de Diego Fernández de León, 1688.

Ramos, Fernão. *Cinema Marginal (1968–1973): A representação em seu limite*. São Paulo: Editora Brasiliense, 1987.

———. "Os novos rumos do cinema brasileiro (1955–1970)." *História do Cinema Brasileiro*, ed. Fernão Ramos, 299–389. São Paulo: Art Editora, 1987.

Ramos, José Mário Ortiz. "O Cinema Brasileiro Contemporâneo (1970–1987)." In *História do Cinema Brasileiro*, ed. Fernão Ramos, 399–454. São Paulo: Art Editora, 1987.

———. "A questão do gênero no cinema brasileiro." *Revista USP* 19 (Sept.–Nov. 1993): 108–13.

Rappaport, Roy A. *Pigs for the Ancestors*. New Haven: Yale University Press, 1969.

Rep, Miguel. *Y Rep hizo los barrios*. Buenos Aires: Página/12, 1993.

Resnick, Claudia C., and Paula Speck. "Quino after Mafalda: a Bittersweet Look at Argentine Reality." *Studies in Latin American Popular Culture* 3 (1983): 79–87.

Rocha, Glauber. *Revolução do Cinema Novo*. Rio de Janeiro: Alhambra/ Embrafilme, 1981.

Rojas-Trempe, Lady. "La alteridad indígena y mágica en la narrativa de Elena Garro, Manuel Scorza y Gioconda Belli." *Alba de América: revista literaria* 9 (1991): 141–52.

Rojo, Grinor. *Muerte y resurrección del teatro chileno, 1973–1983*. Madrid: Michay, 1985.

Rowe, William, and Vivian Schelling. *Memory and Modernity: Popular Culture in Latin America*. London: Verso, 1991.

Sabato, Ernesto. *Tango, disusión y clave*. 3rd ed. Buenos Aires: Editorial Losada, 1968.

Said, Edward. *Orientalism*. London: Penguin, 1978.

Salas, Horacio. "Buenos Aires, mito y obsesión." *Cuadernos hispanoamericanos* 505–07 (1992): 389–99.

Saldías, Adolfo. *Páginas literarias. El Compadrito, su destino, sus barrios, su música*. Buenos Aires: Colección Buen Aire, 1902.

Saltz, Joanne. "Laura Esquivel's *Como agua para chocolate*: The Questioning of Literary and Social Limits." *Chasqui* 24.1 (March 1995): 30–37.

Samper Pizano, Daniel. *Mafalda, Mastropiero y otros gremios paralelos*. Buenos Aires: Ediciones de la Flor, 1986.

Sanday, Peggy Reeves. *Female Power and Male Dominance: On the Origins of Sexual Inequality*. Cambridge: Cambridge University Press, 1981.

Sarlo Sabajanes, Beatriz. *Escenas de la vida posmoderna, intelectuales, arte y videocultura en la Argentina*. Buenos Aires: Ariel, 1994.

———. *Una modernidad periférica: Buenos Aires, 1920 y 1930*. Buenos Aires: Ediciones Nueva Visión, 1988.

Savigliano, Marta E. *Tango and the Political Economy of Passion*. Boulder: Westview Press, 1995.

———. "Whiny Ruffians and Rebellious Broads: Tango as a Spectacle of Eroticized Social Tension." *Theatre Journal* 47 (1995): 83–104.

Sayer, Chloe. *Costumes of Mexico*. Austin: University of Texas Press, 1985.

Schroeder de Oliveira, Luiz Carlos. *Mazzaropi, A saudade de um povo*. Londrina: CEDM Editora, 1986.

Schwartz, Marcy Hellen. "Writing Paris into Contemporary Latin American Narrative: The City Intertex in Manuel Scorza, Bryce Echenique and Futonransky." Ph.D. diss., Johns Hopkins University, 1993.

Schwartz, Marcy Hellen, and Irene Silverblatt. *Moon, Sun and Witches*. Princeton: Princeton University Press, 1987.

Schwarz, Roberto. "Brazilian Culture: Nationalism by Elimination." In *Misplaced Ideas: Essays on Brazilian Culture*, ed. John Gledson. London: Verso, 1992.

Scorza, Manuel. *Cantar de Agapito Robles*. Barcelona: Plaza & Janes, 1984.

———. *Garabombo, el Invisible*. Barcelona: Plaza & Janes, 1984.

———. *El Jinete Insomne*. Barcelona: Plaza & Janes, 1984.

———. *Redoble por Rancas*. Barcelona: Plaza & Janes, 1987.

———. *La tumba del relámpago*. Bogotá: Siglo Veintiuno Editores, 1979.

Segal, Charles. "The Menace of Dionysus: Sex Roles and Reversals in Euripides' *Bacchae*." *Arethusa* 11 (1978): 185–202.

Segal, Lynne. "Changing Men: Masculinities in Context." *Theory and Society* 22 (1993): 625–41.

———. *Slow Motion: Changing Masculinities, Changing Men*. London: Virago, 1990.

Senior Grant, Alder. "La mujer-texto en *Como agua para chocolate*." *Revista de Filología y Lingüística de la Universidad de Costa Rica* 21 (January–June 1995): 47–54.

Simons, Ronald C., and Charles C. Hughes, eds. *The Culture-Bound Syndromes: Folk Illnesses of Psychiatric and Anthropological Interest*. Boston: D. Reidel, 1985.

Simpson, Amelia. *Xuxa: The Megamarketing of Gender, Race, and Modernity*. Philadelphia: Temple University press, 1993.

Slater, Candace. *Dance of the Dolphin: Transformation and Disenchantment in the Amazonian Imagination*. Chicago: University of Chicago Press, 1994.

———. *Stories on a String. The Brazilian Literatura De Cordel*. Berkeley: University of California Press, 1982.

Smith, Paul Julian. "The Language of Strawberry." *Sight and Sound* 4 (1994): 30–34.

Sommer, Doris. *Foundational Fictions: The National Romances of Latin America.* Berkeley: University of California Press, 1991.

Souza, Márcio. *A resistível ascenção do Boto Tucuxi.* Rio de Janeiro: Marco Zero, 1982.

Spivak, Gayatri. *In Other Worlds, Essays in Cultural Politics.* London: Routledge, 1987.

Stam, Robert. *Tropical Multiculturalism: A Comparative History of Race in Brazilian Cinema and Culture.* Durham: Duke University Press, 1997.

Steimberg, Oscar. *Leyendo historietas; estilos y sentidos de un "arte menor."* Buenos Aires: Nueva Visión, 1977.

Taussig, Michael. *Shamanism, Colonialism, and the Wild Man: A Study in Terror and Healing.* Chicago: University of Chicago Press, 1987.

The Dolphin [Ele o Boto]. Dir. Walter Lima Junior. Fox Lorber, 1987.

Tinhorão, José Ramos. *Música Popular: os sons que vêm da rua.* São Paulo: Edições Tinhorão, 1976.

Toussaint, Manuel. "Prólogo." In *La verdadera historia de la China poblana,* ed. José del Castillo Graxeda. Mexico City: Centro Mexicano de Estudios Culturales, 1989.

Tyler, Bruce. "Zoot Suit Culture and the Black Press." *Journal of American Culture* 17 (1994): 21–33.

Valdez, Luis. *Zoot Suit and Other Plays.* Arte Público Press, Houston: 1992.

Vargas Llosa, Mario. *El Pez en el Agua: Memorias.* Barcelona: Seix Barral, 1993.

———. *A Fish in the Water: A Memoir.* Trans. Helen Lane. New York: Farrar, Staus, Giroux, 1994.

———. "Questions of Conquest." *Harper's,* December 1990, 45–53.

Vasconcellos, Gilberto. "A malandragem e a formação da música popular brasileira." In *História Geral da Civilização Brasileira,* vol. 3: *O Brasil Republicano,* ed. Boris Fausto. São Paulo: Difel, 1984.

Vattimo, Gianni. *The Transparent Society.* Trans. David Webb. Baltimore: Johns Hopkins University Press, 1992.

Vattimo, Gianni, and Pier Aldo Rovatti. *Il pensiero debole.* Milan: Feltrinelli, 1988.

Vernant, Jean-Pierre. *Myth and Society in Ancient Greece.* Trans. Janet Lloyd. New York: Zone Books, 1990.

Vieira, João Luiz, and Robert Stam. "Parody and Marginality: The Case of Brazilian Cinema." *Framework* 28 (1985): 20–49.

Vila, Pablo. "Tango to Folk: Hegemony Construction and Popular Identities in Argentina." *Studies in Latin American Popular Culture* 10 (1991): 107–39.

Walker, Barbara G. *The Woman's Encyclopedia of Myths and Secrets.* New York: Harper and Row, 1983.

West, Dennis. "Strawberry and Chocolate, Ice Cream and Tolerance: Interviews with Tomás Gutiérrez Alea and Juan Carlos Tabío." *Cineaste* 21 (1995): 16–20.

Wilden, Anthony. *Man and Women, War and Peace.* London: Routledge and Kegan Paul, [1987] 1993.

Williams, Raymond. *Marxism and Literature.* Oxford: Oxford University Press, 1977.

Wockner, Rex. "Cuban Drags Let Their Hair Down." Online. Available: http://www.qrd.org/qrd/world/wockner/quote.unquote/029-02.22.95.

———. "Cuban Gays Are Out and Precocious." Online. Available: http://www.qrd.org/qrd/world/americas/cuba/out.and.precocious-wockner-05.22.95.

Yúdice, George. "Postmodernity and Transnational Capitalism." In *On Edge. The Crisis of Contemporary Latin American Culture,* ed. Yúdice et al., 1–28. Minneapolis: University of Minnesota Press, 1992.

Zeitlin, Froma I. "The Dynamics of Misogyny: Myth and Mythmaking in the *Oresteia*." *Arethusa* 2 (1978): 149–84.

Zéndegui, Guillermo de. *Todos somos culpables (We're All Guilty).* Miami: Ediciones Universal, 1991.

Zoot Suit [film]. Written and directed by Luis Valdez. Universal Pictures, 1981.

Contributors

Eva Paulino Bueno teaches Spanish and comparative literature at the DuBois campus of the Pennsylvania State University. Her current interests include cultural studies, popular culture, and the work of Amácio Mazzaropi, about whom she has written a book. She has published *Resisting Boundaries, The Suject of Brazilian Naturalism* (1995), as well as several essays in *MLN, Chasqui, Revista de Letras,* and *Revista de critica literaria latinoamericana.*

Terry Caesar is professor of English at Clarion University of Pennsylvania, where, every semester, he teaches freshman composition. He has been awarded a Guggenheim Fellowship, two Fulbrights, and a Northeast Modern Language Book Award for 1996. His recent publications include *Conspiring with Forms* (1990), *Forgiving the Boundaries* (1995), and *Writing in Disguise* (1998), as well as essays that have appeared in *New Literary History, Raritan, South Atlantic Quarterly, Pynchon Notes,* and others.

Jeanne Gillespie is associate professor of Spanish at Southeastern Louisiana University in Hammond. Her research focuses on the representation of women and Amerindians in colonial and twentieth-century Latin American theater and poetry. She is also involved in the project recording, transcribing, translating, and editing oral texts with the Isleño people of Southeast Louisiana. She has published essays on pre-Hispanic literature, colonial Amerindian texts, colonial women writers, and twentieth-century Mexican historical theater.

Nelson Hippolyte Ortega is visiting professor at Ohio University, where he teaches Spanish language and Latin American culture. His most recent research interest is centered on the study of popular culture, especially *telenovelas.* He published *Con un país así* in his native Venezuela.

Héctor D. Fernández L'Hoeste is assistant professor of Spanish at Georgia State University in Atlanta. His academic interests include Latin American cultural studies, film, and media theory, with special concern for urban narratives. He is the author of *Narrativas de representación urbana* (1998) and has published articles on Latin American cinema and theory.

David Swerdlow is associate professor of English at Westminster College in New Wilmington, Pa. In 1993, he was a Fulbright lecturer at the Universidad de Piura in Peru. In addition to articles concerning travel in Peru, he writes poems, many of which have been published in a variety of literary journals.

David William Foster is chair of the Department of Languages and Literatures and Regents' Professor of Spanish, Humanities, and Women's Studies at Arizona State University. His research interests focus on urban culture in Latin America, with emphasis on issues of gender construction and sexual identity, as well as Jewish culture. His most recent publications include *Violence in Argentine Literature; Cultural Responses to Tyranny* (1995); *Cultural Diversity in Latin American Literature* (1994), *Contemporary Argentine Cinema* (1992), and *Gay and Lesbian Themes in Latin American Writing* (1991).

Jerrold Van Hoeg is associate professor of Spanish at the Pennsylvania State University, Fayette. His most recent scholarly interests including Latin American folklore and film. He has written on Caribbean writers and on Chicano theater. He is also involved in the development of distance learning technologies.

James J. Pancrazio teaches Spanish and Latin American culture at Illinois State University, where he is an assistant professor. His academic interests include contemporary Cuban narrative, neo-Baroque and Latin American colonial literature. He is currently writing on the representation of the body in Latin America.

Oscar Lepeley is assistant professor of Spanish at the University of Toledo, where he teaches language and Spanish-American literature. His research is focused on cultural studies and literary productions under censorship. Most of his writing concerns developments in Chilean theater during the military dictatorship of Augusto Pinochet.

Vincent Spina is a poet who also teaches Spanish at Clarion University of Pennsylvania and writes about Latin American literature and culture. His main academic interest is Peruvian literature, especially José María Arguedas, the subject of his work, *El modo épico en Arguedas*. He is currently writing a book about cultural syncretism among indigenous peoples in Ecuador.

Simon Webb has a master's degree in Latin American literature and culture from the Institute of Latin American Studies of the University of London. He is at present working as a contributor and copy editor for the *Mexico City Times*.

Milagros Zapata Swerdlow is a Spanish instructor at Westminster College in New Wilmington, Pa. Educated at the Universidad del Pacífico in Lima, Peru, as well as in the United States, she is currently studying language acquisition theory.

Index